# Mysterious Secrets from Behind the Veil

# Mysterious Secrets from Behind the Veil

*The Worlds Greatest Devastating Deception*

R.A. Mueller

Copyright © 2013 by R.A. Mueller.

| | | |
|---|---|---|
| Library of Congress Control Number: | | 2013907847 |
| ISBN: | Hardcover | 978-1-4836-3341-1 |
| | Softcover | 978-1-4836-3340-4 |
| | Ebook | 978-1-4836-3342-8 |

All rights reserved. No part of this book may be reproduced or transmitted in any form or by any means, electronic or mechanical, including photocopying, recording, or by any information storage and retrieval system, without permission in writing from the copyright owner.

All scriptures are mainly taken from the Old King James Bible, and Apocrypha scriptures are taken from the New English Bible with the Apocrypha.

This book was printed in the United States of America.

Rev. date: 09/27/2013

**To order additional copies of this book, contact:**
Xlibris LLC
1-888-795-4274
www.Xlibris.com
Orders@Xlibris.com
118898

# Contents

Opening Prayer from 1 Samuel 2:1-10..................................................7
Prophetic Scriptures from Isaiah, Malachi, and Mark.....................8
Important Information..............................................................................9

Chapter 1: Who Are We as a People?....................................................11
Chapter 2: Scriptures Used to Prove the Christian Religion Is
the Devil's 1st Born Son's Religion ....................................38
Chapter 3: Who Is the Little Horn of Dan. 7:25 scripture? ............60
Chapter 4: The Ten Commandments Taken from Exodus 20:1-17 ..........84
Chapter 5: Newly Revealed Workings of Our Current World................111
Chapter 6: Proving New Testament Wrong with That of the
Old Testament ......................................................................119
Chapter 7: God's Overall Master Plan................................................142
Chapter 8: Calculations to Pinpoint Certain Occurrences of Events........149
Chapter 9: The Day of the Lord Our God.........................................162

The Closing Prayer....................................................................................169
Important Calculations Determining Past and Future Events .....171
Note Page ...................................................................................................177
Gregorian Calendar Schedule ..............................................................179
Calculating Ages of This World from the End to the Beginning...............181

# 1 Samuel 2:1-10

### To all the Israelites throughout this world

"My heart rejoices in the Lord God, mine horn is exalted in the Lord: my mouth is enlarged over mine enemies; because I rejoice in thy salvation.

There is none Holy as the Lord God: for there is none beside thee: neither is there any rock like our God.

Talk no more so exceeding proudly; Let not arrogancy come out of your mouth: For the Lord is a God of knowledge, and by him actions are weighed.

The bows of the mighty men are broken, and they that stumbled are girded with strength.

They that were full have hired out themselves for bread; and they that were hungry ceased: so that the barren has born seven; and she that has many children is waxed feeble.

The Lord God kills, and makes alive: He brings down to the grave, and brings up.

The Lord God makes poor, and makes rich: He brings low, and lifts up.

He raises up the poor out of the dust, and lifts up the beggars from the dunghill, to set them among princes, and to make them inherit the throne of glory: for the pillars of the earth are the Lord's, and he has set the world upon them.

He will keep the feet of his saints, and the wicked shall be silent in darkness; For by strength shall no man prevail.

The adversaries of the Lord God shall be broken to pieces; out of heaven shall he thunder upon them:

The Lord God shall judge the ends of the earth; and he shall give strength unto his king, and exalt the horn of his anointed."

## Isaiah 25:7

"In this mountain shall the Lord God of hosts make unto all people a feast of fat things, a feast of wines on the lees, of fat things full of marrow, of wines on the lees well refined.

And he will destroy in this mountain the face of the covering cast over all people, and the veil is spread over all nations.

He will swallow up death in victory; and the Lord God will wipe away tears from off all faces; and the rebuke of the people shall he take away from off all the earth: For the Lord God has spoken it."

## Malachi 4:5-6

"Behold, I will send you Elijah the prophet before the coming of the great and dreadful day of the Lord God.

And he shall turn the heart of the fathers to the children, and the heart of the children to their fathers, lest I come and smite the earth with a curse."

## Mark 9:11-12

"And they asked the Holy Messiah, saying, Why say the scribes that Elias must come first?

And he answered and told them, Elias verily cometh first, and restore all things; and how it is written of the Son of man, that he must suffer many things, and be set at nought."

# Important Information

What must take place before the end of this 21st century. 2046.2359 end of 12th age.

Daniel's 12:12 scripture: -<u>1271.4579</u> = (1260 + 30) b. years

= 774.778 Charlemagne attacks the Saxons' place of worship and imposes the christian religion upon our ancestors, known as the Saxons, short version for Isaac's sons of the House of Israel. He placed an image of his christian pagan christ upon the Altar of God, making this Altar of God desolate. He thereafter destroyed this place of worship, known today as the Stonehenge ruins, with the east entrance lining up with the summer solstice sunrise and the west entrance lining up with the winter solstice sunset. This east entrance according to Ezekiel 44:1-3 was used only by God and the King/Prince of the people. The west entrance was used by the Levi priestly family members, where outside was a hanging tree to string up the slaughtered animals and extracted the sacrificial parts of the animals that were to be sacrificed on their Altar of God, and the rest of the animal was cooked in the huge boiling pots located outside this west entrance, for the worshippers to eat. The north and south entrances were for the worshippers to enter and exit. The ones entering via the south entrance had to exit via the north entrance, and the ones entering via the north entrance had to exit via the south entrance, such as passing through. This is also reported in the book of Ezekiel. According to Daniel 8:14 this temple was originally made desolate by Antiochus on the 15th day and the 25th of the 9th month in the year -166.6046 to -166.632 and will be rebuilt and sanctified 2,300 biblical years in the future or 2266.9404 Gregorian years. Therefore, 2266.94 - (-166.6046) = 2100.3354 G. year. Therefore, the end of God's 30-biblical-year reclaiming war at 2046.2358 + Daniel's extra 45 b. yrs. or 44.353 G. yrs. = 2090.5888 G. year. Therefore, the survivors will be gathered up together and led back to the promised land and rebuild the temple and have it sanctified via the blood of a 3-year-old red heifer without spot and without a yoke placed upon her, in 2100.3358 - 2090.5888 = 9.747 Gregorian years. Therefore, subtracting 3.45 for David to gather up the remnant and lead them back to Jerusalem leaves David and the remnant 6.297 years to rebuild the temple and prepare to bring forth sacrifices to the Lord God.

Please be aware of the historical material of Charlemagne sitting on his horse, located at the end of the 2nd chapter and beginning of the 3rd chapter, indicates Charles could have attacked the Saxons' place of worship any time within years 772-775. These attacks by Charlemagne brought alive the countdown of Daniel's 12:11-12 scriptures. My enclosed calculations are now within the year 774.778. Please be aware that this King Saul/Saul called Paul/Charlemagne must show up as the last and next pope of this pagan christian religion 3.5 biblical years prior to God's 30-biblical-year reclaiming world war against the so-called Holy Roman Empire nations and allies. Therefore, we must subtract 33.5 b. years, or 33.02 G. years, off of 2046.2358 to determine when King Saul is due to show up as the next and last pope of the pagan Christian religion, that he in fact is the master builder of, which will be in 2046.2358 - 33.0188 = 2013.217, or Mar. 20th in year 2013, Jerusalem time zone. Therefore, critical time is running out for all the above to occur.

R.A. Mueller

# Chapter 1

# Who Are We as a People?

Gen. 48:5, *"And now thy two sons, Ephraim and Manasseh, which were born unto thee in the land of Egypt before I came unto thee into Egypt, are mine, as Reuben and Simeon, they shall be mine"*. This is Jacob speaking, whose name was changed to Israel as reported in Gen. 35:10. God said unto Jacob, *"Thy name is Jacob; thy name shall not be called any more Jacob, but Israel shall be thy name: and he called his name Israel"*.

In Gen. 48:5, you will notice that Israel adopted these two sons of Joseph as his own; being now the adoptive father and grandfather to them. Before Israel died, Joseph took the two boys to receive, as it turns out, the birthright blessings. Israel placed his right hand on the younger son Ephraim's head and his left hand on the older son Manasseh's head, even crossing his arms to accomplish this, for Joseph, as the custom was, brought Manasseh to the front of Israel's right side and Ephraim to the front of Israel's left side. Upon seeing this, Joseph voiced his objection.

Gen. 48:19-20, Israel stated, *"I know it, my son, I know it: he, Manasseh, also shall become a people, and he also shall be great: but truly his younger brother, Ephraim, shall be greater than he, and his, Ephraim', seed shall become a multitude of nations. And he blessed them that day, saying; in thee shall Israel bless, Saying, God make thee as Ephraim and as Manasseh: and he set Ephraim before Manasseh"*.

What really occurred here was that Ephraim was placed in the position to remove Reuben's status position as the firstborn son of Israel. Because first, although Reuben was responsible in saving Joseph's life from the hands of his brothers, by telling them to cast him into a deep pit for now and rethink about killing him. Reuben instead was hoping to return Joseph back to his father. However, Reuben committed a grievous abominable sin when he slept with Jacob's mistress, which according to God's laws carried the death penalty, but it wasn't implemented because he in fact saved Joseph's life from the hands of his brothers. Reuben received his life for the life he saved. But he, because of his unforgivable sin, lost his birthright status to Joseph's 2nd son, Ephraim; it was swapped with the blessings Ephraim would have received from Joseph. The crossing of Jacob's arms made Manasseh the 13th tribe.

As Moses states in <u>Deut. 33:6</u>, *"Let Reuben live, and not die; and let not his men be few"*. Simeon, because of his actions against Joseph, by going along with his younger brothers while Reuben was absent, sold Joseph to the caravan heading for Egypt, also lost his blessings to the tribes of Joseph.

Please note in <u>Gen. 48:19-20</u>, Israel made two separate nations out of Ephraim and Manasseh. Therefore, we have two great nations on this earth that look like brothers, and one being a multitude of nations, and the other being a single great nation, with the birthright blessings reported below.

<u>Gen. 49:22-26</u>, *"Joseph is a fruitful bough, even a fruitful bough by a well; whose branches run over the wall: The archers have sorely grieved him, and shot at him, and hated him: But his bow abode in strength, and the arms of his hands were made strong by the hands of the Mighty God of Jacob; (<u>from thence is the shepherd, the stone of Israel</u>): Even by the God of thy father, who shall help thee; and by the Almighty, who shall bless thee with blessings of heaven above, blessings of the deep that lies under, blessings of the breasts, and of the womb: The blessings of thy father have prevailed above the blessings of my progenitors unto the utmost bound of the everlasting hills: they shall be on the head of Joseph, and on the crown of the head of him that was separate from his brethren"*.

Also in <u>Deut. 33:13-17</u>, *"And of Joseph he* (Moses) *said, Blessed of the Lord God be his land, for the precious things of heaven, for the dew, and for the deep that couches beneath, and for the precious fruits brought forth by the sun, and for the precious things put forth by the moon, and for the chief things of the ancient mountains, and for the precious things of the lasting hills, and for the precious things of the earth and fullness thereof, and for the good will of him that dwelt in the bush: let the blessings come upon the head of him that was separated from his brethren. His glory is like the firstling of his bullock, and his horns are like the horns of unicorns: with them he shall push the people together to the ends of the earth: and they are the ten thousands of Ephraim, and they are the thousands of Manasseh"*.

Then we have the following blessings that Moses places on the Israelites as a whole; but the majority of these blessings of Moses pertain to the two sons of Joseph, for they have the name Israel put upon them by Jacob. It states as follows in <u>Deut. 33:26-29</u>, *"There is none like unto the God of Jeshurun* (Israelites), *who rides upon the heaven in Thy help, and in his Excellency on the sky. The eternal God is thy refuge, and underneath are everlasting arms: and he shall thrust out the enemy from before thee; and shall say destroy them. Israel then shall dwell in safety alone: the fountain of Jacob shall be upon a land of corn and wine; also his heavens shall drop down dew. Happy, art thou Oh Israel: who is like unto thee, O people saved by the Lord God, the shield of thy help, and who is the sword of thy excellency! And thine enemies shall be found liars unto thee; and thou shall tread upon their high places".*

These two tribes of Joseph are truly a blessed people indeed and are none other than the British Commonwealth of Nations, who are of Ephraim, and the United States of America, who is of Manasseh, and the rest of the tribes of the House of Israel are located in the northwestern corner of Europe, from France, who is Reuben, to Switzerland, Belgium, Denmark, Netherlands, Norway, Sweden, Finland, Iceland, Greenland, Wales, Scotland, Ireland, and whatsoever other lands throughout this world that they have possession of. All these nations are considered relatively wealthy nations, and peoples of the same mindset. All the nations mentioned above are Israelites of the House of Israel. One must not forget that the tribes of Judah and Benjamin are of the House of Judah; the Jewish peoples are also included in their own blessings from God within this 33rd chapter of Deuteronomy and are also included in the above Deut. 33:26-29 blessings. One set of scriptures, along with known historical events, which I have included with this writing, that truly prove that the British Commonwealth of Nations are Ephraim, the United States of America is Manasseh, and Reuben is the French peoples.

Beginning at the predicted punishments due to our ancestors reported in Lev. 26:27-39, *"And if ye will not for all this* (the punishments received from God reported in scriptures of Lev. 26:14-17, 18-20, 21-22, 24-26) *hearken unto me, but walk contrary unto me; Then I will walk contrary unto you also in fury; and I, even I, will chastise you seven times for your sins. And ye shall eat the flesh of your sons, and the flesh of your daughters shall ye eat. And I will destroy your high places, and cut down your images, and cast your carcasses upon the carcasses of your idols, and my soul shall abhor you. And I will make your cities waste, and bring your sanctuaries unto desolation, and I will not smell the savour of your sweet odours. And I will bring the land into desolation: and your enemies which dwell therein shall be astonished at it. And I will scatter you among the heathen, and will draw out a sword after you: and your land shall be desolate, and your cities waste. Then shall the land enjoy her Sabbaths, as long as it lies desolate, and ye be in your enemies' land; even then shall the land rest, and enjoy her Sabbaths. As long as it lies desolate it shall rest; because it did not rest in your Sabbaths, when ye dwelt upon it. And upon them that are left alive of you I will send a faintness into their hearts in the lands of their enemies; and the sound of a shaken leaf shall chase them; and they shall flee, as fleeing from a sword; and they shall fall when none pursues. And they shall fall one upon another, as it were before a sword, when none pursues: and ye shall have no power to stand before your enemies. And ye shall perish among the heathen, and the land of your enemies shall eat you up. And they that are left of you shall pine away in their iniquity in your enemies' lands; and also in the iniquities of their fathers shall they pine away with them".*

Please read the above punishments again and consider what our ancestors went through before they smartened up and realized that when God speaks to them through his servants, and warn them of desolation that will come upon them if they continue in their wicked ways; that God, without any reservations, will bring it to pass as he stated. And we today are as wicked, even more wicked as our ancient ancestors, and will witness first-hand of the desolation God intends to bring upon his people again in the very near future, with the coming world war III, beginning 2016 (.667 yrs) * 366 = Aug. 31st cue., Jerusalem time zone (refer to chapter 8 for precise detail calculations), and described in following scripture:

Jer. 30:7, *"Alas! For that day is great, so that none is like it: it is even the time of Jacob's trouble; but he shall be saved out of it"*.

Only a remnant shall be saved, not the ones who continue to chase after the paganism babylonian christian religion, with all her pagan gods, from their pagan christ, the foundation of this christian religion that Saul/Paul brought forth, and all her other pagan gods—such as the virgin mother, all their canonized saints, with all their images erected throughout their places of worship, even throughout their homes, and even upon their person, with the graven image of a cross with their pagan christ nailed to it and a graven image of some canonized saint on a chain around their neck. We have totally been deceived by this christian religion, and other philosophies, that they have attached themselves and their lives unto. Where all they have to do is study and observe all the ways of the Old Testament and related books written by noted prophets of God, such as also that are in the Apocrypha books.

In the above Lev. 26 chapter in verses 28-35, where God states that he will chastise our ancestors seven times for their sins and will cause the enemy to totally defeat them, and even take the remnants/survivors into the enemies land. In this time period they would lose their freedom and would be slaves to their enemies, the Assyrians/Germans; they in time would lose their language, their culture, and their identity, to the extent they will even be oblivious of who they really are.

God states in Deut. 32:26, *"I said, I would scatter them into corners, I would make the remembrance of them to cease from among men"*.

They also lost their birthright blessings for this time period of seven times. One time is equal to a 360-day year; therefore, the total time period involved is 360 * 7 = 2520 days, but this time period has a scenario of each day representing one biblical year. Therefore, total time period is equal to 2,520 biblical years, or (2520 * 360)/365.25 = 2484 of our calendar years. When the Assyrians defeated the House of Israel, there were two major captivities. The first captivity, called the Galilee Captivity, which occurred in 734 b. cue., and which involved the northern tribes and the tribes east of the river

Jordan, which were the half tribe of Manasseh, the tribe of Gad and the tribe of Reuben; therefore, in 2484 - 734 = 1750 cue., the half tribe of Manasseh was in firm control of developing that single great nation that Jacob predicted he will become, with the developing of the 13 British colonies, along the east coast of the North Americas; and France, who are the Reubenites, were also in firm control of most of the developed lands throughout North America, except for the area Manasseh, of the tribe of Joseph, were in control of. Reuben was at this time, unknown to them or anyone else, was going after the firstborn birthright blessings.

However, in 721 b. cue., a second captivity occurred, called the Samaria Captivity, involving the other half tribe of Manasseh and the tribe of Ephraim. Therefore, in 2484 - 721 = 1763 cue., the British, who consisted of both tribes of Joseph, began in 1750 scrimmaging with France over the developed lands in North America, north of the border, known today as Mexico, which culminated in a 7-year war, beginning in 1755 and ending in 1763, when France signed all her occupied developed lands within this North America land mass over to the British. These lands included Canada and the entire region east of the Mississippi, and France also signed over to the British several islands of the West Indies; the British on a separate deal with Spain received Florida in exchange for Havana and Manila, which the British had captured.

In effect, Reuben lost his birthright blessings to Ephraim, just as Jacob predicted Ephraim was entitled to receive these blessings. This all happened precisely 7 times after they were taken captive by the Assyrians, and to make this more amazing, we had absolutely no idea what and why this was happening as it did, or who we actually were as a people. God was bringing all this about on his own timetable. To top this off, when Jacob/Israel put Ephraim ahead of Manasseh and made two separated tribes/peoples out of them, Manasseh became the 13th tribe of Israel. What makes this so significant is that 13 years after Ephraim won his firstborn birthright blessings from Reuben, Manasseh on July 4, 1776, declared that *"These united colonies are, and of right ought to be, free and independent states".*

This number 13 resonates throughout the history of the United States of America. Such as they started with the 13 British colonies. On the front of the American's seal, there is an eagle with 13 arrows in its left claw, which symbolizes military strength; and in its right claw, an olive branch with 13 leaves and 13 berries, symbolizing a peaceful nation. Over the head of the eagle is a ring of puffy clouds, circled around a cluster of 13 stars meshed together, which symbolizes, believe it or not, the protective cloud God surrounded their ancestors with upon leading them through the desert during the daylight hours, upon redeeming them from Egypt, and in the evening hours, by a column of fire to light up their journey; perhaps this is the message behind the liberty torch. Also in the eagle's mouth, there is a ribbon or banner held in the eagle's beak, with the Latin motto "E Pluribus Unum" ("One out of many")—or one can say, "One out of many Israelite tribes," 13 to be exact. On the chest of the eagle is somewhat of a flag with 13 stripes, which carries over to the modern flag, which still has the 13 stripes. On the back of the United States seal, there is an Egyptian monument, the Great Pyramid with the all-seeing God's eye as its capstone. On the back of the British seal is also an Egyptian monument, the Sphinx; these two monuments represent their Egyptian heritage via their mother, who was the daughter of an Egyptian high priest, that was given to Joseph for his wife by the pharaoh of Egypt. The modern Egyptians are our wandering Gypsies, who also were scattered throughout the world, when God gave their land to the Babylonians in payment for carrying out God's punishment over the House of Judah, because of their wicked ways. Perhaps via the Gypsies' bloodline is where the Americans and the British peoples get their theatrical and musical skills from and their desire to travel around in their camping-out trailers and tents. One has to accept the fact that the 2 tribes of Joseph are indeed an exceptionally talented, skilled, and blessed people. If only they would have directed their exceptional talents, skills, and blessings according to the ways of the Lord our one God; this would have been a different world altogether. A world the majority of us will not experience in our lifetime.

The word 'British' is a combination of two Hebrew words; 'Brit or Briyth' is covenant, and 'ish' is man or people. In other words, the British are the leaders of the covenant people of the House of Israel, and the United States of America, who began with the 13 British (covenant people's) colonies are Manasseh, the brother to Ephraim, who are the British, the recipient of the firstborn status. The title 'Anglo Saxons' means English-speaking sons of Isaac, the word 'Saxons' being a short version of 'Isaac's sons (or sons of Isaac)'. The front of the British seal has a lion and a unicorn reared up on their hind legs, over a throne, with a king's crown between their heads; this unicorn is mentioned in the blessings pertaining to the tribes of Joseph in Deut. 33:17, where it states, *"His glory is like the firstling of his bullock; and his horns are like the horns of unicorns: with them he shall push the people together to the ends of the earth: and they are the ten thousands of Ephraim, and they are the thousands of Manasseh"*.

The British has indeed pushed their peoples to the ends of the world, beginning when the two tribes of Joseph who were together in the British Isles came to discover and settle in the North American lands, then single-handedly spread throughout the rest of the world, bringing about its Commonwealth of Nations, which took a tremendous amount of strength and courage for just one small nation to accomplish. There is absolutely no doubt that God's great hand was fully involved in bringing this about. The lion and the throne, plus the crown, represents the throne of King David, of the tribe of Judah. This throne—with the Stone of Destiny, Lia Fail—and the crown, along with King Zedekiah's daughter that Jeremiah transplanted, from Jerusalem to Northern Ireland, was the first overturning of this throne. The second overturning was to Scotland, and the third overturning was to England; this throne will continue in England until the rightful owner of this throne, God's holy anointed one, King David, will again take possession and return it back to the city of Jerusalem.

This overturning is reported in <u>Ezek. 21:25-27,</u> *"And thou, profane wicked prince of Israel* (Zedekiah), *whose day is come, when iniquity shall have an end; Thus saith the Lord God; Remove the diadem, and take off the crown: this shall not be the same: exalt him that is low, and abase him that is high. I will overturn, overturn, overturn, it: and it shall be no more* (overturned), *until he come whose right it is; and I will give it him".*

Lia Fail, the Stone of Destiny, is the same stone that all the kings of Judah stood beside when they were anointed with oil and declared king. This same stone is the stone Jacob used as a pillow on his way to his mother's brother Laban's place—to avoid the possible wrath of his brother Esau, for allegedly stealing his firstborn birthright blessings—where he dreamt a dream and saw a vision of a stairway to heaven, with angels ascending to heaven and descending from heaven, where God talked to him from the top of the stairs, saying:

<u>Gen. 28:13-15,</u> *"I am the Lord God of Abraham thy father, and the God of Isaac: the land whereon thou liest, to thee will I give it, and to thy seed; And thy seed shall be as the dust of the earth, and thou shalt spread abroad to the west, and to the east, and to the north, and to the south: and in thee and in thy seed shall all the families of the earth be blessed. And, behold, I am with thee, and will keep thee in all places whither thou goest, and will bring thee again into this land; for I will not leave thee, until I have done that which I have spoken to thee of".*

Jacob thereafter erected this stone up as a pillar, anointed it with oil, and called the place Bethel. This stone is located in London's Westminster Abbey, cradled at the bottom of the coronation chair. A peculiar coincidence is that Hebrew reads right to left, while English reads left to right; in reading this name either way, it still reads Lia Fail. The above significant scripture is definitely speaking about us Israelites of today, for we are literally spread all around the world, in all directions, without us even knowing who we are as a people, and who are so defiantly faithless towards their one and only living God, that they are chasing after every false god that they come in contact with and breaking all of God's commandments, God's statutes, God's laws,

God's true judgements, and definitely God's holy Sabbath day, the same day the House of Judah observes. They have lost the knowledge of why they were even born, and believe that everything that comes about is of their own making, being completely ignorant of the power of their one God.

God states in <u>Deut. 32:26-29,</u> *"I said, I would scatter them into corners, I would make the remembrance of them to cease from among men: Were it not that I feared the wrath of the enemy, lest their adversaries should behave themselves strangely, and lest they* (us Israelites) *should say, Our hand is high, and the Lord God has not done all this. For they are nations void of counsel, neither is there any understanding in them. O that they were wise, that they understood this, that they would consider their latter end"!*

The latter devastating end will be upon us, much sooner than we can imagine, beginning in Aug. 31st in year 2016 cue., Jerusalem time zone. We as a people still don't know who we are as a people. How sad to know that we have gone through our entire life not realizing we were of the seed of Jacob/Israel; and we have chased after every pagan god and belief known to mankind, except the one and only true living God of this entire universe, the Lord God of Abraham, Isaac, and Jacob/Israel, our ancient ancestors, who are called the friends of our one God.

There are numerous directional scriptures indicating where they settled; and there are numerous names used in the Bible that interrelate to the House of Israel or the Houses of Joseph, such as their adopted name Israel and such as Joseph, Rachel (mother of Joseph), Samaria (capital city of the House of Israel, situated in the area occupied by Manasseh), their given names Ephraim and Manasseh. The name Jacob usually can be referred to the other remaining tribes of the House of Israel with or without the two tribes of the House of Judah, or even sometimes referring to all 13 tribes together.

<u>Hosea 12:1</u> states, *"Ephraim feedeth on wind, and <u>follows after the east wind".</u>* An east wind blows west. Ephraim must have gone west from the Assyrian nation (Germanized nations).

<u>Ps. 89:25,</u> God states, *"I will set his hand also <u>in the sea".</u>* God has set David's throne <u>in the sea</u> when he transplanted it.

<u>Jer. 3:11-12,</u> God speaking to Jeremiah, *"The backsliding Israel has justified herself more than treacherous Judah. Go and proclaim these words <u>towards the north,</u> and say, return thou backsliding Israel".*

Here Israel is clearly distinguished from Judah. Of course Israel was north of Judah while still in Palestine, but when these words were written by Jeremiah, Israel had been removed from their original location approximately 130 years and had long since migrated north and west of Assyria's original location. In <u>verse 18,</u> in the last days, when the House of Judah will be living amongst the Houses of Israel, as many of them are today, states that *"They* shall come together <u>out of the land of the north</u> to the land I have given for an inheritance unto your fathers". <u>Hosea 11:8 and 10,</u> after saying, *"How shall I give thee up, Ephraim?"* God speaking through Hosea says, *"Then the children shall tremble <u>from the west".</u>*

<u>Jer. 30-31</u> chapters are for consideration in the latter days; <u>verse 31:8</u> states, *"Behold, I will bring them from the north country, and gather them from the coasts of the earth".* Verses <u>2, 4, 9</u> are addressed to Israel; <u>verses 6, 9,</u> to Ephraim; <u>verse 5,</u> to Samaria. <u>Isa. 49:3, 6,12,</u> God referring to the House of Israel, not Judah, saying, *"Behold these <u>shall come from far:</u> and lo, these <u>from the north and from the west;</u> and these <u>from the land of Sinim".</u>* There was no word for 'northwest' in the old Hebrew language, and it is stated as 'north and west.' The Hebrew concordance indicates Sinim to be a distant oriental region. The Vulgate renders Sinim as the Australia and New Zealand area, along with their satellite islands. The same <u>Isa. 49th chapter</u> begins with, *"Listen, O Isles, unto me".* The peoples addressed Israel are called 'O Isles' in the 1st verse and 'O Israel' in the 3rd verse. This can be translated 'coastlands'.

<u>Jer. 31:9-10,</u> locating Israel in the North Country, says, *"I am a father to Israel, and Ephraim is my firstborn. Here the word of the Lord God, O ye nations, and declare it in the <u>Isles afar off".</u> And to be shouted it in <u>"the chief of the nations".</u>*

So finally, today, as in the days of Jeremiah, the House of Israel is in the Isles, which are in the sea, the chief of the nations, northwest of Jerusalem, a coast-dwelling and sea-dominant peoples! Lay a straight line northwest of Jerusalem, across Europe, until you come to the sea, and then to the islands in the sea are the British Isles! This is the home of David's throne and home of Ephraim, Jacob's designated 1st born, and predicted group of nations, and the starting point of Manasseh, Joseph's 1st born and Jacob's predicted single great nation. These are the two tribes of Joseph, the leaders of the rest of the tribes of the House of Israel who are situated at the present time of history in the northwestern corner of Europe, from France, who is Reuben, to Switzerland, Belgium, Netherlands, Denmark, Sweden, Finland, Norway, Iceland, Greenland, and all the nations on the British Isles—such as Scotland, Wales, Ireland, and of course Great Britain with all her peoples scattered around this world throughout her Commonwealth of Nations. And with these the USA *(Manasseh).*

## To what extent have we strayed from the true ways of God?

God states in <u>Jer. 18:5-10,</u> *"O house of Israel, cannot I do with you as this potter? Behold, as the clay is in the potter's hand, so are ye in my hands, O House of Israel.*

*At what instant I shall speak concerning a nation* (the United States of America, or any of the Northwestern European Israelite nations), *and a Kingdom* (the British Empire Kingdom), *to build and to plant it;*

*If it do evil in my sight, that it obey not my voice, then I will repent of the good, wherewith I said I would benefit them"*.

How many terrible disasters must the Lord our one God bring upon our nations and our kingdom, before we come to the realization that God is in total control of whatsoever comes upon our peoples?

Therefore, take heed to listen and obey the voice of the Lord our one God, and keep holy his Sabbaths on the proper day of the week, and on the proper time of day; and all of God's holy yearly events, the same ones the House of Judah observe and keep, <u>minus</u> the drinking of the blood/wine and eating the body/bread ritual, that the House of Judah has also been snared into doing, which is absolutely contrary to the ways of God. For within this cup is the wrath of God.

Read the following scriptures below, where God via Ezekiel is speaking to the House of Judah, and stating that he will cause them to also drink from this abominable wine cup in <u>Ezek. 23:31-34,</u> *"Thou has walked in the way of thy sister; therefore will I give her cup into thine hand. Thus says the Lord God; Thou shall drink of thy sister's cup deep and large: thou shall be laughed to scorn and had in derision; it contains much. Thou shall be filled with drunkenness and sorrow, with the cup of astonishment and desolation, with the cup of thy sister Samaria. Thou shall even drink it and suck it out, and thou shall break the sherds thereof, and <u>pluck off thine own breasts:</u> for I have spoken it, says the Lord God"*.

How many of our young, out-of-control women have removed their own breasts and replaced them with false ones? These young, out-of-control women have been affected by this above scripture and are probably descendants of the House of Judah, that are living amongst the Israelites of the House of Israel.

Therefore, we must return to the ways of God, which are the ways of the Old Testament, and flee as quickly as we can from the christian paganism babylonian religion that Saul/Paul/King Saul, the devil's 1st born son, brought about to lead us astray, to eventually join him in the dark abyss he will occupy with his master Satan.

It makes absolutely no difference what position you have acquired in your lifetime here on earth, or the wealth acquired, or the lack thereof; what truly matters is how you have conducted your life according to the ways of the Lord our one and only God of Israel, the ways that he has instructed us via the books of Moses, written down in the Old Testament for us to read and study. It is never too late to return to the true ways of our one and only true living Lord God. This is one of the reasons I have written this book, as well as giving you advanced knowledge of the disastrous position we find ourselves in, and an early warning of what is about to occur in the very near future. Perhaps some of you are in a position to prepare the nations you represent, for the coming disastrous events that shall, for certain, come against us Israelites, who are at the present time scattered throughout their many countries in all the corners of this planet. Please do not take this warning with a grain of salt. Read this book very thoroughly and consider its content, for your future and the future of your loved ones and the future of your subjects are now in your hands.

King David, God's true Messiah (not Saul/Paul's pagan christ), states in Psalms 16:4, *"Their sorrows shall be multiplied that hasten after another god* (christians' christ): *their drink offerings of blood* (and obviously the eating of the ritual bread/body) *will I* (David) *not offer, nor take their names into my lips"*.

David was very aware that the consumption of any blood whatsoever is contrary to God's laws; and stated as such in Lev. 3:17, *"It shall be a perpetual statute for your generations throughout all your dwellings, that ye eat neither fat nor blood"*.

You don't have to be a rocket scientist to understand the significant importance of this statute, as Lev. 17:10-16 states, *"Whatsoever person there be of the house of Israel, or of the strangers that sojourn among you, that eats any manner of blood; I will even set my face against that person that eats blood, and will cut him off from among his people. For the life of the flesh is in the blood: and I have given it to you upon the altar to make an atonement for your souls: for it is the blood that makes an atonement for your soul. Therefore I said unto the children of Israel, No person of you shall eat blood, neither shall any stranger that sojourn among you eat blood. And whatsoever man there be of the children of Israel, or of the strangers that sojourn among you, which hunts and catches any beast or fowl that may be eaten* (classified clean beasts or fowl); *he shall even pour out the blood thereof, and cover it with dust. For it is the life of the flesh; the blood of it is for the life thereof: whosoever eats it shall be cut off. And every person that eats that which died of itself, or that which was torn with beasts, whether it be one of your own country, or a stranger, he shall both wash his clothes, and bathe himself in water, and be unclean until the evening: then shall he be clean. But if he wash not, nor bathe his flesh; then he shall bear his iniquity"*.

In other words, whatsoever diseases that are within the flesh is within the blood and the fat; putting anyone that eats meat with the blood residue within it and the fat trimmings in and upon it, at risk of contracting whatsoever diseases that may be within this meat, in some future time. Even via a blood transfusion, that has been screened by our, know it all scientists, with all their sophisticated equipment. Instead of curing the sick, we are indeed spreading all sorts of various diseases throughout the population and are then left trying to control all these diseases with scores of powerful devastating drugs that play havoc with the body and mind. Where do you think all these birth deformities are coming from? This is what we get for trying to play God. Wake up, people! You have been deceived. Are we that naive to trust our medical establishment, bringing about a so-called cure which requires us to break God's all important blood and fat laws? The answer is yes, and the results are all around us, with the population displaying the devastating, ugly, crippling, deadly diseases. We keep asking ourselves, Why? Not only are we eating the blood and the fat of the flesh, but we are also consuming classified unclean animals, fowls, sea creatures, and insects; animals, fowl, sea creatures, and insects, that we are not even to touch their dead carcasses. Why? Why? We stare at one another in amazement. Wake up, people! Study the statutes and laws of God Almighty, <u>that are good for us,</u> and <u>whereby we ought to live in,</u> which are written in the books of Moses. And at the same time study God's great commandments, which we are blatantly demolishing continuously, and study God's great judgements of how to run a great nation and its people, of which we haven't got a clue in doing. Refer to chapter 4 for precise information.

We are at the present time following <u>Ezek. 20:24-26</u>, where God states, *"Because they* (our ancient Israelite ancestors) *had not executed My Judgments, but had despised My Statutes, and had polluted My Sabbaths, and their eyes were after their father's idols. Wherefore I gave them <u>also</u> statutes that were <u>not</u> good, and judgments whereby they should <u>not</u> live; And I polluted them in their own gifts* (christmas, easter, saint day events, gifts and goodies; even the helloween gifts and goodies), *in that they caused to pass through the fire all that opens the womb* (unwanted firstborn via abortions, etc.), *that I might make them desolate, to the end that they might know* (come to realize) *that I am the Lord their Only God"*.

God will bring everyone that refuses to conform to his ways, to total desolation. Our educational system omitted the teachings to us of the true ways of God, and we so-called highly educated society have wasted our lives in total falsehood, in things that mean absolutely nothing. Thanks to our christian religious leaders, <u>the wolves in sheep's clothing,</u> devouring our spirits/minds with all their falsehood and evil ways.

The following scriptures are illustrating what the unbelievers, who refuse to conform to God and his ways, the ways of the Old Testament, will have to endure for their stubborn and rebellious ways:

<u>Isa. 8:21-22,</u> *"And they shall pass through it* (coming world war III, and the follow up of Daniel's extra 45 biblical years), *hardly bestead and hungry: and it shall come to pass, that when they shall be hungry, they shall fret themselves, and curse their king and their God, and look upward. And they shall look unto the earth;*

*and behold trouble and darkness, dimness of anguish; and they shall be driven to darkness".*

Pro. 1:24-32, *"Because I have called, and ye refused; I have stretched out my hand, and no man regarded; But ye have set at naught all my counsel, and would none of my reproof: I also will laugh at your calamity; I will mock when your fear cometh; When your fear cometh as desolation, and your destruction cometh as a whirlwind; when distress and anguish cometh upon you.*

*Then shall they call upon me, but I will not answer; they shall seek me early, but they shall not find me: For that they hated knowledge, and did not choose the fear of the Lord God: They would none of my counsel: they despised all my reproof. Therefore shall they eat of the fruit of their own way, and be filled with their own devices. For the turning away of the simple shall slay them, and the prosperity of fools shall destroy them".*

Deut. 32:15-38, *"But Jeshurun* (Israelites) *waxed fat, and kicked: thou art waxen fat, thou art grown thick, thou art covered with fatness; then he forsook God which made him, and lightly esteemed the Rock* (God) *of his salvation. They provoked him to jealousy with strange gods* (christian pagan gods)*, with abominations provoked they him to anger. They sacrificed unto devils, not to God; to gods whom they knew not, to new gods that came newly up, whom your fathers feared not. Of the Rock* (Lord God) *that begat thee thou art unmindful, and hast forgotten God that formed thee. And when the Lord God saw it, he abhorred them, because of the provoking of his sons, and of his daughters. And he said, I will hide my face from them, I will see what their end shall be: for they are a very forward generation, children in whom is no faith. They have moved me to jealousy with that which is not God; they have provoked me to anger with their vanities: and I will move them to jealousy with those which are not a people* (terrorists); *I will provoke them to anger with a foolish nation* (Iraq, Iran, North Korea, Syria, etc.)*. For a fire is kindled in mine anger, and shall burn unto the lowest hell, and shall consume the earth with her increase, and set on fire the foundations of the mountains. I will heap mischiefs upon them. They shall be burnt with hunger, and devoured with burning heat, and with bitter destruction: I will also send the teeth of beasts upon them, with the poison of serpents of the dust. The sword outside, and terror within, shall destroy both the young man and the virgin, the suckling also with the man of gray hairs. I said, I would scatter them into corners, I would make the remembrance of them to cease from among men* (today we don't even know who we are as a people): *Were it not that I feared the wrath of the enemy, lest their adversaries should behave themselves strangely, and lest they* (us modern day Israelites, of the remnant, of House of Israel, the 10 lost tribes) *should say, Our hand is high, and the Lord God has not done all this. For they are nations void of counsel, neither is there any understanding in them. O that they were wise, that they understood this, that they would consider their latter end! How should one chase a thousand,*

*and two put ten thousand to flight, except their rock* (God) *had sold them, and the Lord God had shut them up? For their rock* (pagan christ/god) *is not as our Rock* (Lord God), *even our enemies themselves being judges. For their vine is of the vine of Sodom, and of the fields of Gomorrah: their grapes are grapes of gall, their clusters are bitter: Their wine is the poison of dragons, and the cruel venom of asps. Is not this laid up in store with me, and sealed up among my treasures? To me belongeth vengeance, and recompense; their* (our) *foot shall slide in due time: for the day of their calamity is at hand, and the things that shall come upon them make haste* (beginning Aug. 31st, 2016. *For the Lord God shall judge his people, and repent himself for his servants, when he sees that their power is gone, and there is none shut up or left. And He* (God) *shall say, where are their gods, their rock* (pagan christ/god, including their canonized so-called saints) *in whom they trusted, which did eat the fat of their sacrifices, and drank the wine of their drink offerings? Let them rise up and help you, and be your protection".*

Then God tells us in verse 39, *"See now that I, even I, am he, and there is no god with me: I kill, and I make alive; I wound, and I heal: neither is there any that can deliver out of my hand".*

The christians are all relying on their pagan christ that Saul/Paul brought about, and all their so-called canonized saints, that they pray to, serve, and worship, as if they have the power, as a true God, to save them, which will be in vain:

Amos 8:18-20 states, *"Woe unto you that desire the day of the Lord God! To what end is it for you? The day of the Lord is darkness, and not light. As if a man did flee from a lion, and a bear met him; or went into the house, and leaned his hand on the wall, and a serpent bit him. Shall not the day of the Lord be darkness, and not light? Even very dark, and no brightness in it?"*

This is the coming world war III, beginning Aug. 31st of 2016 cue. and ending 2046.2358 Mar. 27th, Jerusalem time zone. (Refer to chapter 8 for complete calculations.)

For we are told in Jer. 51:6-7, *"Flee out of the midst of Babylon* (confused christian religion), *and deliver every man his soul; be not cut off in her iniquity; for this is the time* (end-time world war III, beginning in our year of 2016.667 on Aug. 31st cue., the beginning of God's 30-biblical-year reclaiming period of us Israelites that take this warning, and flee from this paganism babylonian christian religion, or any other non-Old Testament beliefs, before it is to late) *of the Lord God's vengeance; he will render unto her a recompense. Babylon has been a golden cup in the Lord God's hand that made all the earth drunken: the nations have drunken of her wine; therefore the nations are mad* (upon their pagan idols)*".*

This wine cup is the same wine cup that all the christian organizations throughout this world are using in their ritual, called communion, drinking the blood/wine of their pagan christ and eating the body/bread of this same pagan christ, which this pagan christ demands his followers to perform.

This is also the same wine cup that God gave to Jeremiah in 25:15-17, *"For thus saith the Lord God unto me; Take the wine cup of this fury at my hand, and cause all the nations, to whom I send thee, to drink it. And they shall drink, and be moved, and be mad, because of the sword that I will send among them. Then took I the cup at the Lord God's hand, and made all the nations to drink unto whom the Lord God had sent me".*

This so-called christ is none other than King Saul himself. Refer to 2 Esdras 2:42-46 where it states, *"I, Ezra, saw on Mount Zion a crowd too large to count, all singing hymns of praise to the Lord. In the middle stood a very tall young man, taller than all the rest, who was setting a crown on the head of each one of them; he stood out above them all. I was enthralled at the site, and asked the angel, 'Sir, who are these?' He replied, 'They are those who have laid aside their mortal dress and put on the immortal, those who acknowledged the name of God. Now they are being given crowns and palms'."* In verse 47 he is told, *this tall young man is the Son of God.* Yet we have in 2 Esdras 2:10-14, where it states, *God has rejected Israel as a people and shall give the land of Israel to another people from the east.* Also in 2 Esdras 1:24 it states, *"What am I to do with you, Jacob? Judah, you have refused to obey me. I will turn to others nations; I will give them my name, and they will keep my statutes".*

It definitely appears to me as if these above scriptures are added to this book of Ezra. There is absolutely no way God will break his promises he made with our fore-fathers, and choose Gentile or Heathen nations instead. This tall young man is none other than King Saul with the evil spirit still upon him, masquerading as the real Son of God, this is that chief anti-Messiah at work again, who John refers to in 1 John 2:18, that must come at the end. These 1st two chapters of Esdras have been altered or even added to this book.

The real Messiah of God makes his appearance in the 13th chapter of this same book, where it states, 2 Esdras 13:40, *"Then you, Ezra, saw him collecting a different company, a peaceful one. They are the ten tribes* (the remnant of the House of Israel) *which were taken off into exile in the time of King Hosea, whom Shalmaneser, king of Assyria took prisoner. He deported them beyond the river, and they were taken away into a strange country. But then they resolved to leave the country populated by the Gentiles and go to a distant land never yet inhabited by man, and there at last to be obedient to their laws, which in their own country they failed to keep".*

This land is where they lived and were known as the tribes of Saxons. The same lands where Charlemagne/King Saul set upon their Altar of God, an image of himself as the christians' pagan christ, and thereafter destroyed their place of worship, bringing Daniel's 7:20, 7:25, 12:7 and 12:11 alive, as well as Ezekiel 20:24-26 and Rev. 12:17, where we received the statutes and judgements that are not good for us and whereby we should not live. This false christian babylonian religion was brought about with God's approval via the hands of Saul Paul/King Saul in the New Testament times; because us Israelites were so intent in following falsehood, that God basically stated that he will give to us exactly what we wanted, to teach us a lesson we will never forget, and bring us to total desolation.

This is reported in Ezek. 20:24-26, *"Because they* (our ancestors) *had not executed my Judgments, but had despised my Statutes, and had polluted my Sabbaths, and their eyes were after their father's idols. Wherefore I gave them also statutes that were not good* (via the christians' so-called holy events) *and judgments* (via our inept justice system), *whereby they should not live; And I polluted them in their own gifts* (christmas, easter, saint day events, even the helloween, gifts and goodies), *in that they caused to pass through the fire all that opens the womb* (aborted firstborn), *that I might make them desolate, to the end that they might know* (or realize) *that I am the Lord their God".*

With the use of the word also in this above set of scriptures, it's telling us that God never took away the statutes and judgments and his holy Sabbath days from us, for they are still available to us in the books of Moses, and throughout the rest of the books of the Old Testament, and even in the books of the Apocrypha; if only we would flee from this falsehood, and observe and keep only God's statutes and judgments, which are good for us and whereby we should live in. God left this choice up to us, to continue in our destructive ways and receive eternal death and the hell fires, or flee from this destructive path and return to his true ways, and gain eternal life with him and his Holy Messiah, King David, as reported below.

Ezek. 37:24-25, *"And David my servant shall be king over them; and they all shall have one shepherd: they shall also walk in my Judgments, and observe my Statutes, and do them. And they shall dwell in the land that I have given unto Jacob my servant, wherein your fathers have dwelt; and they shall dwell therein, even they, and their children, and their children's children forever: and my servant David shall be their prince forever".*

Therefore, the answer to the title of this chapter, "Who are we as a people" is quite evident that we are the descendants of the ancient Israelites of the House of Israel, that God gave to us via Ezek. 20:24-26, and Dan. 7:25, statutes and judgments that are not good for us, and whereby we ought not to live in, and a different Sabbath day of the week, and different time of the day, all contrary to the ways of God; as it is stated in Dan. 7:25, where the little horn thinks to change times and laws of God; this horn is none other than King Saul, with the evil spirit still upon him, which makes him associated with the devil.

God states in <u>Deut. 32:26,</u> *"I said, I would scatter them into corners, I would make the remembrance of them to cease from among men"*.

Even though it appears God has completely rejected us as a people; he has indeed blessed us beyond any other peoples on this earth, with all the birthright blessings given to us via Jacob's and Moses's predictions of <u>Gen. 49th and Deut. 33rd</u> chapters. But all the punishments that we receive in our lifetime are of our own makings, for as you should realize by now, that we are living our lives contrary to the ways of God and, in doing so, will be subject to the curses that follow. If you eat the blood and fat of the animals, and consume unclean animals, of which we are not even to touch their dead carcasses, sooner or later, the adverse effects will be evident upon your health, or upon your children, such as birth defects, etc. Or if you continue chasing after false gods, and completely ignore the true God of Israel, and/or put these false gods ahead of the true God, such as praying to God for whatsoever, but ask it of God in the name of Saul/Paul's pagan christ/another god, which is the same as giving this false god power over the true God. This prayer of yours would be using God's name in vain, which is breaking God's 3rd commandment.

This is the same action Saul/Paul brings about in his legitimizing scripture in <u>Acts 13:35,</u> *"Wherefore he (God) said also in another Psalm* (to Saul/Paul's christ), *Thou shalt not suffer thine Holy One to see corruption"*.

Here Saul/Paul has God speaking to Saul/Paul's christ, which gives Saul/Paul's pagan christ power <u>over</u> God, for it would be up to Saul/Paul's christ whether God would be subject to the corrupting powers of the grave, for God would be referring to himself as "thine Holy One". This scripture in taken from <u>Ps. 16:10,</u> where it is David speaking to God, not the other way around, and David states, *"For thou wilt not leave my soul in hell; neither wilt thou suffer thine Holy One to see corruption"*. Here David is referring to himself as "thine Holy One", which is giving the power to God, whether David would see the corrupting powers of the grave. You will also notice that Saul/Paul doesn't use the first part of this scripture, which eliminates the first person pronoun "my", indicating David, who wrote this Psalm, is referring to himself. Saul/Paul also omits to even tell his audience which Psalm he was referring to; he just states, *"In another Psalm"*, knowing full well what they would have discovered by checking up on him, or perhaps they would have been just as blind as we are today and allowed to be deceived as we have become.

Therefore, if you want to receive God's total blessings, you must worship him only, serve him only, pray to him only, and live your life according to his ways only. There is no ins, ands, or buts, about it. This is God's direct commandments to his people. Read the first three commandments, and then consider what Deut. 32:39 is relating to you when God states, *"There is no God with me"*. What part of no, don't you understand?

Isa. 42:17 states, *"They shall be turned back, they shall be greatly ashamed, that trust in graven images, that say to the molten images, Ye are our gods"*. The christian religion is loaded with graven images of all their many canonized saints, virgin mother, lady Fatima, and of course their pagan imaginary christ/another god.

Isa. 43:10-11 states, *"Ye are my witnesses, saith the Lord God, and my servant* (David) *whom I have chosen: that ye may know and believe me, and understand that I am he: before me there was no God formed, neither shall there be after me. I, even I, am the Lord God; and beside me there is no saviour"*.

David even states in Ps. 2:8, *"Salvation belongeth unto the Lord God: thy blessing is upon thy people"*.

God's people are the ones who observe and keep his ways—such as his weekly holy Sabbath day, not on the 1st day of the week, Sunday, but the 7th day of the week, Friday, just before sunset, to Saturday just after sunset, the proper day and time of the day of the week.

God states in Gen. 31:13-14, *"Speak unto the children of Israel, saying, Verily my Sabbaths ye shall keep: for it is a sign between me and you throughout your generations; that ye may know that I am the Lord God that does sanctify you. Ye shall keep the Sabbath therefore; for it is Holy unto you: every one that defiles it shall surely be put to death: for whosoever does any work* (or engage in any pleasurable activities) *therein, that soul shall be cut off from among his people"*.

Those individuals that keep God's holy Sabbath day properly, by refraining from all your works and pleasures, and use this day to study God's ways via the Old Testament books and prove all scriptures from the New Testament books to that of the Old Testament books, which is the source of all God's ways, and conduct their lives according to the ways of God, will indeed reclaim their lives from the pits of hell. Even though your previous lives have been completely contrary to the ways of God; that door to receive God's Salvation to an eternal life with him and his Holy Messiah, King David and company is still open towards us, for God sacrificed his only begotten son, King David, to wash us clean with his shed blood, only if we do our part and change ourselves and our ways according to the ways of God, and flee from this babylonian paganism false christian religion, that Saul/Paul brought forth, with his pagan christ/another pagan god., and all his pagan ways, to deceive us all. God has left the choice up to us; it's as simple as this.

This Saul/Paul is none other than King Saul with the evil spirit still upon him, which God placed upon him after rejecting him as king over our ancient ancestors; because he broke God's direct command to eradicate all the

Amalekites with their animals and material goods, including valuables such as gold, silver, etc. He allowed his followers to take of the choice animals, gold, silver and pleasant things, because he feared the people more than he feared the Lord God; and he also kept their king alive.

Just as we today, fearing what your friends, family, business colleagues and acquaintances may think or say about you; being completely ignorant that it is from God only we may receive an everlasting life, after the present temporary life expires. Who cares what your associates think or say about you? Isn't your eternal life the most important goal for you to achieve? How can you or anybody let this gift slip through your fingers, by dwelling on what individuals may think or even say about you? Perhaps this is the same desire they have, but like you, they also are afraid what others may think or say about them. We must act upon achieving our desires, and not cowardly hide behind our vain excuses.

The following are writings from 2 Esdras 7:75-87, portraying what becomes of our spirit and soul upon our death, as this Apocrypha book states in the New English Bible, with all of the Apocrypha books.

*"Then Esdras said, If I have won your favour, my Lord, make this plain to me: At death, when every one of us gives back his soul, shall we be kept at rest until the time when you begin to create your new world, or does our torment begin at once? I will tell you that also, the angel replied. But do not include yourself among those who have despised my laws; Do not count yourself with those who are to be tormented. For you have a treasure of good works stored up with the Most High, though you will not be shown it until the last days. But now to speak of death: When the Most High has given final sentence for a man to die, the spirit leaves the body to return to the One who gave it, and first of all to adore the glory of the Most High. But for those who have rejected the ways of the Most High and despised his law, and who hate all that fear God, their spirit enter no settled abode, but roam thence forward in torment, grief and sorrow. And this for seven reasons. First, they have despised the law of the Most High. Secondly, they have lost their last chance of making a good repentance and so gaining life. Thirdly, they can see the reward in store for those who have trusted the covenants of the Most High. Fourthly, they begin to think of the torment that awaits them at the end. Fifthly, they see that angels are guarding the abode of the other souls in deep silence. Sixthly, they see that they are soon to enter into torment. The seventh cause for grief, the strongest cause of all, is this: At the sight of the Most High in his glory, they break down in shame, waste away in remorse, and shrivel with fear remembering how they sinned against him in their lifetime, and how they are soon to be brought before him for judgment on the last day".*

*"And for those who have kept to the way laid down by the Most High, this is what is appointed for them when their time comes to leave their mortal bodies. During their stay on earth they served the Most High in spirit of constant hardship*

*and danger, and kept to the letter of the law, given to them by the Lawgiver. Their reward is this: <u>First</u> they shall exult to see the glory of God who will receive them as his own, and then they shall enter into rest in seven appointed stages of joy. Their <u>First joy</u> is their victory in the long fight against their inborn impulses to evil, which have failed to lead them astray from life into death. Their <u>second joy</u> is to see the souls of the wicked wandering ceaselessly, and the punishment in store for them. Their <u>third joy</u> is the good report given of them by their Maker, that throughout their life they kept the law with which they were entrusted. Their <u>fourth joy</u> is to understand the rest, which they are now to share in the storehouses, guarded by angels in deep silence, and the glory waiting for them in the next age. Their <u>fifth joy</u> is the contrast between the corruptible world they have escaped and the future life that is to be their possession, between the cramped laborious life from which they have been set free and the spacious life which will soon be theirs to enjoy forever and ever. Their <u>sixth joy</u> will be the revelation that they are to shine like stars, never to fade or die. With faces radiant as the sun. Their <u>seventh joy</u>, the greatest joy of all, will be the confident and exultant assurance which will be theirs, free from all fear and shame, as they press forward to see face to face the One whom they served in their lifetime, and from whom they are soon now to receive their glory".*

"*The joys I have been declaring are the appointed destiny for the souls of the just. The torments I described before are the sufferings appointed for the rebellious".*

Therefore, we Israelites of the House of Israel, of the 10 lost tribes, in order to gain eternal life, must change our lives and flee from this babylonian paganism christian religion that Saul/Paul built, and the foundation of this religion is his imaginary pagan christ, as stated in <u>1 Cor. 3:10-11.</u> And flee from all other beliefs that do not agree with the books of the Old Testament. Your eternal life is within your own hands. Take the initial step and throw away all the graven images, pictures, symbols of your pagan gods—and yes, even that medal of some pagan canonized saint or/and cross on a chain with or without Saul/Paul's pagan imaginary christ nailed to it. Also that picture you have and worship of the christians' pagan imaginary christ, or the virgin mother, or of some canonized saint, or of Melchizedek, who is reported in the New Testament as one without father or mother; but one can't trust any statements that come from the New Testament, particularly if they come from Saul called Paul's writings, or even the 4 gospel books, for they are littered with inconsistencies. Even the true apostle books of James; Peter 1 and 2; John 1, 2, and 3; and the book of Jude, which are also corrupted with the name of Paul's imaginary pagan christ—these must be proved via the Old Testament, the same precaution must be exercised with the book of Revelation. It's as if someone got a hold of the originals and manipulated them. That someone definitely was Saul/Paul and his associates, for he was much younger than the true apostles, for when they put Stephen to death, which was most likely King David, God's Holy Messiah, that they laid the clothing at the feet of a young man, whose name was Saul, the leader of the band of soldiers, and later bartered for his clothing amongst themselves. This is the same Saul who infiltrated into the ranks of the true apostles and then changed his name to Paul, his first deceptive move. This Saul called Paul/King Saul reported in the first book of Samuel/the next and last pope of the christian religion due to be crowned as the last pope or as he will originally be as the Archbishop of Canterbury, leader of the High Anglican Church of England on Mar. 20th of year 2013, called false prophet reported in Rev. 19:20, with miraculous powers. This Justin Welby with his miraculous powers will make his move to gain control over the Roman Christian's throne and join the two Christian religions into one group. He will also claim to be the Christ of God and prove it via his miraculous works. This Justin in times past may have been Charles Martel (Charlemagne's grandfather) plus Charlemagne, who with his French and German forces, imposed his pagan Christian religion upon our Israelite ancestors in the years 774 to 804 cue., which was the beginning of Daniel's 12:11 scripture. He also spent a whole winter in the Vatican, as he claims, fixing up the scriptures, no doubt according to his way of thinking, and Saul called Paul, the builder of the Christian religion as stated in 1 Cor. 3:10-11. He also, with his Roman force (soldiers) crucified God's Holy Messiah, King David. He also was King Saul, the 1st king of our ancient Israelites, reported in the 1st book of Samuel. Plus he is also the Christian's imaginary pagan Christ, who is in fact the devil's 1st born son, it is him that is referred to in Rev. 1:5 as being the 1st born, but it really means of the devil's 1st born son.

Bringing forth a writing about Charlemagne, from the Cauldron of Europe, page 28, it states:

*"Charles Martel lived for nearly ten years after Poitiers but passes almost wholly from our sight even though quite evidently he kept the firmest of grips on the kingdom., It is tantalizing in the extreme to know so little about this man who had a personality so formidable as to impose his will upon an army at its most vulnerable moment, the moment of victory. Judging by a vicious little story put about by clerics he lacked a certain respect for the Holy Church.*

*A prelate of St. Denis, where Charles Martel was buried, after a vision opened his tomb. There was no human corpse inside, only a black, winged dragon which rushed out and flew away. But at about the time of his death there was born to his son Pippin, a child, a boy. He, too, was a bastard as had been Charles Martel. He, too, was given the simple, all-embracing name of 'Man'—Carl. Later, after the boy indeed became a man, and the man became an emperor, those who toyed with the heresy of the transmigration of souls were free to wonder whether the soul of Charles Martel might not, at his death in 742c.e., have entered the body of Charlemagne".*

Throughout the historical material about Charlemagne it states that no one knew the exact date of Charlemagne's birth, and he withheld this knowledge from even his close acquaintances and didn't even want to talk about it. I urge you to read all of the historical material on Charlemagne and get a better picture of this extraordinary man, and you will have better understanding of the scripture in <u>1 Sam. 9:2,</u> *"Kish had a son, whose name was Saul, a choice young man and a goodly* (well proportioned)*: and there was not among the children of Israel a goodlier person than he: from his shoulders and upward he was higher than any of the people".* This same description is also in <u>1 Sam. 10:23-24.</u>

This is the same picture one gets from the historical material of Charlemagne. *"He had a broad and strong body of unusual height, but well proportioned; for his height measured seven times the length of his foot. His skull was round, the eyes lively and rather large, the nose was more than average length, the hair gray but full, the face friendly and cheerful. Seated or standing, he thus made a dignified and stately impression even though he has a thick, short neck and a belly that protruded somewhat; but this was hidden by the good proportion of the rest of his figure. He strode with firm steps and held himself as a man; he spoke with a higher voice than one would have expected of someone of his build".* <u>Deut. 4:12-19, 23-24,</u> *"And the Lord God spoke unto you out of the midst of the fire: ye heard the voice of the words, but saw no similitude; only ye heard a voice. And he declared unto you his covenant, which he commanded you to perform, even ten commandments; and he wrote them upon two tables of stone. And the Lord God commanded me at that time to teach you statutes and judgments, that ye might do them in the land whither ye go over to possess it. Take ye therefore good heed unto yourselves; for ye saw no manner of similitude on the day that the Lord God spoke unto you in Horeb out of the midst of the fire: Lest ye corrupt yourselves, and make you a graven image, the similitude of any figure, the likeness of male or female, the likeness of any beast that is on the earth, the likeness of any winged fowl that flies in the air, the likeness of any thing that creeps on the ground, the likeness of any fish that is in the waters beneath the earth: And lest thou lift up thine eyes unto heaven, and when thou see the sun and the moon, and the stars, even all the host of heaven, should you be driven to worship them, and serve them, which the Lord thy God has divided unto all nations under the whole heaven".*

*"Take heed unto yourselves, lest ye forget the covenant of the Lord your God, which he made with you, and make you a graven image, or the likeness of anything, <u>which the Lord thy God has forbidden thee</u>".*

It is absolutely plain that any religion that displays images of their pagan gods is of total falsehood. Therefore, flee from all falsehood and return to the ways of God, the ways of the Old Testament, and save your eternal life alive, for there is life after our initial death, with this life being only a temporary trial period.

I pray that God will open your eyes, unplug your ears and clear your mind and allow you to see, hear and understand his truths, and spur your interest to continue reading this writing no matter how strange it may appear to whatever you have been subjected to throughout your years. Always keep within your mind that God has given you all the false beliefs you have been subjected to, the statutes and judgments and false sabbath days, that are <u>not</u> good for us, and whereby we should <u>not</u> live, as stated in <u>Ezek. 20:24-26,</u> because our ancients refused to live up to the covenant that they made with their one God; so God gave to them exactly what they wanted, which will bring them and us, their offspring, to total desolation. But we can reverse the outcome by returning back to the ways of the Old Testament as best we can. There is no new covenant as Saul/Paul claims in the New Testament, nor has there ever been. The same Old Covenant is still in force, and always has been. The one difference that the New Testament brought forth was the shedding of the Holy Messiah's blood, who was King David, and definitely not Paul's pagan imaginary christ, to eliminate the shedding of the animal's blood in making an atonement for our past, present, and even future sins, only if we return back to the ways of the Lord our only God of Israel, the ways of the Old Testament. This sacrifice eliminates the need to use animal sacrifices to attain God's salvation to an eternal life with him and his holy ones.

Another scripture that corresponds with the above Ezekiel scripture is <u>Dan. 7:25,</u> where God states, *he will put them* (remnant of the House of Israel, mentioned in <u>Rev. 12:17)</u>, *into the horn's hand* (the christian pagan religion via the hands of King Saul) *for 1260 days* (of biblical years, or 1241.9 of our years). This all happened in the year 774 cue. on Oct. 10th, when Charlemagne attacked the Saxons' place of worship and set the abomination, the christian pagan christ, which was of himself, upon their Altar of God, that made this altar desolate, forcing the Saxons to worship this pagan christ as a God; he later destroyed their place of worship, that brought an end to any sacrifices they have performed.

All this action by Charlemagne and his forces brought alive <u>Dan. 12:11,</u> *"And from the time that the daily sacrifice shall be taken away, and the abomination that makes the altar desolate is set up, there shall be a thousand two hundred and ninety days"* (biblical years).

All biblical scholars and christian leaders are still waiting for this to happen in some future time, being completely ignorant that this already happened in the year 774 cue. by Charlemagne. This time frame is the same as <u>Dan. 12:7,</u> where the *"time, times, and an half"* (3½ biblical years, where each day represents a biblical year), or 1,260 biblical years, plus the 30 biblical years, which is God's reclaiming period of us Israelites, to match the same number of years it took Charlemagne to fully impose the christian pagan religion upon the Saxons, *"When he shall have accomplished to scatter the power of the holy people* (us Israelites), *all these things shall be finished"*. This totals to the same 1,290 days, of biblical years, or a total of 1271.46 of our Gregorian years. This is telling us, our civilizations, shall be totally finished in 774.778+ 1271 = 2046.2358 in the month of Mar 27th, which is the end of the 12th age. Then followed with 45 days, of biblical years, of nothingness; fulfilling Dan. 12:12, *"Blessed is he that waits, and comes to the thousand three hundred and thirty five days* (of biblical years)".

This period of time is also mentioned in Hosea 3:4, *"For the children of Israel shall abide many days without a king, and without a prince, and without a sacrifice, and without an image, and without an ephod, and without teraphim"*.

Then followed by Hosea 3:5, *"Afterword shall the children of Israel return, and seek the Lord their God, and* DAVID *their king* (not Saul/Paul's pagan imaginary christ); *and shall fear the Lord God and his goodness in the latter days* (of biblical years)".

After these 45 days, of biblical years, God will gather the survivors of the House of Israel and the House of Judah and lead them back to the Promised Land, just as he did when he redeemed the Israelites from Egypt approximately 3,500 biblical years ago. This is reported in Jer. 16:14-16, and Jer. 50:17-20, and many other scriptures throughout the Old Testament.

At the present time we are still within the Jer. 16:13 scripture; which states, *"Therefore will I cast you out of this land* (the promised land) *into a land that ye know not, neither ye nor your fathers* (the present lands we are now living in throughout this world); *and there shall ye serve other gods day and night* (the christians' pagan imaginary christ, all the so-called canonized saints, even the devil himself, via the observance of the helloween, there is absolutely nothing hallowed in this event, reason I spelled it as such); *where I will not show you favour"*.

The christian leaders, from the pope, and all the way down to the clergy person are the reported wolves dressed up in sheep's clothing, eager to devour the spirit/mind of whomever comes in contact with them, for their master Satan and his 1st born son King Saul, the builder of this christian religion; and at the present time, has a stranglehold on us all, even though we may not attend any of their places of worship, we via our minds/spirits are being devoured by participating in all their so-called holy events, etc., and turning our backs on God's reported holy events, from his holy Sabbath weekly day, just before sunset Friday to just after sunset Saturday, and all the other reported Old Testament holy events; to the eating of classified unclean animals, to consuming the blood of the flesh and the fat, even administrating blood transfusions by the thousands every day of the year, even being ignorant of all the clean and unclean laws of God, as well as all of God's other laws. Is it any wonder our society is in such a mess.

It is very difficult to follow respective dates in the Bible as accurate because the 360-day year (12 months of 30 days each) was actually 5.25 days off the solar calendar. Therefore, ever so often the Hebrew calendar had to add approximately 19 or so days to their calendar to catch up to the solar calendar year. Therefore, it was very seldom accurate.

When King Jeroboam uncovered the golden calves for the House of Israel to worship instead of the Lord their God in the month of Aug. in the year 910 b. cue., 116 days or so into the 10th age. He created a precedent for the House of Israel to continue over the centuries to chase after pagan gods instead of their one and only true living Lord God, the creator of this entire universe and everything in it, on it, and under it, including mankind. Read <u>Deuteronomy chapter 32</u> depicting the course we have followed over the centuries and where God states in verses <u>36-40</u>, *"For the Lord God shall judge his people, and repent himself for his servants, when he sees that their power is gone, and there is none left. And He shall say, Where are their* (pagan) *gods, their rock* (christians' pagan christ, virgin mother, numerous saints) *in whom they trusted, which did eat the fat of their sacrifices, and drank the wine of their drink offerings? Let them rise up and help you, and be your protection. See now that I, even I, am He, and there is no god with me: I kill, and make alive; I wound, and I heal: neither is there any that can deliver out of my hand. For I lift up my hand to heaven, and say, I live forever".*

There are no other Gods, for He is the only God. But us Israelites, God's chosen people, have turned their backs on the Lord their only God and are following the example King Jeroboam brought about. God, through his prophets, warned his people of the House of Israel that he will bring punishments upon them in an attempt to persuade them to return back to his ways, outlined for us via the Old Testament and other notable books via the true apostles in the Old and New Testaments along within the Apocrypha books. These warnings began in the book of <u>Lev. 26:18, 24, 28, 33</u> to our eventual defeat by the Assyrians in the years 734-721 b. cue., and after the Babylonians became world powers, our ancestors eventually received their freedom and migrated north, northwest and west from the Assyrian lands, they did indeed return to the ways of God even building a place of worship and even performed sacrificial feats on God's Altar. This place of worship today is known as the Stonehenge ruins. The proof of this is the fact that the east entrance lines up with the summer solstice sunrise, indicating this entrance being of great importance as indicated in <u>Ezekiel 44:1-3</u>, the entrance that God entered this place of worship and the entrance the King/

Prince of the people entered and exited, and where the King/Prince ate his meals. This gate was to be kept closed at all times. The west entrance of secondary importance lines up with the winter solstice sun setting, which was only used by the priestly Levi's family members, where they prepared and brought in the sacrificial animal parts to offer upon God's Altar, and outside where they cooked in huge boiling pots, the animal meat for the worshippers to eat. They had a hanging tree at a short distance from this west entrance to string up the slaughtered animals, to skin, clean and extract the animal parts to offer upon the altar and cut up the animal for whatever other purpose. The north and south entrances were for the rest of the worshippers. The ones who entered via the north entrance had to exit via the south entrance, and the ones entering via the south entrance had to exit via the north entrance, such as passing through. God through Ezekiel brought our ancient ancestors back again after the Babylonians became the world dominate power. God put it into these Israelites to migrate away from the German area and return back to his way. God even deposited the Prophet Ezekiel amongst them, and no doubt Ezekiel had a major role in bringing them back. He even warned these Israelites via demonstrations of what will come upon them and their future children via the cutting of his hair and dividing his hair into three lots and bringing various disasters against each lot, even against the small 4th lot that he placed into his apron. This all represents what we can expect via the coming 30-biblical-year world war III, and the extra 45 b. year period after the war. Where only one tenth survive out of the one-third that enter into this disastrous 45-biblical-year period. This above takes place after God allowed the devil's 1st born son King Saul/Saul called Paul/Charlemagne to build his pagan christian religion in the New Testament times and then impose his christian pagan religion upon our ancestors in the years 774 to 804 cue. for 1,260 biblical years as reported in Dan. 7:25, not for our good, but as a punishment upon us as mentioned in the following <u>Ezekiel 20:24-26</u> scripture, *"Because they had not executed my Judgments, but had despised My Statutes, and had polluted My Sabbaths, and their eyes were after their fathers' idols. Wherefore I gave them <u>also</u> statutes that were <u>not good</u>, and judgments whereby they should <u>not</u> live; And I polluted them in their own gifts, in that they caused to pass through the fire* (our incinerators) *all that opens the womb, that I might make them desolate, to the end that they might know* (come to realize) *that I am the Lord God* (bringing all this destruction upon us because of our wicked ways)*"*.

This, believe me, it's the pagan christian religious ways that we are trapped within that Charlemagne imposed upon us, via our ancestors in the year 774.778 on Oct. 10th, and completed all his atrocities before sunset. When he attacked their place of worship and set upon their Altar of God an image of himself (the christian' christ), and forced the people to worship it, killing whomever refused. This act made this altar desolate as Dan. 12:11 states. He thereafter destroyed this place of worship, which brought an end to any further sacrifices. Bringing Daniel's above-mentioned scripture alive, and the countdown of 1,290 days of biblical years began. This consists of 1,260 biblical years or 1241.8891 of our Gregorian years we will be within his hands via his pagan christian religion, and 29.5688 years of world war III that God will reclaim us back, matching the same number of years it took Charles to fully impose his pagan christian religion upon our ancestors. Therefore, 774.778 + 1241.8891 = 2016.667 time expires, at which time world war III begins, and ends on 2046.236 in Mar. These 2 atrocities against the Saxons' place of worship and God's Altar, brought alive Dan. 12:7 and 11 scriptures, and the countdown continues, to the point we have from late spring of year 2006 approx. 10 plus years until WWIII begins in 2016.667 against our arch-enemy, the so-called Holy Roman Empire nations with their allies, hidden today within the EURO conglomerate of nations. But before this war begins, the builder of this pagan christian religion, King Saul/Saul called Paul/Charlemagne/next and last pope/false prophet with miraculous powers mentioned in Rev. 19:20 will make his reappearance and be crowned in 2013.217, for 3 ½ biblical years or 1,260 days to bring his atrocities upon us. After his time expires, King David, God's true Holy Messiah will put him to his final death. After this God will begin to reclaim his people back with a 30-biblical-year world war, against our nemeses the so-called Holy Roman Empire with their allies, as I stated above, matching the same number of years it took Charlemagne to fully impose his pagan christian religion upon our Saxon ancestors, the 1st lot to have the christian religion imposed upon them, their children of today, will be the 1st to be reclaimed, the last ones the christian religion was imposed upon, their children of today will be the last ones to be reclaimed. This is why Daniel added 30 to 1,260 to get 1,290. Therefore, it is vital to break away from this most paganism christian religion this world has ever witnessed and return back to the Lord your only God. Continue reading this book to get a clear picture of what truly occurred over the many years, you will be amazed. This above-mentioned 30-biblical-year WWIII will be God's reclaiming us Israelites from the hand he put us via our ancestors into this mouthy arrogant individual's hand, mentioned in Dan. 7:20-25 scriptures for 1,260 biblical years, matching the same number of biblical years it took Charlemagne to fully impose his pagan christian religion upon our ancestors in the years 774.778 Oct. - 804.3468 May.

# Chapter 2

# Scriptures Used to Prove the Christian Religion Is the Devil's 1st Born Son's Religion

<u>Cor. 3:10-11</u> proves Saul/Paul is the builder of the christian religion. As he states, *"According to the grace of God which is given unto me, as a wise masterbuilder, I have laid the foundation, and another builds thereon. But let every man take heed how he builds thereupon. For other foundation can no man lay than that is laid, which is Jesus Christ"*.

There is no disputing it that this scripture proves Saul who is called Paul is the builder of this christian religion that we have been snared by, ever since God put us into the hand of the little horn of <u>Daniel's 7;20 and 25</u>, for a time period of 1,260 biblical years or 1241.8891 of our calendar years. This horn *"that had eyes, and a mouth that spoke very great* (boasting, bragging) *things, whose look was more stout* (bigger, taller, etc.) *than his fellows"*. Was none other than King Saul/Saul called the apostle Paul, with the evil spirit still upon him. Did he not go on a rampage, destroying many of the Jewish synagogues and killing many of the people worshipping their one God? This act by it-self, proves he did indeed have the evil spirit upon him, in order to commit these atrocities upon his <u>own people</u> of the House of Judah.

The following 2 scriptures that are connected to Saul/Paul, proving it is indeed the christian religion that he is the master builder of:

<u>Acts 11:26</u>, *"The disciples were called christians first in Antioch"*. This is the area that Saul/Paul and Barnabas went to preach the gospel of their christ, *"They assembled themselves with the church for a whole year and taught many people"*.

The second time is when Saul/Paul is trying to defend himself, in front of Agrippa; why the Jewish followers of James, the religious leader of the true followers of the true Messiah of God, wanted to kill him. Agrippa says in <u>Acts 26:28</u>, *"Almost thou persuadest me to be a christian"*.

The third and last time the word christian is used in the Bible is when Peter is using it in <u>1 Peter 4:16,</u> stating: *"But let none of you suffer as a murderer, or as a thief, or as an evildoer, or as a busybody in other men's matters. Yet if any man suffer as <u>a christian</u>* (will suffer), *let him not be ashamed; but let him glory God on this behalf. For the time is come that judgement must begin at the house of God, and if it first begin at us, what shall the end be on <u>them</u>* (christians) *that obey not the Gospel of God"*(but the gospel of their pagan christ)?

It is absolutely obvious that Peter is condemning the christian religion while speaking to his Hebrew audience, otherwise, why would he be using the word christian? Who were at this time preaching the gospel of Saul/Paul's pagan christ, and who were obviously at this time in history, separated from the ranks of the true followers of God and his true Holy Messiah, King David, who will be the future king of, not only the Jews, but of all the dispersed Israelites throughout the entire world, such as the 10 lost tribes of the House of Israel, with many of the levis, the priestly family tribe, for Jacob in <u>Gen. 49:7</u> states, *"Cursed be their* (Simeon's and Levi's) *anger, for it was fierce; and their wrath, for it was cruel; I will divide them in Jacob, and scatter them in Israel"*.

The name Jacob in this scripture is referring to the House of Judah, plus the tribes of the House of Israel <u>minus</u> the 2 tribes of Joseph. Where the use of the name Israel is referring <u>only</u> to the houses of Joseph, for did not Israel put his name Israel upon the heads of Ephraim and Manasseh, reported in the following scripture?

<u>Gen. 48:16,</u> *"The Angel which redeemed me from all evil, bless the lads; and let my name be named on them, and the name of my fathers Abraham and Isaac; and let them grow into a multitude <u>in the midst of the earth</u>"*.

Is not most of the major countries of the British Commonwealth of Nations, and the United States of America, situated <u>in the midst of the earth,</u> basically separated from most of the nations of this world via the oceans and seas? Is there any doubt that they are the 2 tribes of Joseph, with the fabulous birthright blessings given to them by their adoptive father-grandfather Israel?

King David, God's true Messiah, knew, as did his followers, he was indeed destined to become our future king, when he was sacrificed by God in the New Testament times, shedding his blood as in a lamb brought to the slaughter, to atone for our past, present, and even our future sins, to a certain degree. This sacrifice does not atone for the many heinous crimes against God and humanity. This christ that Saul/Paul brought about is not even a real individual, but only an imaginary figure, whom Saul/Paul gave the <u>title</u> of the true <u>Messiah,</u> as a <u>name</u> to his imaginary individual, which means <u>holy anointed one</u> and interpreted from the Greek language into the English language, <u>christ</u>; and combines it with the sacrificial act that God brought about; with the name Jesus, meaning saviour from the Greek language. What Saul/Paul is doing here is giving all the credit to his pagan imaginary christ, and none of it to God Almighty, for Saul/Paul states that we now receive salvation from this imaginary christ of himself.

David in Ps. 3:8 states, *"Salvation belongeth unto the Lord God:"*

Ps. 89:26 states that it will be David who will cry onto God, *"Thou art my father, my God, and the rock of my salvation".*

Isa. 12:2 states, *"Behold, God is my salvation; I will trust, and not be afraid: for the Lord JEHOVAH is my strength and my song; he also is become my salvation".*

In Acts 13:33-37, Saul/Paul is attempting to legitimize his imaginary individual as God's true Messiah with the use of Ps. 2:7, 16:10, and Isa. 55:3. These so-called legitimizing scriptures from Acts are as follows:

Vrs. 33: *"God has fulfilled the same unto us their children, in that he has raised up Jesus again; as it is also written in the second Psalm, Thou art my son, this day have I begotten thee".*

Vrs. 34: *"And as concerning that he raised him up from the dead, now no more to return to corruption, he said on this wise, I will give you the sure mercies of David".*

Vrs. 35: *"Wherefore he said also in another Psalm, Thou shall not suffer Thine Holy One to see corruption".*

Vrs. 36: *"For David, after he had served his own generation by the will of God, fell on sleep, and was laid unto his fathers, and saw corruption".*

Vrs. 37: *"But he, whom God raised again, saw no corruption".*

## These scriptures from the source are as follows:

Psalm 2:7, *"I will declare the decree: the Lord God has said unto me; Thou art my son; this day have I begotten thee".*

Psalm 16:10, *"For thou will not leave my soul in hell; neither will thou suffer Thine Holy One to see corruption".*

Isa. 55:3, *"Incline your ears, and come unto me: hear, and your soul shall live; and I will make an everlasting covenant with you, even the sure mercies of David".*

On examining the scriptures used by Saul/Paul in attempting to legitimize his christ, you will notice all the 1st person pronouns within these scriptures, which proves David is speaking of himself and not his seed. Please notice Saul/Paul omits to use the first portion of these scriptures, which have the 1st person pronouns, connecting David to the rest of the scripture, and is referring to himself as *"Thine Holy One"* in Ps. 16:10. Also you will notice that Saul/Paul has the wrong individual doing the speaking in this Ps. 16:10

scripture, such as God speaking to Saul/Paul's pagan christ, which would give his pagan christ power over God. For it would be up to Saul/Paul's christ whether God would see the corrupting powers of the grave. With David doing the speaking to God, it would be up to God whether David would see the corrupting powers of the grave.

This is a prime example to illustrate what happens when we are praying to God, in His Holy Name, and asking for certain favors of whatsoever, and then finishing the prayer with "in the name of, Saul/Paul's christ, I ask these favors". This is exactly the same as giving Saul/Paul's imaginary christ power over God. No wonder none, if any, of our prayers are ever answered. For this is using God's name in vain.

Isa. 42:8 states, *"I am the Lord God: that is my name: and my glory will I not give to another, neither my praise to graven images"*.

Our christian religious organizations are loaded with graven images of Saul/Paul's pagan christ, virgin mother, and numerous saints canonized by the leader/pope of the christian religion; being completely ignorant of the fact that saints are not canonized, but are God's chosen obedient living individuals of the tribes of Israel, the covenant obedient ones. This is illustrated as such in Dan. 7:25, where it states, *"And he* (the horn) *shall speak great words against the Most High, and shall wear out the saints of the Most High"*,

Notice the saints are living, but obedient ones of the Most High. They are not individuals that one should pray to, serve, and worship as a god, as the christians continually do. This is breaking God's first and second commandments. As stated in Ex. 20:4-6, Lev. 26:1, Deut. 4:16-19, Deut. 4:23. *"Thou shall not make unto thee any graven images, or any likeness of anything that is in the heavens above, or that is in the earth beneath, or that is in the water under the earth. Thou shall not bow down thyself to them, nor serve them: For I the Lord Thy God am a jealous God, visiting the iniquities of the fathers upon the children unto the third and fourth generations of them that hate me; and show mercy unto thousands of them that love me, and keep my commandments"*.

Making graven images of the christians' imaginary pagan christ and all their so-called canonized saints, virgin mother, lady Fatima, etc., is no way of keeping the covenant our ancestors made with God, but is in fact breaking his 1st and 2nd commandments. Even God's true Messiah, King David, is not to be worshipped, prayed to, and served as a God, for he is only a human being, just as you and I are; and proven with scriptures taken from, Ps. 2:7, Ps. 16:10, that I have quoted above, along with Ps. 30:3, Ps. 49:15, Ps. 89:18-27, and Ps. 118:17-18; they state as follows:

Ps. 30:3, *"O Lord God, thou has brought up my* (David's) *soul from the grave: thou has kept me* (David) *alive, that I* (David) *should not go down to the pit"*.

Ps. 49:15, "*But God will redeem my* (David's) *soul from the power of the grave: For he shall receive me*".

Ps. 89:17-18, 26-27, "*For the Lord God is our defence: and the Holy One of Israel is our King. Then thou spoke in vision to Thy Holy One, and said, I have laid help upon one that is mighty; I have exalted one chosen out of the people. I have found* David *my servant; with my Holy oil have I anointed him* (David): *With whom my hand shall be established: mine arm also shall strengthen him* (David).

*He* (David) *shall cry unto me, Thou art my father, my God, and the rock of my salvation. Also I will make him* (David) *my firstborn, higher than the kings of the earth*".

Ps. 118:17-18, "*I* (David) *shall not die, but live, and* declare the works of the Lord God (our witness). *The Lord God has chasten me* (David) *sore: but he has not given me* (David) *over unto death*".

Please notice all the 1st person pronouns that are in the Psalms David wrote, proving that David is definitely referring to himself and not his seed. To believe Saul/Paul's christ is the true Messiah of God is believing an assumption and sooner or later will make an ass out of you and whoever else believes this assumption. David is/was that witness that shall *"declare the works of the Lord God"*. Definitely not Paul's christ, as stated in Rev. 1:5. David was/is God's firstborn and will be King of kings of the earth as stated in the above Ps. 89:26-27 scriptures, proving again Rev. 1:5 false. King Saul, Saul/Paul, via Charlemagne, did indeed alter the scriptures to suit his purpose.

Isa. 55:4 states, "*Behold I have given him for a* witness *to the people, a leader and a commander to the people*".

David was a leader and a commander in his original generation and is now a witness of the works of God after reappearing as the true Messiah, in the New Testament times, to shed his blood, as in a sacrificial lamb, brought to the slaughter, to make atonement for our past, present, and even future sins, to a certain degree; but in order to take advantage of David's shed blood, we must return to the ways of God—such as observing and keeping God's holy Sabbath day on the 7th day of the week, not on the christians' 1st day of the week, and also on the proper time of a day, from just before sundown Friday to just after sundown Saturday, not the christians' time of a day, from midnight to midnight. We must also observe and keep all of God's designated yearly holy events, mentioned in the Old Testament books. We must destroy and cast away all our graven images of whatsoever, and pray to, serve, and worship only the Lord our God, and no one or anything else. For this would be keeping the covenant our ancestors made with the Lord our God.

As stated in Deut. 4:14-19, 23-24, "*Which the Lord thy God has forbidden thee*". To bring about any images of whatsoever, and then worship the individual or thing that these images represent, is breaking God's first and second commandments. <u>For the Lord thy God is the only God; there are no other so-called gods.</u>

Also stated in <u>Ps. 89:26-27</u>, which is written by Maschil of Ethan the Ezrahite, using the name "David", that will cry to God, *"Thou art my father, my God, and the rock of my salvation. Also I (God) will make him (David) my firstborn, higher than the kings of the earth"*. Not Saul/Paul's pagan christ mentioned in <u>Rev. 1:5</u>. I am stating again, there can only be one firstborn from the dead and one King of kings. Being that the Old Testament is the source of God's ways, it proves <u>Rev. 1:5</u> is wrong. By changing the name jesus christ to David, God's Holy Messiah, would correct Revelation's scripture. Being David is the real Messiah, he must not be worshipped as a god, for he is only a human being, just as we are.

In <u>Acts13:33 & 37</u>, Saul/Paul uses the phrase <u>*"raised up again"*</u>. This can only mean that his christ had a previous birth, life, death, and redemption. You can search the Bible from the first to the last page, and you will not find Saul/Paul's pagan imaginary christ with a previous birth, life, death, and redemption. The only person in the entire Bible that had a previous birth, life, death, and redemption is none other than King David, proven by the scriptures of <u>Ps. 2:7, 30:3, 49:15, 89:18-27,</u> and <u>118:17-18</u>, which I quoted above.

Also in <u>Acts 13:36</u> Saul/Paul states, when David fell on sleep, he was laid with his fathers and was subject to the corrupting powers of the grave. David in the same scriptures quoted above, refutes Saul/Paul's statement.

In <u>Acts 13:34</u> above, Saul/Paul is attempting to legitimize his pagan imaginary christ when he claims, God said to Saul/Paul's imaginary pagan christ, *"I will give you the sure mercies of David"*.

This scripture comes from <u>Isa. 55:3</u>, and quotes as such; *"Incline your ears, and come unto me: hear, and your soul shall live; and I will make an everlasting covenant with you, <u>even the sure mercies of David</u>"*.

Please note that this above scripture refers to "anyone" whom submits to the ways of God; therefore, there is no way Saul/Paul can use this scripture to legitimize his pagan imaginary christ/another god.

You will also notice in <u>Acts 13:35,</u> that Saul/Paul uses the phrase *"in another Psalm"*. What is he hiding from his audience? Surely a person of his intelligence would know the Psalm he is in fact quoting word for word. Should he not refer the number of this Psalm to his audience, so they can reprove his quote with the source, which are the books of the Old Testament?

God states in <u>Prov. 1:23,</u> *"Turn you at my reproof: behold, I will pour out my Spirit unto you, I will make known my words unto you"*.

This is a promise made to you by God himself, that if you will take the time and make the effort to prove all things, never taking the word as being the gospel truth from anyone's lips. God's spirit will come upon you, and make known his words unto you, such as giving great understanding of his words to you. I myself can testify to this statement as a fact, for the day that I truly wanted to know what the Bible was all about and started to study it, beginning with the Old Testament, which is, as I mentioned above, the source of God's ways; jotting down interesting scriptures and reproving them with many other alike scriptures via the references received from various scriptures within the Old Testament. I spent every Sabbath day, from just before sundown Friday to just after sundown Saturday, the proper time of God's holy Sabbath day, the same day the Jewish people of the House of Judah observe and keep, which is the 7th day of the week, and before I realized it, God's Holy Spirit was upon me, and was slowly but surely giving me greater and greater understanding of his words as the days, weeks, months and even years went along. God has given me an understanding completely different to what the christian religion has imbedded within my mind over the many years of being a christian. I am at the present time, actually ashamed to even admit I use to be a christian, and went along with all their so-called holy events and days. I now consider myself as an Old Testament observer and keeper to the best of my ability.

This scripture that Saul/Paul is referring to when he uses the phrase *"in another Psalm"* is in fact Ps. 16:10, the only place it can be found in the Old Testament. Saul/Paul's reason for not referring it to his audience is the fact that he has the wrong individual doing the speaking, such as God speaking to Saul/Paul's pagan christ/another god, which is giving Saul/Paul's pagan christ/another god, power over God; where in Ps. 16:10, it is David speaking to God: which gives God power over David, for David, the speaker, is referring to himself, as *"Thine Holy One"*.

Saul/Paul also has another reason to hold it back from his audience, for within this same 16th Psalm is a scripture that condemns this another god that Saul/Paul brought about, that demands his followers to drink of his blood, and obviously eat of his body. Sure it is only wine and bread; but in one's mind, it is indeed the blood and flesh of their pagan imaginary christ/another god.

This scripture is Ps. 16:4, which states, *"Their sorrows shall be multiplied that hasten after another god* (the christians' pagan imaginary christ): *their drink offerings of blood* (and obviously the eating of his body/bread), *will I* (David) *not offer, nor take up their names into my lips"*.

David is well aware that consuming the blood of any flesh is totally against God's blood laws, as well as eating the human flesh. Saul/Paul pulls the same stunt when he uses the scripture of Isa. 55:3; knowing full well that he cannot hope to legitimize his pagan imaginary christ/another god with a scripture that refers to <u>anyone</u> that submits to God's ways. Notice, Saul/Paul does not tell his audience where he took this <u>Isa. 55:3</u> scripture from. Saul/Paul just states in <u>Acts 13:34</u>, *"He (God) said on this wise", "I will give you the sure mercies of David"*.

This <u>Ps. 16:4</u> scripture, proves that this communion ritual of drinking the blood, and obviously eating of the body is totally against the laws of God. Sure it is only bread and wine, but within one's mind it is indeed his body and blood.

<u>Lev. 3:17, 7:23-27</u> states, *"It shall be a perpetual statute for your generations throughout all your dwellings, that you eat neither fat nor blood. Moreover ye shall eat no manner of blood, whether it be of foul or of beast, in any of your dwellings. Whatsoever soul/person it be that eats <u>any manner of blood</u>, even that soul/person shall be cut off from his people"*.

Proving that Saul/Paul's pagan christ/another god is of falsehood. All the information from the above scriptures; proves Saul/Paul is a liar, a deceiver, and a thief by using David's scriptures that only refer to King David: to override David as the true Messiah with his pagan imaginary christ/another god. This action also makes him "that chief anti-christ/<u>Messiah</u>" John refers to below:

<u>1 John 2:18,</u> *"Little children, <u>it is the last time</u>; and as ye have heard <u>that antichrist (Messiah)</u> shall come, even now are there <u>many antichrists (Messiahs)</u>; whereby we know that <u>it is the last time</u>"*.

This last time John is referring to is actually of a set period of time of the ages of this world that we live in. For in <u>2 Esdras 14:11-13</u>, of the Apocrypha books, the angel told Ezra that the whole time of this world is in 12 divisions/ages, and that there are only 2½ divisions remaining. John no doubt is referring to the end of the 10th age on 74.9834 cue. in Dec. 24th. An age or division is equal to 1,000 biblical years or 985.62628 of our calendar years. For this 10th period began 985.62628 - 74.9834 = 910.64288 b. cue. 116 days prior to King Jeroboam the first king of the breakaway tribes, called the House of Israel, whose reign began in the year 921 b. cue.; and on the 10th year of his reign on Aug. 15, 911 b. cue, beginning after sundown, presented two golden calves for the members of the House of Israel to worship as their pagan gods, mainly because, due to continuous war between the House of Judah and the House of Israel, were expelled from participating in the religious activities within the temple; therefore, Jeroboam arranged to hold his so-called holy event a month later on the 15th at sunset of Friday, onward, matching the Jewish time table, according to our equivalent Gregorian Calendar of year 2003 of the 8th month; this action also signified a standard set for his future inheritors of his throne, and the future pagan worshipping that the peoples of the House of Israel will continue doing thereafter, even unto our present years of today, which is totally against the ways of God, and which they are to this very day upon their reign over the Houses of Israel; known today as the British Commonwealth of Nations, the United States of America (the two tribes of Joseph), France (Reuben), and the Northwestern European nations (the rest of the lost 10 tribes of Israel). This worshipping of these golden calves, set up by Jeroboam, began a month after the House of Judah expelled the peoples of the House of Israel, from their land and from entering the temple and participating in the years major worshipping rituals. This action of unveiling these golden calves set a precedent for the House of Israel to chase after paganism. The end of the 10th age, and the beginning of the 11th age, would then be in 985.62628 - 910.64288 = 74.9834, which would be after the complete destruction of the temple in Jerusalem, and the end of the pursuing war against the Roman forces, and the last time of the 10th age, John is referring to in his above scripture. This also tells us the angel was speaking to Ezra after 910.64288 - (985.62628/2) = 417.82974 b. cue.

Ezek. 11:15, *"Son of man, thy brethren, even thy brethren, the men of thy kindred* (of the tribe of Levi), *and all the house of Israel wholly, are they unto whom the inhabitants of Jerusalem have said, Get you far from the Lord God: unto us is this land given in possession".*

This happened when the worshippers from the breakaway tribes of the House of Israel in the year 911 b. cue. on the 14th day of the 7th month, were turned away from participating in the Feast day services within the temple. Therefore, Jeroboam had 2 golden calves crafted, erected a house of worship at Bethel, <u>made priests out of the lowest of the people</u>, <u>who were not of the tribe of Levi</u>, and presented these 2 golden calves for the people to worship as their new gods; which caused the people to sin against the Lord God. Just as the christians are sinning against the Lord our God, by worshipping all their graven images of their pagan gods—such as their pagan christ/another so-called god and all their so-called saints, even allowing whomever to be their priests, ministers, etc.

1 Kings 12:32-33 states, *"And Jeroboam ordained a feast in the eighth month, on the fifteenth day of the month, like unto the feast that is in Judah, and he offered upon the altar. So did he in Bethel, <u>sacrificing unto the calves</u> that he had made: and he placed in Bethel the priests of the high places which <u>he had made</u>. So he offered upon the altar which <u>he had made in Bethel</u> the fifteenth day of the eighth month, even in the month which he had devised of his own heart; and ordained a feast unto the children of Israel: and he offered upon the altar, and burnt incense".*

This also tells us that the peoples of the House of Israel will be, more than likely, worshipping pagan gods up to, and including into the reclaiming period of us Israelites by our Lord God in the years of our calendar 2016.667 to 2046.2358 cue. The survivors/remnant of this coming 3rd world war, and of the 45 biblical years to follow, will emerge a remnant that will be gathered up and lead back to the promised land, just as stated below:

Jer. 16:14-15, *"Therefore, behold, the days come, saith the Lord God, that it shall no more be said, The Lord God lives, that brought up the children of Israel out of the land of Egypt; But, the Lord God lives, that brought up the children of Israel from the land of the north, and from all the lands whither he had driven them: and I will bring them again into their land that I gave unto their fathers".*

Therefore, we are indeed very close or even upon the threshold of the entrance into the next world to come. This destruction of the temple in Jerusalem, in the New Testament times, took place shortly after the death of God's true Holy Messiah, King David, for in Dan. 9:27, it states, *"He (God's Messiah, King David) shall confirm the covenant with many for one week (7 biblical yrs): and in the midst of the week (1,260 days) he shall cause (via the shedding of the Messiah's blood) the sacrifice and the oblation to cease, and for the overspreading of abomination he shall make it desolate, even until the consummation, and that determined shall be poured upon the desolate".*

In other words, the shedding of David's blood only eliminated the ritual of shedding the blood of an animal, to acquire the forgiveness of our sins; it did not affect the covenant, it confirms that the covenant is still binding upon us.

Dan. 9:26 states, *"After 62 weeks shall Messiah be cut off, but not for himself: and the people of the prince that shall come, shall destroy the city and the sanctuary, and the end thereof shall be with a flood, and the end of the war desolation's are determined".* This scripture also tells us the death of the Holy Messiah, King David, could have occurred 3 ½ biblical years or 1,260 days before the end of year 73 and the beginning of year 74, as well as the complete destruction of the temple.

Here again Daniel's scripture is talking about the end, most likely not only about the end of the destruction of the temple and of the war, but also toward the end of the 10th age period of this present world. The word "flood" in the above scripture is referring to a flood of arms (weapons). Therefore, the final 2 ages of time will come to an end in 2000 * (360/365.25) + 74.9834 = 2046.2358 cue. on Mar. 27th from sunset of previous day.

Dan. 12:7 states, *"I heard the man clothed in linen, which was upon the waters of the river, when he held up his right hand and his left hand unto heaven, and sware by him that lives forever that it (the period of being in the horn's hand) shall be for a time, times, and an half; and when (the 30-biblical-year time period God takes to reclaim the Israelites back from the horn's hand) he shall have accomplished to scatter the power of the Holy people, all shall be finished".* End of our civilizations.

This 3 ½ times, corresponds to the same times of Dan. 7:25, where God states he will put them (the remnant of the House of Israel), corresponding to <u>Rev. 12:17,</u> *where the devil being wroth with the woman (Zion), that gave birth to the man child, and because God and the earth protected the woman from the face of the serpent, he went to make war with the <u>remnant</u> of her seed, which keep the commandments of God and his testimonies)* into the little horn's hand for 3 ½ times.

In this above scripture a time is equal to one biblical year of 360 days. Therefore, 3 ½ times is equal to 3.5 * 360 = 1260 days (biblical years). Therefore, 1260 * 360/365.25 = 1241.8891 years of our Gregorian calendar. According to <u>Dan. 7:25 and 12:7,</u> this <u>remnant of the House of Israel</u> will be in the hands of this little horn for 1241.8891 of our calendar years. In our calendar year of 774.778 (Oct. 10th from sunset of previous day) is the exact period of time God began putting our ancestors, of the House of Israel, into the hands of this emerged little horn, when "Karl-the-man", called Char-le-magne by the French, on behest of the christian pope, or most likely his own initiative, began to impose the christian religion upon all the tribes that lived in the areas that he ruled over. All the tribes, except the Saxon tribes, submitted to the christian religion, for the Saxons, according to <u>Rev. 12:17,</u> at this particular time in history, were keeping the commandments of God and his testimonies.

<u>2 Esdras 13:41-42,</u> confirms this, *"But then they resolved to leave the country populated by the Gentiles and go to a distant land* (the present area where the Northwestern European nations are located) *never yet inhabited by man, and there <u>at last to be obedient to their laws,</u> which in their own country* (the land of Israel) *they had failed to keep".*

This word <u>Saxons</u> is a short version for the <u>"sons of Isaac</u> (or <u>Isaac's sons)"</u>. For in <u>Gen. 21:12,</u> God tells Abraham, *"In Isaac shall thy seed be called".* <u>Anglo Saxons</u> means <u>English-speaking</u> <u>sons of Isaac</u>, where the word <u>Anglo</u> meaning <u>English</u> in the German language; the name <u>British</u> is a combination of two Hebrew words meaning <u>covenant man/people.</u> This is basically telling us that the British and its Commonwealth countries are Jacob's predicted group of nations given to Ephraim, the second son of Joseph. And the United States of America, which began with the 13 British (<u>covenant people's</u>) colonies, is Jacob's predicted single great nation given to Joseph's firstborn son Manasseh. These two peoples are the leaders of the House of Israel, the "<u>remnant</u>" referred to in <u>Rev. 12:17.</u> The rest of the House of Israel are located in the northwest corner of Europe, such as France (Reuben), Switzerland, Belgium, Netherlands, Denmark, Sweden, Finland, Norway, Greenland, Iceland, Scotland, Wales, Ireland and whatever other lands they have control of, and which are of the most prosperous nations of this world; all with the same mindset, except that of the tribe of Reuben who is still struggling with the loss of their 1st born birthright blessings and status to Ephraim of the tribes of Joseph.

However, in the fall of 774 cue., Oct. 10th from sunset of previous day, "Karl the man"/Char le magne, via a French and German force, attacked the Saxons' place of worship and set up a statue/image of the christians' pagan christ upon their Altar of God, even perhaps the shroud with the image of the face of the christians' christ, which was/is in reality an image of the face of King Saul/Saul called Paul/Charlemagne, and will be the image of the <u>last</u> and <u>next</u> pope of the christian religion, and proceeded to force the Saxons in attendance to worship this pagan imaginary christ; and killed those who refused to worship his pagan christ. He thereafter destroyed their place of worship. Refer to <u>2 Esdras 2:43-47</u> which is one of many obvious alterations to chapters 1 and 2 or even the whole of these two chapters being added, with chapter 3 being the real beginning. For the Holy Messiah makes his entrance in chapter 13.

In the book of Amos are a couple of scriptures that point towards proving the above statements, where <u>Amos in 7:9 and 16</u> states, *"And the high places of <u>Isaac</u> shall be desolate, and the sanctuary of <u>Israel</u> shall be laid waste; and I will rise against the house of <u>Jeroboam</u> with the sword".*

The names of <u>Isaac</u> and <u>Israel</u> are referring to the <u>sons of Isaac</u> (or <u>Isaac's sons</u>) of the <u>House of Israel,</u> led by the two tribes of Joseph who were given this name <u>Israel</u> by their adoptive father/grandfather, Jacob/Israel. The House of Jeroboam is referring to the House of Israel.

*"Now therefore hear thou the word of the Lord God: Thou sayest, Prophesy not against Israel, and drop not thy word against the <u>house of Isaac</u>".*

Amos in these scriptures is definitely prophesying of a time in the future, when God's sanctuary will be laid waste. This is also verified in <u>Ezek. 24:21,</u> *"Speak unto the <u>house of Israel,</u> Thus saith the Lord God; Behold, I will profane my sanctuary, the excellence of your strength, the desire of your eyes, and that which your soul pitieth; and your sons and your daughters whom <u>ye have left</u> shall fall by the sword".* This is the same sanctuary referred to in the scriptures of Amos. Notice the use of the name <u>Isaac</u> by Amos, which is pointing to a time when these Israelites will be referred to as <u>"sons of Isaac</u> (or <u>Isaac's sons</u>)". This is exactly what the name <u>Saxons</u> means.

Also notice in <u>verse 13,</u> Amaziah the priest says to Amos, *"But prophesy not again any more at Bethel: for it is the <u>king's chapel</u>, and it is the <u>king's court</u>".*

Notice it is not God's sanctuary, but a place to worship the golden calves that Jeroboam brought forth for the peoples to worship as <u>1 Kings 12:31-32</u> states, *"And Jeroboam made an house of high places, and <u>made priests of the lowest of the people, which were not of the sons of Levi</u>. And Jeroboam ordained a feast in the 8th month, on the 15th day of the month, like unto the feast that is in Judah,* *and he offered upon the altar. So did he in Bethel, sacrificing unto the calves that he had made: and he placed in Bethel the priests of the high places which <u>he had made</u>"*.

When reading any of the material on "The Saxon Wars", one must keep in mind that a biased christian wrote this material years later; even referring these Saxons to faithless heathens; yet here we have Charles attacking 'their' place of worship; even taking their very young children captive and placing them in christian monasteries, and thoroughly brain-washed in the christian beliefs for future leaders. Enclosed at the beginning of chapter 3 is a page portraying Charlemagne sitting on his horse, and verifying our ancestors performed sacrifices to our one God.

These two actions brought about by Charlemagne, which is reported in <u>Dan. 11:30-39.</u> In verse <u>31</u> it says, *"And arms shall stand on his part, and they shall pollute the sanctuary of strength, and shall take away the daily sacrifice, and they shall place the abomination that makes the altar desolate"*.

The biblical scholars and christian leaders believe this action was brought about by Antiochus Epiphanes, or if not, they believe this will happen in some future date; but this is absolutely false, for the scriptures of <u>Dan. 8:9-14,</u> describes Epiphanes actions. These so-called highly educated deceived individuals are still waiting for this action that makes the altar desolate, to be set up, in some future date; being completely ignorant it has already happened approximately 1,250 biblical years ago, from this first correction date of this writing in late spring of year 2006 cue., when Charles set a statue/image of the christians' pagan christ upon the Saxons' Altar of God. And they have been spreading this deception unto their followers for many years now. Talk about the blind leading the blind. And we as a people deserve everything that comes upon us, because we have believed all these lies without proving whether their statements had any validity.

The leader in <u>Dan. 11:30-39 scriptures</u> *"had a strange god whom his fathers knew not, whom he shall acknowledge and increase with glory, and honour with gold, silver, pleasant stones and things"*.

This strange god is none other than the christians' <u>imaginary</u> christ. According to <u>Dan. 12:7 and 7:25,</u> these Saxons will be in the hand of this christian religion that Charles imposed upon them for 1,260 days (of biblical years) or 1241.8891 from sunset of previous day of our years. After this time expires, God <u>must</u> reclaim our ancestor's children back, of whom we are, for this is exactly what God is implying. It took 30 biblical years for Charles to fully impose this christian religion upon our ancestors; therefore, it will also take God 30 biblical years to fully reclaim us back.

This is why in <u>Dan. 12:7,</u> the 30 biblical years are included in the end section that states, *"And when he shall have accomplished to scatter the power of the Holy people, all these things shall be finished"*.

This totals to the 1260 + 30 = 1290 biblical years; the same timetable mentioned in <u>Dan. 12:11</u>. These 1,290 biblical years calculates to 1271.4579 of our Gregorian years. Therefore, 774.778 +1271.4579 = 2046.2359 cue. *"all these things shall be finished"*. Other words, this will be the end of our civilization as we know it.

This matches the same year the end of the 12th age of this world expires; by using the date when the temple in Jerusalem was destroyed and the war expired, which was 74.9834 cue. at sunset of Dec. 24th, plus 2,000 biblical years, which is 1971.2525 of our calendar years; adds up to 2046.2358 cue. on Mar. 27th from sunset of previous day, marks the end of world war III and the beginning of the 45 biblical years that the survivors must live through, for <u>Dan. 12:12</u> states, *"Blessed is he that waits, and comes to the 1335 days* (of biblical years)*"*, before God gathers the remnant together, and leads them back to the promised land, which is verified below, via King David and his faithful soldiers which is verified below:

<u>Jer. 16:15,</u> *"The Lord God lives, that brought up the children of Israel from the land of the north, and from all the lands whither he had driven them: and I will bring them again into their land that I gave unto their fathers"*. And where the true Messiah of God, King David, will be their king, prince, and shepherd. As stated below:

<u>Ezek. 37:24-25,</u> *"David my servant shall be king over them; and they all shall have one shepherd: they shall also walk in My Judgments, and observe My Statutes, and do them. And they shall dwell in the land that I have given unto Jacob my servant, wherein your fathers have dwelt; and they shall dwell therein, even they, and their children, and their children's children forever: and my servant David shall be their prince forever"*.

Not some glorified pagan imaginary christ that Saul/Paul conjured up in the New Testament times; and a new period of 400 years, according to <u>2 Esdras 7:28-29,</u> will begin, with King David being their special king, under God himself. After 400 years they will all begin to die off to finish the 13th age of this world, which than is followed up with the 14th age which is God's holy Sabbath day of 1,000 biblical years. Just as God's holy Sabbath day (7,000 to 7999.99 biblical years), began upon Adam and Eve being evicted from the Garden of Eden at the end of the 6th day/age. With the completion of the 14th age God's recreation period of a new heaven and earth begins; and followed by the great Judgement Day of all the individuals who have ever lived. Those individuals that believe King David is God's true Messiah, and <u>FLEE</u> from following this Babylonian paganism christian religious ways and any other non-Old Testament ways, and convert back to the ways of the Old Testament, which is the ways of God's instructions for us to live our lives on this earth, which is only a trial period to qualify for God's salvation to an eternal life, will definitely have a very good chance to receive God's salvation to an eternal life; or fail and receive eternal damnation:

Salvation is a promise from God himself, as stated in the quoted scripture of <u>Isa. 55:3,</u> to whoever submits to the ways of God. *"Incline your ear, and come unto me: hear, and your soul shall live; and I will make an everlasting covenant with you, even the sure mercies of David".*

<u>Pro. 1:33,</u> *"But whoso hearkens unto me shall dwell safely, and shall be quiet from fear of evil".*

<u>Chapters of Ezekiel 18 and 33,</u> also tell us how to receive eternal life after death. But the time is running out, for God's reclaiming period begins on 2016.667 on Aug. 31st from sunset of previous day, Jerusalem time zone. Don't be a fool and leave it to the last second, for it may be too late.

<u>Pro. 1:23-32,</u> *"Turn you at my reproofs: behold, I will pour out my Spirit unto you, I will make known my words unto you.*

*Because I have called, and ye refused; I have stretched out my hand, and no man regarded; But ye have set at naught all my counsel, and would none of my reproofs: I will mock when your fear comes; When your fear comes as desolation, and your destruction comes as a whirlwind; when distress and anguish comes upon you: Then shall they call upon me, but I will not answer; they shall seek me early, but they shall not find me: For that they hated knowledge, and didn't choose the fear of the Lord God:*

*They would none of my counsel: they despised all my reproofs. Therefore shall they eat of the fruit of their own ways, and be filled with their own devices. For the turning away of the simple shall slay them, and the prosperity of fools shall destroy them".*

<u>Ezek. 12:25 states,</u> *"For I am the Lord God: I will speak, and the word that I will speak shall come to pass; it shall be no more prolonged: <u>For in your days, O rebellious house</u>, will I say the word, and will perform it, says the Lord God".*

We have been in 'our days' ever since the collapse of the Soviet Union. We, Israelites, have never been in such control of world affairs, as we are at this present time of history; therefore, <u>the time is ripe for God to say the word</u> and bring about the predicted visions of total disasters to occur, not only upon us Israelites, but also upon this whole earth. This same scenario we have today, also occurred before the 1st and 2nd year world wars, we were then also in <u>'our days'</u>, and we were in firm control of world affairs. What happened thereafter, <u>God spoke the word,</u> and brought upon us the devastating world wars; bringing us down from our high perch. And the weapons in those days that was furbished and polished, and given into the hands of our enemies (<u>Ezek. 21:9-15</u>), the Germanized nations (Assyrians), of the Holy Roman Empire as it existed in those days, and their allies, with the flying rockets sent over the English Channel, plus their supersized battleship, the Bismarck;

that caught the British totally by surprise, and brought them down to their knees. Mr. Winston Churchill, God's servant, warned the British government some years before hand, but they didn't take his warning serious, thinking Mr. Churchill was nothing more than a complaining windbag.

This book is again bringing forth, what truly is, the <u>last warning</u> of our civilization, where God again is about to hand over a weapon that shall be furbished and polished, so it can be handled, and given to the <u>slayer</u> (the so-called Holy Roman Empire conglomerate of nations, hidden within the European Union of Nations, with the aid of their allies) of our Israelite peoples, to make a <u>great slaughter</u> of our modern Israelites of today. Please take the time to read <u>Ezek. 21:9-15</u>; and check out what <u>verse 14</u> tells us, *"That this sword will be <u>doubled</u> the 3rd time* (doubled in <u>intensity</u> for this 3rd and <u>last</u> world war)". Or as <u>verse 12</u> states, *"Cry and Howl, son of man: for <u>it shall be upon my people</u>, it shall be upon <u>all the princes of Israel:</u> terrors by reason of the sword <u>shall be upon my people"</u>.* And as verse 15 states, *"I have set the point of the sword against <u>all their gates</u>, that their hearts may faint, and their ruins be multiplied: Ah! It is made bright, it is wrapped up for the <u>great slaughter</u>".*

One of the two major countries in the revival of this so-called Holy Roman Empire, hidden today within the European Union of Nations, will again be the German nations, who throughout history was the major country; when Charlemagne imposed the christian religion upon the Saxon tribes with a 30-biblical-year war; when God used this nation, his sword, to give us as <u>Ezek. 20:24-26</u> states, statutes and judgements that are <u>not good for us</u> and <u>whereby we ought not to live,</u> via the christian religion Charles (disguise of King Saul, with the evil spirit still upon him) imposed upon our ancestors, the <u>Celtic Saxon people;</u> and when the 1st and 2nd world wars occurred, for Germany is the hub of all these European countries, and because he is also God's sword, that God uses to discipline us Israelites, because of our evil ways.

<u>Isa. 10:5-6,</u> *"O Assyrian, the rod of mine anger, and the staff in their hand is mine indignation. I will send him against an hypocritical nation* (us Israelites), *and against the people of my wrath will I give him a charge, to take the spoil, and to take the prey, and to tread them down like the mire of the streets".* <u>Verse 10,</u> tells us why: *"As my hand has found the kingdoms of the <u>idols,</u> and whose <u>graven images</u> did excel them of Jerusalem and Samaria".*

As I am implying, that the christian religion is the most paganism religion that has ever existed, and we <u>naive</u> Israelites are chasing after all our so-called other gods that our graven images represent; from our pagan imaginary christ, to all of our more than 200 pagan canonized saints, to even the pagan virgin mother, lady fatima, etc. But this coming world war III, the German nation will be in partnership with the country Greece. No doubt greatly influenced by the Greek Catholic religion, sister to the Roman Catholic religion.

Zech. 9:12-17, *"Turn you to the stronghold, ye prisoners of hope: even today I declare that I will render <u>double</u> unto thee; when I have bent Judah for me, filled the bow with Ephraim, and raised up thy sons, O Zion, against thy sons, O Greece, and made thee as the sword of a mighty man.*

*And the Lord God shall be seen over them, and his arrows shall go forth as the lightning: and the Lord God shall blow the trumpet, and shall go with whirlwinds of the south. The Lord God of Hosts shall defend them; and they shall devour, and subdue with sling stones; and they shall drink, and make a noise as through wine; and they shall be filled like bowls, and as the corners of the altar.*

*And the Lord their God shall save them in that day as the flock of his people: for they shall be as the stones of a crown, lifted up as an ensign upon his land. For how great is his goodness; and how great is his beauty! Corn shall make the young men cheerful, and new wine the maids".*

Also <u>Hab. 1:5-7</u> states, *"Behold ye* (Israelites) *among the heathens, and regard, and wonder marvellously: For I will work a work in '<u>your days</u>', which ye will not believe, though it be told you. For, lo, I raise up the <u>Chaldeans,</u> that bitter and hasty nation, which shall march through the breadth of the land, to possess the dwelling places that are not theirs. They are terrible and dreadful: their judgment and their dignity shall proceed of themselves".*

The terrorists of today are mostly of the Chaldean peoples that God is bringing against us, because of our evil ways. As I have been stating all along, every action that happens on this earth is brought about by God. We must change our ways, away from this paganism christian religion, and revert back to the ways of the Old Testament, God's ways, with the statutes, judgements, ordinances, and commandments, <u>that are good for us</u> and <u>by which we ought to live our lives,</u> and to <u>keep God's holy Sabbath day</u> on the 7th day of the week, <u>not</u> on the christians' 1st day of the week. We must get rid of all falsehood, such as all our graven and painted images of whatsoever, for there is only <u>one God</u> and none other. Even God's Holy Messiah, King David, is not to be worshipped as a God, for he is a human being just as you and I are. Wake up, people! For we have been deceived to believe falsehood that has been forced upon us via the christian religion and other vain philosophies. There is only <u>one true way,</u> as there is only <u>one true gospel,</u> as there is only <u>one true God.</u> The gospel of the christians' christ is of total falsehood.

Also consider in <u>Dan. 10:14,</u> the angel spoke to Daniel, saying, *"Now I am come to make thee understand what shall befall thy people <u>in the latter days:</u> for yet the vision is for many days* (of biblical years)*".* After telling Daniel what will happen towards the coming of the end, and at the end, Daniel is told in <u>Dan. 12:4 & 9,</u> *"Shut up the words and seal the book <u>till the time of the end";</u>* <u>verse 9</u>

confirms that the words are closed up and sealed till the time of the end. In other words, no one will be able to unseal these end-time scriptures until the time of the end is upon us.

    I am here to announce that we are now in the time of the end, for I have been given the keys to unseal all Daniel's vital sealed scriptures and many other scriptures throughout the Old Testament and New Testament; and those keys are within this writing. As I have stated earlier, our so-called highly educated religious scholars and religious leaders are still waiting for the abomination that makes the Altar of God desolate, to be set up in some future date, being completely ignorant that this action has already occurred approximately 1251.5 biblical years ago and counting from late spring of the year 2006 cue. This action was brought about by Charlemagne on Oct. 10th from sunset of previous day in year 774 cue., and believe it or not, he is the reappearance of King Saul, with the evil spirit still upon him, that God gave him, after rejecting him from being king over the Israelites. This was his 2nd reappearance; his 1st reappearance was Saul and called Paul in the New Testament times. Did he not go on a rampage and destroy many of the Jewish places of worship throughout their land, killing many worshippers in the process? These were his own people he was killing, and then after he and his forces crucified King David, God's true Messiah, he infiltrated the ranks of the true apostles, led by James, and became that chief anti-Messiah/wolf, dressed up in sheep's clothing, devouring the minds/spirits of his followers, with all his false teachings about his imaginary pagan christ and ways, as John is referring to in 1 John 2:18, that 'that chief anti-Messiah' must come first before the end comes—just as your christian priests, ministers, clergy persons, etc., being 'the many anti-Messiahs' amongst us as the wolves dressed up in sheep's clothing, devouring our minds/spirits with all their falsehood, even all the way up to, and including, the pope are doing. Can you expect Saul/Paul to behave any different because he returned by the name "Karl"? Read the historical material on Charlemagne, and you will find that he also was a very tall impressive looking individual, just as King Saul, who was taller than any of his fellow countrymen, from his shoulders upward. The material states that Charles had a broad and strong body of unusual height, being 7 times the length of his foot, which would make him, more than likely, a 6.4 footer or so. (But after paleontologists measured his bones, it was their determination that he was approx. 6 foot 4 inches tall.) However, we will all find out the truth when he reappears as the next and last pope of his christian high Anglican religion that he is the master builder of, for he will also be claiming that he is in fact the Son/Christ of God, and that the christians' images are of himself (2 Esdras 2:42-47). It also states, *"Seated or standing, he made a dignified and stately impression"*. He was not only head of the Roman Empire, as it existed in his days; but he was also in charge of even the christian religion, for the emperor selected the pope in those days. This never changed until 74.9834 + 985.62628 = 1060.6096 on Aug. 10th from sunset of previous day, when the leaders of the christian religion assembled and made a decree to select their own pope. Believe it or not, the presenting and the signing of this decree was precisely at the end of the 11th age and the beginning of the 12th age of this world. Charles in his time was able to take full advantage of his position; imposing "his" christian religion, that he was the master builder of, as stated in <u>1 Cor. 3:10-11</u>, upon our ancestors, the Saxon tribes, living in the area that he ruled over. The French to this day, claim he was one of them. King Saul was an Israelite of the tribe of Benjamin. Saul called Paul was an Israelite of the tribe of Benjamin. This Charles the Great, being the same person, was an Israelite of the tribe of Benjamin. The French are Israelites of the tribe of Reuben. Which reinforces their claim to a certain degree; but Charlemagne's sole purpose was to advance "his" christian religion, mainly upon the Israelites of the House of Israel, with a lot of help from the tribe of Reuben.

Fulfilling <u>Ezek. 20:24-26</u> scriptures, where God states, *"Because they had not executed My Judgements, but had despised My Statutes, and had polluted My Sabbaths, and their eyes were after their fathers' idols. Wherefore I gave them* <u>*also*</u> *statutes that were* <u>*not good*</u>*, and judgements whereby they should* <u>*not live*</u>*; and I polluted them in their own gifts* (via all the christian events) *in that they caused to pass through the fire all that opens the womb* (aborted 1st born via our incinerators) *that I might make them desolate, to the end that they* <u>*might know*</u> (come to realize) *that I am the Lord God"*.

All the above is in the overall master plan of our God of Israel, to bring us to total desolation, because of our continuous evil ways. He gave us statutes, laws, commandments, and judgements that are <u>good for us</u> and whereby we <u>should live in</u>; and they are still available to us via the instructions in the books of Moses. But we humans think we know a better way to live our lives, so God basically is giving to us exactly what we are asking for, statutes, laws, commandments and judgements that are <u>not</u> good for us and whereby we ought <u>not</u> to live; and all these ways are in the christian religion that King Saul as Saul called Paul built, even a different Sabbath day, and these ways will bring us to total desolation, if we don't smarten up and return to the good ways, and acknowledge that there is "<u>only one God</u>" in this entire universe that has brought everything into existence. For us humans to chase after all our pagan gods, as the christians do, is an insult to our <u>one God</u>. But he is still there to embrace you; but only if you prove to him you are a worthy being, just as a father is willing to embrace his rebellious son that he loves. You either conform to his ways, or you are on your own, and must face God's great wrath that shall no doubt come upon the rebellious ones as indicated below:

Micah 5:10-14, *"And it shall come to pass in <u>that day</u>* (the reclaiming time period of 30 biblical years), *says the Lord thy God, that I will cut off thy horses out of the midst of thee, and I will destroy thy chariots: And I will cut off the cities of thy land, and throw down all thy strong holds: And I will cut off witch-crafts out of thine hand: and thou shall have no more soothsayers: Thy <u>graven images</u>* (pictures/trinkets of the christians' pagan imaginary christ, virgin mother, all the canonized saints, etc.) *also will I cut off, thy <u>standing images</u>* (statues of all above-mentioned pagan other so-called gods) *out of the midst of thee; and thou shall no more worship the works of thine hands. And I will pluck up thy groves out of the midst of thee: so will I destroy thy cities"*. And if you refuse to comply; you end up where King Saul will be, in the abyss of the devil's domain. This life is only a trial period, to receive a glorious eternal life with our <u>one God</u>, or a life of total extinction after a prolonged period of extreme damnation with your master Satan. The choice is now in your hands.

<u>Micah 6:8</u> states, *"He has showed thee, O man, what is good; and what does the Lord thy God require of thee, but to do justly, and to <u>love mercy</u>* (on the victims, <u>not</u> on the criminals as we in our society are doing), *and to walk humbly with the Lord thy God?"* To walk humbly with your <u>one God</u>, you <u>must</u> keep the first 4 commandments, that relate to God himself, and keep the covenant that our ancestors made with 'The Lord our God'; by worshipping <u>only</u> the Lord God and <u>no one else or anything whatsoever</u>, such as the christians' pagan imaginary christ, virgin mother, canonized saints, etc. We are not to make graven, painted or standing images of the above-mentioned pagan so-called other gods; not even an image of what we may think God looks like. We are <u>forbidden</u> to do this, as <u>Deut. 4:23 states</u>. We are not to use God's name in vain, such as praying to God for certain favours of whatsoever, but asking it of God in the name of the christians' pagan imaginary christ, another so-called god; or some pagan canonized saint, virgin mother, etc. God <u>will not</u> answer this prayer. Nor are we to make any graven, painted images of anything whatsoever to pray to, and serve, as if they are real gods. God forbids us to do this. We <u>must</u> keep holy God's Sabbath day; <u>not</u> on the christians' first day of the week, Sunday; but on God's 7th day of the week, just before sundown Friday to just after sundown Saturday, the proper day and time of this day. No one has the right to change this day to any other day, to suit their own purpose. For this is a sign between God and his chosen obedient people. Everyone that continues to ignore this vital covenant and the commandments are expelling themselves from being of God's people. The choice is now, again, in your hands. Please notice in <u>Dan. 9:27</u>, the Messiah came to <u>confirm</u> the covenant, not to eliminate it.

There is no new covenant made with us Israelites, when God sacrificed his only begotten firstborn Son, King David. The only difference between God and his people, us dispersed Israelites, is the fact that we are no longer required to sacrifice an animal, in shedding its blood to atone for our sins, and then place these sins on the head of the second animal, which was a goat, that was then set free in the wilderness. This ritual was performed once a year on the Day of Atonement.

God's ultimate sacrifice of shedding the blood of his only begotten Son, replaced this animal sacrifice; and on the Day of Atonement we are to keep this ultimate sacrifice within our minds, and thank the Lord our only God for this great sacrificial act, for no greater sacrifice could God have brought about, than to sacrifice his only begotten Son; that's how great God loves his people, the children of Abraham, Isaac, and Jacob, whom he called Israel. But this doesn't set us free to ignore the original covenant that our ancestors made with the Lord our God. We are still bound to this covenant, <u>like it or not</u>, we are required to fear our <u>one God</u>, and not to fear any other so-called gods, as our christian paganism religion preaches, nor bow down yourselves to them, nor pray to them, nor serve them, nor sacrifices to them, nor make any graven/standing/painted images of them. As stated below:

<u>2 Kings 17:35-39,</u> *"But the Lord God, who brought you up out of the land of Egypt with great power and a stretched out arm, <u>him shall ye fear</u>, and <u>him shall ye worship</u>, and <u>to him shall you do sacrifice</u>. And the <u>Statutes</u>, and the <u>Commandments</u>, and the <u>Ordinances</u>, and the <u>Laws</u>, which <u>he wrote for you</u>, <u>ye shall observe to do forevermore;</u> and ye shall <u>not</u> fear other gods. But <u>the Lord your God ye shall fear;</u> and <u>he shall deliver you out of the hands of your enemies</u>".*

Notice the underlined word 'forevermore', which definitely tells us that this covenant is not a part time covenant, but a covenant for all times. Please "again" notice in <u>Dan. 9:27,</u> the Messiah came to <u>confirm</u> the covenant, not to eliminate it.

Please consider the following scriptures from <u>Jer. 11:3-5,</u> *"Thus saith the Lord God of Israel; <u>Cursed</u> be the man that obeys not the words of this covenant, which I commanded your fathers in the day that I brought them out of the land of Egypt, from the iron furnace, saying, <u>Obey my voice,</u> and do them* (the words of the covenant) *according to all which I commanded you: so shall ye be my people, and I will be your God: That I may perform unto your fathers, to give them a land flowing with milk and honey, as it is this day".* <u>Vr. 8,</u> *"Yet they obeyed not, nor inclined their ear, but walked every one in the imagination of their evil heart: therefore I will bring upon them* (the attached curses to) *all the words of this covenant, which I commanded them to do; but they did them not".* <u>Vrs. 10-11,</u> *"They* (us modern day Israelites) *are turned back to the iniquities of their forefathers, which refused to hear my words; and they went after other gods to serve* them: *The House of Israel and the House of Judah have broken my covenant which I made with their fathers*. Therefore thus saith the Lord God, Behold, I will bring evil upon them, which they shall not be able to escape; and though they shall cry unto me, I will not hearken unto them".

Pro. 1:23-33, "Turn you at my reproof: behold, I will pour out my spirit unto you, I will make known my words unto you. Because I have called, and ye refused; I have stretched out my hand, and no man regarded; But ye have set at naught all my counsel, and would none of my reproof; I also will laugh at your calamity; I will mock when your fear comes; When your fear comes as desolation, and your destruction comes as a whirlwind; when distress and anguish comes upon you,

Then shall they call upon me, but I will not answer; they shall seek me early, but they shall not find me: For that they hated knowledge, and did not choose the fear of the Lord their God: They would none of my counsel: they despised all my reproof. Therefore shall they eat of the fruit of their own way, and be filled with their own devices. For the turning away of the simple shall slay them, and the prosperity of fools shall destroy them.

But whoso hearkens unto me shall dwell safely, and shall be quiet from fear of evil".

This is exactly what I performed when studying the Bible, on God's holy Sabbath day, sunset Friday to sunset Saturday, not only reading these many scriptures, but also writing them down with other look alike scriptures that related to them, giving me a greater understanding of what these scriptures were relating to me. As a result I found it necessary to bring forth this book, in order to keep a record of what I have learned from studying the Bibles from various sources and to pass this knowledge to the public interested in knowing the real truth, not from my lips or any other lips that believe they know the truth, but with this book where the individual can check the knowledge within this book with whatever sources they may have or find, by following the above-mentioned scripture, to reprove all things. And I am absolutely sure God will also give to you complete knowledge of his ways, just as the Lord God Almighty has given unto me.

# Chapter 3

# Who Is the Little Horn of Dan. 7:25 scripture?

2 Cor. 7:14, 9:2-4, 10:8, 13-16, and 11:16-17, proves Saul/Paul is a boaster. They are as follows:

"For if *I have boasted* any thing to him of you, I am not ashamed; but as we speak all things to you in truth, even so *our boasting*, which I made before Titus, is found a truth".

"For I know the forwardness of your mind, for which *I boast of you* to them of Macedonia, that Achaia was ready a year ago; and your zeal has provoked very many. Yet have I sent the brethren, lest *our boasting* of you should be in vain in this behalf; that, as I said, ye may be ready"; Lest haply if they of Macedonia come with me, and find you unprepared, we (that we say not, ye) should be ashamed in this same *confident boasting*".

"For though *I should boast* somewhat more of our authority, which the Lord has given us for edification, and not for your destruction, I should not be ashamed:"

"But we will not *boast of things* without our measure, but according to the measure of the rule which God has distributed to us, a measure to reach even unto you. For we stretch not ourselves beyond our measure, as though we reached not unto you: for we are come as far as to you also in *preaching the gospel of christ*: Not *boasting of things* without measure, that is, of other men's labours; but having hope, when your faith is increased, that we shall be enlarged by you according to our rule abundantly, to preach the gospel in the regions beyond you, and not to *boast* in another man's line of things made ready to our hand".

"I say again, Let no man think me a fool; if otherwise, yet as a fool receive me, that *I may boast myself a little.* That which I speak, I speak it not after the Lord, but as it were foolishly, in this *confidence of boasting*".

James 4:16 states, "But now you rejoice in *your boastings:* All such rejoicings *is evil*". Which is proving to us that this so-called Apostle Paul is not a true apostle but is a false apostle, who is in fact bringing about a false religion, called the christian religion, with a pagan imaginary christ and false doctrine mainly about this false pagan imaginary christ of his; as he states in the above underlined scripture: *"preaching the gospel of christ"*.

James 3:5-6 is talking about the tongue amongst our members *that boasts great things.* James no doubt is referring to Saul/Paul and his close associates. James is even referring to Saul/Paul *as a vain man* in 2:20, because Heb. 11:17 and 31, and other scriptures within Saul/Paul's writings, states that by faith only, without works, Abraham and Rahab the harlot were justified. And in other scriptures within Saul/Paul's writings, such as in Eph. 2:8-9, *"For by grace are ye saved through faith; and that not of yourselves: it is a gift of God: not of works, lest any should boast"*. Saul/Paul's statements are absolutely false, they do not agree with Ezek. chapters 18 and 33, where works are the requirements to receive God's salvation.

James in 2:21-26 states, *they were justified by their works with their faith. Faith without works is dead, being alone, as the body without the mind/spirit is dead.*

This book of James is mainly a rebuttal of Saul/Paul's teachings. Notice the phrase *boasting great things.* This is the same phrase used in Dan. 7:20-25, where the emerged little horn on the 10 horned beast *spoke great boasting things/words* against the Most High. This horn also was more stout than his fellows; just as *King Saul was higher than his country folks, from his shoulders upward, and that there was none like him among all the people,* as 1 Sam. 10:23-24 states.

The following are comparable scriptures from various Bibles to prove that King Saul, Saul called Paul, the little emerging horn in Dan. 7:20 & 25, the leader (Charles the Great, or Charlemagne) in Dan. 11:30-39, and even the leader/pope of verses 40-45, *"who will plant the tabernacles of his palace between the seas in the glorious holy mountain"*, which may very well be the catalyst that brings about the dreaded 30 biblical years of the 3rd world war, which will be God's reclaiming period of his people of the House of Israel; and also the false prophet in Rev. 19:20 & 20:10 is the same person, Saul, the first king of the Israelites, who was rejected by God, and who than received an evil spirit from God upon him, which troubled him, and thereafter prophesied falsely.

* Acts 7:58, *"And the witnesses laid down their clothes at a young man's feet, whose name was Saul"*.
* 1 Sam. 9:2, *"And Kish had a son, whose name was Saul, a choice young man, and a goodly: and there was not among the children of Israel a goodlier person than he: from his shoulders and upward he was higher than any of the people"*. (KJB; some Bibles include the word handsome)
* 1 Sam. 10:23-24, *"And they ran and fetched Saul thence: and when he stood among the people, he was higher than any of the people, from his shoulders and*

upwards, that _there is none like him among all the people_". (KJB; New World Translation and New International Bible use the word _taller_)
* Dan. 7:20, "Even of that horn that had eyes, and a mouth that spake very great things, whose look was more stout than his fellows". (KJB)

- "Even that horn that had eyes and _a mouth speaking grandiose things, and the appearance of which was bigger than that of its fellows_". (NWT)
- "The horn that looked more imposing than the others, and a mouth that spoke boastfully". (NIB)
- "The horn that had eyes, and a mouth speaking proud words and appeared larger than the others". (NEB)
- "The horn looked greater than the others. It had eyes and a mouth that kept bragging". (NCV)
- "A mouth that spoke arrogant things, and which appeared greater than its fellows". (DSSB)
- "That horn which had eyes and a mouth uttering great boasts, and which was larger in appearance than its associates". (NASB)
- "The mouth that spoke proud words, and seemed stronger than his fellows". (MTB)
- Dan. 7:25, "And he shall _speak great words against the Most High_, and shall wear out the saints of the Most High, and think to change times and laws (of God)". (KJB)
- "And he will _even speak words against the Most High_, and he will harass continually the Holy Ones. And he will intend to change times and laws". (NWT)
- "_He shall hurl defiance at the Most High_, and shall wear down the saints of the Most High. He shall plan to alter the customary times and laws". (NEB)
- "And he will _speak out against the Most High_, and wear down the saints of the Highest One, and he will intend to make alterations in times and in law". (NASB)
- "He shall _speak words against the Most High_, shall oppress the Holy Ones of the Most High, and shall think of changing the times and the laws". (DSSB)
- "He shall _vaunt himself against the Most High_, and harass the saints of the Most High; he shall plan to alter the sacred seasons and laws". (MTB)

* Dan. 11:36, "And the king shall do according to his will; and he shall _exalt himself, and magnify himself_ above every god, and shall speak marvellous things against the God of gods, and shall prosper till the indignation be accomplished: for that that is determined shall be done". (KJB)

* "And the king will actually do according to his own will, and he will <u>exalt himself and magnify himself</u> above every god; and against the God of gods he will speak marvelous things. And he will certainly prove successful until the denunciation will have come to a finish; because the things decided upon must be done". (NWT)
* "The king will do what he chooses; he will <u>exalt and magnify himself</u> above every god and against the God of gods he will utter monstrous blasphemies. All will go well for him until the time of wrath ends, for what is determined must be done". (NEB)
* "Then the king will <u>do as he pleases, and he will speak monstrous things against the God of gods;</u> and he will prosper until the indignation is finished, for that which is decreed will be done". (NASB)

- "And the king shall do according to his will; he shall <u>exalt himself and magnify himself</u> above every god, and shall speak astonishing things against the God of gods. He shall prosper till the period of wrath is accomplished; for what is determined must take place". (DSSB)
- "The king shall <u>do as he pleases, he shall uplift himself and exalt himself over every god, uttering amazing vaunts against the God of gods;</u> he shall prosper till the wrath divine has run its course, for what has been decreed must be fulfilled". (MTB)
- In this <u>Dan. 11th chapter,</u> we have this king exalting himself above every god, and speaks great monstrous blasphemies against the Most High God, nor does he regard any god, as <u>verse 37</u>, tells us; yet <u>verse 38</u> states that *in his estate shall he honour the god of forces; and a god whom his fathers knew not,* <u>shall he honor with gold, silver, and precious stones and pleasant things</u>.
- This is that same christ/another god that he brought forth in the New Testament times. This is also the same so-called another god of the woman/religion mentioned in <u>Rev. 17th chapter,</u> which has upon her forehead a name written, *mystery, babylon the great, the mother of harlots and abominations of the earth.* In <u>verse 3,</u> this woman/religion sits upon a scarlet-coloured beast, so-called Holy Roman Empire, hidden within the European Union of Nations, full of names of blasphemy, having seven heads and ten horns. This is the same beast in <u>Dan. 7:20,</u> with the 10 horns. Also this woman/religion and the pagan christ/another god whom he honours, which his fathers, his Israelite ancestors knew not, he honours with gold, silver, and precious stones and pleasant things, just as this woman-religion in <u>Rev. 17,</u> was arrayed in purple and scarlet colour, and decked with gold, precious stones, and pearls, and having a golden cup/

communion cup, in her hands full of abominations and filthiness of her fornication:

Only a totally deceived individual can't see the connection between this King Saul's christ/another god and this woman/christian religion that he is the master builder of, for Saul/Paul's deceptive veil is still upon them and will have to be removed by God himself, when they, the <u>remnant</u>, will be led back to the promised land of Israel, after God's 30 biblical years of reclaiming period expires in 2046.2358 cue. and the expiration of the 44.353 Gregorian years of nothingness in 2090.5888 cue. on Aug. 2nd from sunset of previous day.

<u>Isa. 25:6-8</u> states, *"And in this mountain shall the Lord God of hosts make unto all people a feast of fat things, a feast of wines on the lees, of fat things full of marrow, of wines on the lees well refined. And he will destroy in this mountain <u>the face of the covering cast over all people, and the</u> (deceptive) <u>veil that is spread over all nations.</u> He will swallow up death in victory; and the Lord God will wipe away tears from off all faces; and the rebuke of his people shall he take away from off all the earth: for the Lord God has spoken it".*

<u>1 Sam. 16:4</u> tells us *"that the Spirit of God departed from Saul, and an evil spirit from the Lord troubled him".*

This evil was still on him when he reappeared as this Saul called Paul in the New Testament times. As you can now hopefully see, that this little horn is none other than King Saul in person, with the evil spirit still upon him. Saul's destiny was to put God's Holy Messiah, King David, to death as a lamb brought to the slaughter, shedding his blood to atone for the sins of God's people, and in doing so opened the way for us obedient ones to receive God's salvation to an eternal life. For no greater sacrifice could God bring about, than to sacrifice "His only begotten son" to atone for our sins. King Saul was finally able to put King David to death, but only by design of God's divine master plan. This King Saul, as we are all aware of, tried several times to put David to death in their original generation. It is absolutely fitting that God chose King Saul to have the job to carry out this great sacrifice for him, and in effect handing over all God's obedient ones to his adversary, King David. For King Saul is the devil's 1st born son, the son of perdition. Saul/Paul-King Saul's job was also to bring about a new religion, which is called the christian religion, with his imaginary pagan christ as the stumbling block to lead God's people astray. God's Holy Messiah is not Paul's christ but is none other than King David, God's choice, to be king over the future Israelites, and indeed over all the peoples of the future world.

This pagan christ that Saul/Paul brought about was in reality <u>himself</u>, and proven as such in the first two chapters of <u>2 Esdras 2:42-47</u>, which states,

*"In the middle* (of a large gathering of Gentile and heathen followers*) stood a very tall young man, taller than all the rest, who was setting a crown on the head of each one of them; he stood out above them all"*. Is this not the same as 1 Sam. 2:9 and 10:23-24? Where it states, *"And Kish had a son, whose name was Saul, a choice young man, and a goodly: and there was not among the children of Israel a goodlier person than he: from his shoulders and upward he was higher than any of the people"*. Are not these scriptures referring to the same person? This 2 Esdras 2:47 scripture refers to this tall young man as God's Son. Read the first two chapters of 2 Esdras; and you will find that a large part of these two chapters are definitely altered or even wholly being added within this book. Chapter 3 is the unaltered continuation of this book.

The Holy Messiah comes on the scene in the 13th chapter, where in vrs. 32-33 states, *"My Son* (King David*) will be revealed, whom you saw as a man rising from the sea"*. Vrs. 39-40 states, *"Then you saw him collecting a different company, a peaceful one. They are the 10 tribes which were taken off into exile in the time of King Hoshea, whom Shalmaneser king of Assyria took prisoner* (in the years 734-721 b. cue.)*"*.

## **This is proven by scriptures below**

Jer. 30:9, *"But they shall serve the Lord their God, and David their king, whom I will raise up unto them"*.

Ezek. 34:23-24, *"And I will set up one shepherd over them, and he shall feed them, even my servant David; He shall be their shepherd; And I the Lord will be their God, and David a prince among them; I the Lord God have spoken it"*.

Ezek. 37:24-25, *"And David my servant shall be king over them; and they shall all have one shepherd: They shall also walk in My Judgments, and observe My Statutes, and do them. And they shall dwell in the land that I have given unto Jacob my servant, wherein your fathers have lived, and they shall dwell therein, even they, and their children, and their children's children forever: and my servant David shall be their prince forever"*.

Hosea 3:5, *"Afterword shall the children return, and seek their God, and David their king; and shall fear the Lord God and his goodness in the latter days"*.

If these above-quoted scriptures do not convince you that David will be the end-time Messiah of God, and our future prince, shepherd, and king, there is nothing more to say. For these scriptures are speaking about the time period after all 12 ages of this world expires in the year of 2046.2358 cue., which is at the end of God's reclaiming period of us Israelites that recognize David as being God's Holy Messiah, who was indeed sacrificed by God, as a lamb brought to the slaughter, shedding his blood to make atonement for our past, present, and even future sins, to a certain degree. As I stated above, Saul/Paul, who is none other than the reappearance of King Saul, with the evil spirit still upon him, was chosen by God to shed David's blood to make atonement for our past, present, and even future sins, to a certain degree. Individuals think they can live their lives completely ignoring God's Old Testament instructions and still take advantage of David's shed blood to receive God's salvation, to an eternal life, after their initial death from this temporary life here on earth. But they are completely mistaken. For all one has to do is read all of <u>Ezekiel's chapters of 18 & 33,</u> and you will find that there are works to be performed in order to take advantage of David's shed blood, to receive God's salvation to an eternal life. Do not allow anyone to deceive you in believing otherwise, for your eternal life is in your hands.

<u>Proverbs 1:22-32,</u> *"How long, ye simple ones, will ye love simplicity? And the scorners delight in their scorning, and fools hate knowledge? Turn you at my reproof: behold, I will pour out my spirit unto you, I will make known my words unto you".*

*"Because I have called, and ye refused; I have stretched out my hand, and no man regarded; but ye have set at naught all my counsel, and would none of my reproof: I also will laugh at your calamity; I will mock when your fear comes; when your fear comes as desolation, and your destruction comes as a whirlwind; when distress and anguish comes upon you".*

*"Then shall they call upon me, but I will not answer; they shall seek me early, but they shall not find me: for that they hated knowledge, and did not choose the fear of the Lord God: they would none of my counsel: they despised all my reproof".*

*"Therefore shall they eat of the fruit of their own way, and be filled with their own devices. For the turning away of the simple shall slay them, and the prosperity of fools shall destroy them".*

*"But whoso hearkens unto me shall dwell safely, and shall be quiet from fear of evil".*

## <u>Other sets of scriptures that verify God's laws and testimonies are still in force are as follows:</u>

<u>Isa. 8:16-17 and 20,</u> *"Bind up the testimony, seal the law among my disciples. And I will wait upon the Lord God, that hides his face from the house of Jacob, and I will look for him".*

*"To the law and to the testimony: if they speak not according to <u>this word</u>* (God's laws and testimonies) *it is because there is no light in them".*

# To those people that take the above information lightly, the following scriptures are a warning:

<u>Isa. 8:21-22,</u> *"And they shall pass through it* (the reclaiming time period, beginning (2016.667 on Aug. 31st from sunset of previous day, Jerusalem time zone) *hardly bestead and hungry; and it shall come to pass, that when they shall be hungry, they shall fret themselves, and curse their king and their God, and look upward. And they shall look unto the earth; and behold trouble and darkness, dimness of anguish; and they shall be driven to darkness".*

<u>Ezek. 11:21,</u> *"But as for them whose heart walks after the heart of their detestable things and their abominations, I will recompense their way upon their own heads".*

Our real problem began when Saul, of the tribe of Benjamin, of the Israelites, a citizen and soldier of the Roman Empire, with his band of mainly Roman soldiers, put King David, God's true Messiah to death, and thereafter penetrated into the group of the true Apostles, led by James; to bring about his teachings of a different gospel of his (Saul/Paul's) imaginary pagan christ, taking the title of the true Messiah, King David, whom he and his forces put to death, and gave this title to his imaginary figure, as a name; hence the name Jesus Christ, interpreted from the Greek language, into English. The Jewish followers of the true Messiah, King David, found out that Saul/Paul was preaching a new gospel, not of God, but of his imaginary pagan christ; and made an oath, that they will neither eat nor drink till they have killed him. But he received protection from the Roman's puppets ruling over the Jewish nation. Saul/Paul no longer preached his gospel to the Jewish people, but only to the Gentiles, as it is to this day, However, by design of God's plan via the actions of Charlemagne, gave us Israelites, of the <u>remnant (Rev. 12:17)</u>, of the House of Israel, of the ancient Saxon tribes, into the hands of Saul/Paul's christian religion for a time period of 1,260 days (of biblical years) or1241.8891 of our calendar years, which was planned in an early summer month of the year 772 cue., and will begin to end with a 30-biblical-year war against this same 4th world empire and their allies in the year 774.778 + 1241.8891 = 2016.667 on Aug. 31st from sunset of previous day, slightly more than 10 years from late spring of year 2006 cue., for this 30-biblical-year world war is God's reclaiming period, of us modern Israelites from this pagan christian religious hand; matching the time it took Charles to fully impose this pagan christian religious hand upon our ancient ancestors. Reading the historical information about Charlemagne's physical appearance, where it states;

*"He had a broad and strong body of <u>unusual height</u>, but well proportioned; <u>for his height measured seven times his feet.</u> His skull was round, the eyes lively*

*and rather large, the nose was more than average length, the hair gray but full, the face friendly and cheerful. Seated or standing, he thus made a dignified and stately impression even though he has a thick, short neck and a belly that protruded somewhat; but this was hidden by the <u>good proportion of the rest of his figure.</u> He strode with firm step and held himself as a man; he spoke with a higher voice than one would have expected of someone of his build".*

He was indeed a very tall, goodly, impressionable looking person, just as <u>1 Sam. 9:2 and 10:23-24 states,</u> *"And he, Kish, had a son, whose name was Saul, a choice young man, and a goodly: and there was not among the children of Israel a goodlier person than he: from his shoulders and upwards he was higher than any of the people".*

*"And they ran and fetched him thence: and when he stood among the people he was higher than any of the people from his shoulders and upwards. And Samuel said to all the people, See ye him whom the Lord God has chosen, that there is none like him among all the people? And all the people shouted, and said, God save the king".*

Compare the two sets of quotations of <u>Charlemagne</u> and <u>King Saul</u>; are they not the same person, the emerged little horn recorded in <u>Dan. 7:20 & 25</u> scriptures, that God stated he will put <u>them</u> into his hands for 1,260 days, of biblical years? God put our Saxon ancestors into this horn's hand via the christian religion, that <u>Saul called Paul</u> is the master builder of, and believe it or not, all three are the same person, with the evil spirit still upon him, that he received from God, after being rejected as king of the Israelites.

This is what the Bible along with our historical material discloses to us, if we really go after the truth. Even in the scriptures of <u>Ezek. 20:24-26,</u> proves that we are in this false religious hand when it states: *"Because they had not executed My Judgments, but had despised My Statutes, and had polluted My Sabbaths, and their eyes were after their father's idols. Wherefore I gave them <u>also</u> statutes that were <u>not good</u> for them, and judgments whereby they should <u>not live in</u>; and I polluted them in their own gifts* (christmas, easter, saint day events, even the helloween event, gifts and goodies), *in that they caused to pass through the fire* (incinerators) *all that open the womb, that I might make them desolate, to the end that they might know* (come to realize) *that I am the Lord God".* (Who has brought all this desolation upon us, because of our continuous evil ways.)

Our Saxons ancestors, when Charles imposed this christian religion upon them, received these statutes and judgements, and false Sabbath day, and different time of a day, <u>that are not good for us,</u> and <u>whereby we ought not to live,</u> and we are at the present time in history, dominated by all these changes, brought upon us by the little horn's disciples, the leaders of the christian organizations, that are contrary to God's ways.

This world will not change its ways even if it recognizes the truth; therefore, it is left up to ourselves to flee from this paganism christian religion before it is too late and follow the ways of the Old Testament, which is God's ways. Because our ancient ancestors polluted God's holy Sabbaths, God states that He will pollute us in our own gifts, in that they caused to pass through the fire all that open the womb, that He might make us desolate, to the end that we might come to realize that all this evil is brought upon us by God himself, because of our continuous evil ways.

These gifts and goodies are what we receive in the christian events, such as the christmas, easter, saint day events, and believe it or not, even the helloween event; there is absolutely nothing hallowed in this event; reason I spelled it as such. We are being brainwashed with these gifts and goodies, which keeps us observing and carrying them on from one generation to another, and in doing so, we are being polluted with all the pagan gods that come along with these events.

We should by now come to a realization that this little horn that emerged on the 10 horned beast is none other than King Saul in person, with the evil spirit still upon him. This horn was the builder of this christian religion, and will be the <u>next and last</u> king/pope of this christian religion (<u>2 Esdras 12:10-34)</u>, and will come on the scene March 20th in 2013, 1,260 days prior to Aug. 31st of 2016. He will more than likely take the name Saul Paul I, or even Saul Paul II, for this will be the second time he will physically be the leader of this christian religion, known as the High Anglican of the Church of England when he again takes the reign as the <u>next and last pope</u> of all the christian religions he in fact built in the New Testament days. For he will be putting down Pope Francis after he gets settled as the archbishop of the High Anglican Church of the Church of England. For he is the right head of the eagle mentioned in 2 Esdras 11, of the Apocrypha books and who devours the head on the left, who is at the present time the newly elected Pope Francis of the Roman Catholic religion. For he via the christian religion and the <u>beast (</u>the <u>last revival</u> of the so-called Holy Roman Empire, hidden within the European Union Conglomerate Countries, and with their allies) that he will be directing, will be destroyed by God's true Messiah, King David and his forces as stated below. Also refer to chapter 5, where the angle interprets Ezra's vision in a dream.

<u>Rev. 19:20,</u> which states, *"And the beast was taken, and with him the false prophet that wrought miracles before him, with which he deceived them that had received the mark of the beast, and them that worshipped <u>his image.</u> These both were cast alive into a lake of fire burning with brimstone"*.

"His image" in the above scripture is referring to the false prophet as the pagan christ, and the "false prophet" is referring to none other than Saul called Paul, King Saul in person, with the evil spirit still upon him, and the sign of the beast is the keeping of the Sunday or the 1st day of the week as the holy day, where the sign of God is the keeping of the 7th day of the week, from just before sunset Friday to just after sunset Saturday. This last pope/false prophet will be a very tall individual, just as King Saul, was a head taller than his country folks, and with the evil spirit still upon him, he will be an arrogant, boasting, imposing, and probably a handsome impressionable individual, and according to Rev. 19:20, will be able to work miracles. This false prophet will come on the scene, after he disposes of this present Pope Frances. For further information to prove the above critical statement, refer to chapter 5, where the angel in 2 Esdras 12:10-34, gives Ezra the interpretation of his vision, where the three heads of the eagle represents the last three kings/popes of the christian religious body of the so-called Holy Roman Empire, and the Church of England hidden today within the European Union of Nations.

In Dan. 7:25 is where God tells us that He will put us into the leader/horn's hand of this christian religion for 1,260 days (of biblical years). This scripture is in conjunction with Rev. 12:17 scripture, where *"the devil was wroth with the women* [Zion] *that gave birth to the man child* (and because God and the earth protected the woman), *the devil went to make war with the remnant of her seed, which keep the commandments of God and his testimonies"*.

This remnant is not of the House of Judah; but is of the House of Israel, the 10 lost tribes. The tribes that were defeated by the Assyrian nation; and the survivors/remnant were taken into the Assyrian lands and were ruled over by them. This Assyrian nation is known today as the German speaking nations. These 10 lost tribes of the House of Israel were known as the Saxon tribes, who were residing north and west of the area of these German speaking nations.

Dan. 7:25 became a reality when Charles the Great in a winter month of the year 774.778 cue. on Oct. 10th from sunset of previous day, began to impose the christian religion upon these Saxon tribes that he ruled over. One of his first major actions was to advance upon the Saxons' place of worship, called the Irminsul, in the historical literature of "The Saxon Wars". This name Saxons is a short version or slang of Isaac's sons (or sons of Isaac). In Gen. 21:12, God tells Abraham that his seed shall be called after Isaac.

This Irminsul, according to the historical material, was a tall column of wood erected on the Holy Heath (a holy patch of earth) which was honoured as the symbolic bearer of the universe. Caution must be taken upon reading this historical literature, for on this Holy Heath was in fact an erected altar, whereupon they offered sacrifices to God. This place today is what we are calling the Stonehenge ruins, located in England. The initial proof is the east entrance lines up with the summer solstice sunrise, indicating this entrance of major importance as indicated in Ezekiel 44:1-3, where only God and the

King/Prince are the only ones that used this entrance, and where the King/Prince of the people ate his meal. The west entrance lines up with the winter solstice sun setting, giving it of secondary importance. This entrance was only used by the Levi priestly family members where outside a short distance away was in fact a hanging tree located outside their place of worship where they strung up the sacrificial animal to prepare it for the sacrifice. These Saxons were not tree worshippers as some of these writings indicate. Again we are dealing with a deceived christian's mind, not able to separate truth from obvious lies. This was in fact the remnant taken prisoner when the Israelites were defeated by the Assyrians/Germans in the years 734 to 721 b. cue., and taken into their lands and put to work as slaves, and the work they performed, they were named after. My last name is Mueller and my male ancestor was put to work grinding grain, the English equivalent is Miller. However, my mother's last name is Degelman, this is a Hebrew word meaning Flagman, even stated as such on the internet. The only ones allowed to carry the Hebrew flag was of the priestly family of the tribe of Levi. It appears that I have been chosen by God to bring forth His truths within this book. To my knowledge all God's prophets were of the priestly family of the tribe of Levi. I urge you to read this book and prove it with the Old Testament books and the Apocrypha books, particularly of 2 Esdras, but be cautious with chapters 1 and 2, for they have been tampered with or wholly added to this book of 2 Esdras by none other than King Saul/Saul called Paul the builder of the christian religion/Charlemagne/the devil's 1st born son/the next and last pope of the christian religion, who spent a whole winter in the Vatican fixing up the scriptures, naturally according to his way of thinking. Whose hand God put us sinful Israelites into, as reported in Daniel's 7:25 for 1,260 biblical years. We have been within his hand ever since Charlemagne imposed it upon our Saxon ancestors, not for our good, but for our punishment as reported in Ezekiel 20:24-26, which is the pagan christian religion. The christian leaders and religious scholars are still looking for these two abominations to come about in some future time, being completely ignorant this has already happened in the year 774.778, Oct. 10th from sunset of previous day.

In Ex. 20:26, God states, *"Neither shall thou go up by steps unto mine altar, that thy nakedness be not discovered thereon".*

The christian organizations from the Catholics to most of the breakaway protestants have altars with steps leading up to it, a breaking of God's commandment. This is probably why the author of "The Saxon Wars" doesn't even mention the Saxons' Altar of God, on the Holy Heath, for it had no steps leading up to it, per God's commandment. This historical writing also calls these Saxon tribes as faithless heathens; yet here we have Charles attacking 'their' place of worship; a totally biased writing to be sure. This writing is definitely written by a deceived christian many years later.

Therefore, because we do not have the Saxons' point of view in any writings, we must assume that the actions Charles took upon their place of worship and the people, mirrored the action Antiochus Epiphanes took upon the temple in the city of Jerusalem, where on the 15th of the 9th month Kislev he set up the abomination of desolation on God's Altar, his own altar, and on his own altar placed upon it his pagan god Jupiter Olympius, making God's Altar desolate, and forced the Jewish worshippers to worship his pagan god, killing whomever refused. 10 days later he sacrificed a pig on God's Altar, and forced the people in attendance to eat this unclean animal. This action not only defiled God's Altar for the second time, but also defiled the whole sanctuary. And according to Dan. 8:14, this sanctuary will not be fully cleansed until a time period of 2,300 days (of biblical years) expires. This action occurred in our calendar year of 166.605 b. cue. Therefore, this sanctuary will be finally cleansed, the proper way, from the vision concerning *"the daily sacrifice, and the transgression of desolation, to give both the sanctuary and the host to be trodden under foot"* as Dan. 8:13 states: 2,300 days, of biblical years, is equal to 2300 * 360/365.25 = 2266.9404 - (-166.3954) = 2100.3358 of our Gregorian calendar year, May 1st from sunset of previous day, and the temple shall be completely rebuilt, with a new altar *"and be cleansed and sanctified via the blood and ashes of a red heifer without spot and wherein is no blemish, and upon which never came yoke"*, as stated in Numbers 19:2: in our calendar year of 2100.3358 cue. Having only 2090.5888 - 2100.3358 = 9.747 Greg. years to gather up his flock and lead them back to the land of Israel in 3.45 Greg. years and still have the allotted time of 6.297 Greg. years to rebuild the temple after the 45 biblical years of nothingness expires in 2090.5888, reported in Daniel's 12:13 scripture, that the survivors will have to endure before they are gathered together and lead back to the promised land; recorded in Jer. 16:14-21. This allows David to gather his flock in 9.747 - 6.297 = 3.45 years, a time frame equal to that of King Saul's time to enforce his christian religion upon us for the last 3.45 years, upon him showing up in 2013.217 on Mar. 20th in year 2013 from sunset of previous day, Jerusalem time zone.

In Dan. 11:30-39, describes Charles's actions against the Saxons' place of worship. Verse 31 states, *"And they shall pollute the sanctuary of strength, and shall take away the daily sacrifices, and they shall place the abomination that makes the altar desolate"*. A statue/image of this jesus christ that Saul/Paul-Charlemagne-King Saul brought about as his another god, was set on the Saxons' Altar of God: which was in the image of himself.

Also in 2 Esdras 13:39-46, adds to the above verification, when it states, *"Then you saw him* (God's Holy Messiah, King David*), collecting a different* *company, a peaceful one. They are the ten tribes* (House of Israel), *which were taken off into exile in the time of King Hoshea, whom Shalmaneser king of Assyria took prisoner. He deported them beyond the river, and they were taken away into a strange country. But then* (after many years) *they resolved to leave the country populated by the gentiles and go to a distant land never yet inhabited by man, and <u>there at last to be obedient to their Laws,</u> which in their own country* (the promised land) *they had failed to keep. As they passed through the narrow passages of the Euphrates, the Most High performed miracles for them, stopping up the channels of the river until they had crossed over. Their journey through that region, which is called Arzareth, was long, and took a year and a half. They have lived there* (the present area of the Northwestern European nations) *ever since, until this final age".* This is where Manasseh migrated from to form their single great nation, United States of America.

The above Anglo Saxons, 10 tribes referred to in the above <u>2 Esdras</u> scriptures are the Israelites of the House of Israel that Shalmaneser took prisoner, and they did indeed return to be obedient to God's covenant; and it was their Altar of God that Charlemagne set the abominable image of the christians' christ; making this altar desolate; and thereafter destroyed this place of worship; bringing an end to their sacrificial feasts, and the morning and evening sacrifices, that they definitely were performing.

These actions brought alive <u>Dan. 12:7-12 scriptures</u>. Two sets of scriptures verify these above <u>Daniel's</u> and <u>2 Esdras's</u> scriptures, such as <u>Ezek. 24:21,</u> and <u>Amos 7:9,</u> that are definitely referring to the House of Israel/Isaac in a future time.

<u>Ezek. 24:21,</u> *"Speak unto the house of Israel, Thus saith the Lord God; Behold, I will profane my sanctuary, the excellency of your strength, the desire of your eyes, and that which your soul pitieth; and your sons and your daughters whom ye have left shall fall by the sword".* This is spoken by Ezekiel after God took him to where the remnant of the House of Israel resided, after migrating west and north west from the Assyrian controlled lands.

<u>Amos 7:9,</u> *"And the high places of Isaac shall be desolate, and the sanctuary of <u>Israel</u> shall be laid waste; I will rise against the house of Jeroboam* (Israel) *with the sword".* This is talking about the same sanctuary as the above Ezekiel scripture is referring to, for *"the high places at Bethel were the king's chapel and the king's court",* as referred to in <u>Amos 7:13,</u> where they *"sacrificed to the golden calves"* (not to the Lord God).

This above destruction on God's Altar and God's Sanctuary, occurred when Charles imposed his pagan christian religion upon the tribes of Isaac in the year 774.778 or Oct. 10Th from sunset of previous day, of our Gregorian calendar, and the countdown of <u>Dan. 12:7 and 11</u> scriptures of the 1,260 plus 30 biblical years began.

<u>Psalms 16:4</u> states, *"Their sorrows shall be multiplied that hasten after another god: Their drink offerings of blood* (and obviously their eating of his body*), will I* (David) *not offer, nor take up their names into my lips".*

This is a Psalm written by David; notice all the 1st person pronouns. This can only mean that it is David who is condemning this ritual of this <u>another god,</u> which is the drinking of his blood and eating of his body that the christians' pagan christ demands his followers to perform. Needless to say, this ritual is totally against God's commandment to consume the blood of <u>any flesh,</u> as stated below:

<u>Lev. 7:26-27,</u> *"Moreover ye shall ear no manner of blood, whether it be of fowl or of beast, in any of your dwellings. Whatsoever soul-person it be that eats <u>any manner of blood,</u> even that soul-person shall be cut off from his people"* (from the eternal life to come).

However, Charles continued on, no doubt to force the worshippers to acknowledge his pagan another god, and on refusing to serve, and worship this, another god; brought upon them Charles's wrath, which was death. Erecting of this statue/image upon their altar, was the abomination that made this altar desolate, as reported below:

<u>Dan. 12:11,</u> *"And from the time the daily sacrifice shall be taken away, and the abomination that makes desolate is set up, there shall be 1290 days* (of biblical years)*".*

This action that Charles brought about and the action that Antiochus brought about are two separate and distinct events. <u>Dan. 8:9-14</u> is referring to Antiochus's event, and <u>Dan. 11:30-39</u> is referring to Charles's event, and states as follows: *"For the ships of Chittim shall come against him; therefore he shall be grieved, and return, and have indignation against the Holy Covenant; so shall he do; he shall even return, and have intelligence with them that forsake the Holy Covenant* (the French leaders)*, and arms shall stand on his part, and they shall pollute the sanctuary of strength, and shall take away the daily sacrifice, and they shall place the abomination* (their pagan jesus christ) *that makes the altar desolate. And such as do wickedly against the covenant shall he corrupt by flatteries: but the people that do know their God shall be strong and do exploits. And they that understand among the people shall instruct many: Yet they shall fall by the sword, and by flame, by captivity, and by spoil, <u>many days</u>* (30 days, of biblical years, plus even throughout the entire 1,260 days, of biblical years, of being in this little horn's hand): *Now when they shall fall, they shall be helped with a little help; but many shall cleave to them with flatteries. And some of them of understanding shall fall, to try them, and to purge, and to make them white, <u>even to the time of the end</u>: because it is yet for a time appointed. And the king shall do according to his will; and he shall <u>exalt himself,</u> and <u>magnify himself</u> above every god, and <u>shall speak marvelous things against the God of gods,</u> and shall prosper till* *the indignation be accomplished: for that that is determined shall be done. Neither shall he regard the god of his fathers, nor the desire of woman, nor regard any god: for <u>he shall magnify himself above all</u>. But in his estate shall he honour the god of forces: <u>and a god whom his fathers knew not shall he honor with gold, silver, and with precious stones, and pleasant things</u>. Thus shall he do in the most strong holds with <u>a strange god, whom he shall acknowledge and increase with glory</u>: and he shall cause them to rule over many, and shall divide the land for gain".* How much <u>stranger</u> can an imaginary god of <u>himself</u> be?

I myself am not surprised to discover Charles was in fact the reappearance of King Saul in person for the second time. For he reigned from 772 to 836, a span of 64 years, and according to the above scripture, *"he shall <u>exalt himself,</u> and <u>magnify himself</u> above every god, even the God of gods shall he speak marvelous things against".* This statement matches that of <u>Dan. 7:25,</u> where *"<u>the little horn shall speak great marvelous words against the Most High</u>",* who is in fact God of any other so-called gods. This leader has *"no desire of women, nor regard for any god".* However, *"he has a <u>strange god,</u> whom he shall acknowledge and increase with glory".* This *"<u>strange god</u>"* definitely is his pagan 'imaginary' christ, <u>of himself,</u> that he conjured up in the New Testament times. King Saul as we all know, was an Israelite of the tribe of Benjamin, and according to the above quoted scripture, this god of his, his fathers of the Israelite tribes, knew not, which he honoured with gold, silver, with precious stones and pleasant things. You can be certain that his fathers did not even hear of his jesus christ. Also compare <u>Rev. 17:4-5,</u> with the above quoted scripture, where this leader, Charles, honours his god with *"<u>gold, silver, precious stones, and pleasant things</u>".*

Revelation's 17 scriptures it states, *"And the woman was arrayed in purple and scarlet colour, and <u>decked with gold and precious stones and pearls</u>, having <u>a golden cup in her hand</u>* (christians' communion cup) *full of abominations and filthiness of her fornication: And upon her forehead was a name written,* MYSTERY, BABYLON THE GREAT, THE MOTHER OF HARLOTS AND ABOMINATIONS OF THE EARTH".

This woman is in fact the mother of all the Protestant Christian religions. The Roman Catholic religion, which Saul/Paul brought about to preach the gospel of this <u>pagan imaginary christ</u> of himself.

This man, King Saul will appear for the third time as the <u>last pope</u> of the christian religion. One can say that this King Saul is in fact working triple time to win control over the Israelites, and indeed over all the nations of this world. The struggle between the first two kings over control of the tribes of Israel and the Gentile nations is not over as yet, and we all know who will win this struggle.

This time period of 1,290 days (of biblical years), refers to <u>Dan's 7:25,</u> 1,260 days, of biblical years, of time period that God states. *"He will put them* (the <u>remnant</u> of the House of Israel, referred to in <u>Rev. 12:17,</u> when the devil went out to make war with the remnant of her seed) *into his hands"*, plus the 30 days, of biblical years, it will take God to reclaim us back from this christian religious hand, matching the same time period it took Charles to fully impose his christian religion upon the Saxon tribes. This same time period is reported in Dan. 12:7, which states, *"That it shall be for a time, times, and an half* (1,260 days, of biblical years);*"* That the remnant of the House of Israel will be in the horn's hand. And the 30 days, of biblical years, of God's reclaiming time, *"to have accomplished to scatter the power of the Holy people, all these things shall be finished"*.

We of the House of Israel, the British Commonwealth of Nations, the United States of America (the two tribes of Joseph), and the Northwestern European nations (France, Switzerland, Belgium, Netherlands, Denmark, Norway, Sweden, Finland, Wales, Ireland, Scotland, Greenland, and Iceland) are considered the holy people in this and other scriptures within the Bible, and of course, the Jewish people of the House of Judah. Therefore, 774.778 + (1260 * 360/365.25) = 2016.667 on Aug. 31st from sunset of previous day cue., God will begin to reclaim us, of the House of Israel, of the above-mentioned nations, back from the hands of the little horn/King Saul, the master builder and leader/pope of the christian religion. God will take 30 days, of biblical years, or 29.5688 years of our calendar, matching the same time it took Charles to fully impose the christian religion upon our ancestors. This will be world war III, and is described below:

Jer. 30:7, *"Alas! For that time is great, so that none is like it: It is even the time of Jacob's trouble; but he shall be saved out of it"*. Only 1/3rd of all the Israelites will be saved out of it, and they must try to stay alive in the 45 days, of biblical years, a period of total desolation, where only one out of ten will survive, and will be the blessed ones gathered up and led back to the promised land as stated in the following scriptures.

Therefore, *"all shall be finished"*, as Dan. 12:7 states, *"When he shall have accomplished to scatter the power of the Holy people, all these things shall be finished"*.

Therefore, 2016.667 + 29.5688 = 2046.2358 cue., *"all these things shall be finished"*. Matching the same time set when all 12 ages of this world/civilization will come to an end.

Dan. 12:12 states, *"Blessed is he that waits and comes to the 1335 day,* of biblical years*"*.

In other words, there will be a 45-biblical-year period after the war, that the survivors will be living in a desolate land, trying to stay alive, for this war came upon us as stated:

Jer. 16:17-18, *"For mine eyes are upon all their ways: they are not hid from my face, neither is their iniquity hid from mine eyes. And first I will recompense their* iniquity and their sin <u>double</u>; because they have defiled my land, they have filled my inheritance with their detestable and abominable things".

Followed by Jer. 16:16, "*Behold, I will send for many fishers, saith the Lord God, and they shall fish them; and after will I send for many hunters, and they shall hunt them from every mountain, and from every hill, and out of the holes of the rocks*".

Then Jer. 16:14-15, follows, "*Therefore, behold, the days come, says the Lord God, that it shall no more be said, THE LORD GOD LIVES, that brought up the children of Israel out of the land of Egypt; But, THE LORD GOD LIVES, that brought up the children of Israel from the land of the north, and from all the lands whither he had driven them: and I will bring them again into their land that I gave unto their fathers*".

The survivors/remnant of this coming devastation period will again, after the 45 biblical years of nothingness, be gathered up together and led back to the promise land to rebuild the temple and live with God's Messiah, King David, who will be their prince, shepherd, and king with our great God.

2 Esdras 7:26-38, "*Listen! The time shall come when the signs I have foretold will be seen; the city which is now invisible shall appear and the country now concealed be made visible. Everyone who has been delivered from the evils I have foretold shall see for himself my marvellous acts. My son the Messiah* (King David) *shall appear with his companions and bring 400 years of happiness to all who survive. At the end of that time, my son the Messiah shall die, and so will all mankind who draw breath. Then the world shall return to its original silence for seven days as at the beginning of creation, and no one shall be left. After seven days the age, which is not yet awake, shall be roused and the age which is corruptible shall die. The earth shall give up those who sleep in it, and the dust those who rest there in silence; and the storehouses shall give back the souls entrusted to them. Then the Most High shall be seen on the Judgment seat, and there shall be an end of all pity and patience. Judgment alone shall remain; truth shall stand firm and faithfulness be strong; requital shall at once begin and open payment be made; good deeds shall awake and wicked deeds shall not be allowed to sleep. Then the place of torment shall appear, and over against it the place of rest; the furnace of hell shall be displayed, and on the opposite side the paradise of delight. Then the Most High shall say to the nations that have been raised from the dead: Look and understand who it is you have denied and refused to serve, and whose commandment you have despised. Look on this side, then on that: here are rest and delight, there fire and torments. That is what he will say to them on the Day of Judgment*".

Therefore, it is absolutely imperative that we as human beings to search out the scriptures and prove all things with the source, about our creator, God Almighty, and who his Holy Messiah really is, and avoid being led astray by Saul/Paul's pagan christ/another god, which is the stumbling block recorded in your Bible, along with all the other idols/images of their saints, virgin mother, etc., that they set up, for their members to serve them, pray to them, and worship them as gods.

Ezek. 14:3-8, *"Son of man, these men have set up their idols in their heart, and put the stumbling block of their iniquity before their face: should I be enquired of at all by them? Therefore speak unto them, and say unto them; Thus saith the Lord God; Every man of the house of Israel that sets up his idols in his heart, and puts the stumbling block of his iniquity before his face, and comes to the prophet; I the Lord God will answer him that comes according to the multitude of his idols; That I may take the house of Israel in their own heart, because they are all estranged from me through their idols. Therefore say unto the house of Israel, Thus says the Lord God; Repent, and turn yourselves from your idols; and turn away your faces from all your abominations. For every one of the house of Israel, or the stranger that sojourneth in Israel, which separates himself from me, and sets up his idols in his heart, and puts the stumbling block of his iniquity before his face, and comes to a prophet to enquire of him concerning me; I the Lord God will answer him by myself; And I will set my face against that man, and will make him a sign and a proverb, and I will cut him off from the midst of my people; and ye shall know that I am the Lord God".*

2 Kings 17:35-41, *"With whom the* LORD GOD *had made a covenant, and charged them, saying, Ye shall not fear other gods, nor bow yourselves to them, nor serve them, nor sacrifice to them: But the Lord God* (only, Isa. 26:13*), who brought you up out of the land of Egypt with great power and a stretched out arm, him* (only, 1 Sam. 12:24) *shall ye fear, and him* (only, 1 Sam. 7:4) *shall ye worship, and to him* (only, Ex. 22:20*) shall ye do sacrifice. And the Statutes, and the Ordinances, and the Law, and the Commandments, which he wrote for you, ye shall observe to do for evermore; and ye shall not fear other gods* (christians' christ and saints, etc.*). And the covenant that I have made with you ye shall not forget; neither shall ye fear other gods. But the Lord your God* (only, 1 Sam. 12:24) *ye shall fear; and he shall deliver you out of the hand of all your enemies".*

*"However, they did not hearken, but they did after their former manner. So these nations feared the Lord God. And served their graven images, both their children, and their children's children: as did their father's, so do they unto this day".*

We modern Israelites are doing the same by accepting this christian religion and all her pagan gods, with all their pagan so-called holy days and events, which are all contrary to God's Old Testament ways.

Isa. 42:8-9, *"I am the Lord God: that is my name: and my glory will I not give to another, neither my praise to graven images. Behold, the former things are come to pass, and new things do I declare: before they spring forth I tell you of them".*

I myself am disclosing to you, in this final writing, in this year of 2006, what and when God's great wrath will be upon us in the very near future, beginning at Aug. 31st from sunset of previous day in the year 2016 cue. for the <u>two acts</u> that brought about the countdown of <u>Dan. 12:7 and 11</u>, occurring in the area of the tribes of Israel, of the House of Israel, occupied lands, with God's reclaiming period of us Israelites, the children of our ancient ancestors, the Saxon tribes, from the hands of King Saul, disguised as Charlemagne, who began imposing this christian religion upon our ancient ancestors in a winter month of the year 774.778 Oct. 10th from sunset of previous day cue. This is the little horn's hand that God put us in for 1,260 days, of biblical years, or 1241.8891 of our Gregorian years. The beginning of God's reclaiming period is at the expiry date of this 1,260 days, of biblical years. This place of worship was this <u>Stonehenge site</u> that Charlemagne and his forces destroyed after he placed an image of his christian pagan christ, which was of himself, upon God's Altar, making this Altar of God desolate, and forced the worshippers to worship his pagan christ, killing whomever refused, he thereafter destroyed this place of worship, bringing an end to any future animal sacrifices. These two abominable actions brought alive <u>Dan. 12:7 and 11</u> scriptures. Our religious scholars and christian leaders are still waiting for these two abominable actions to come about in some future time, being completely ignorant Charlemagne performed these actions in the year 774.778 cue. Now we have these many foolish and ignorant Archaeologists currently digging throughout this area. Even the east opening should have been an initial clue which is lined up to receive the summer solstice sun rising, an opening that only God and the king/prince of the people was allowed to enter and exit as indicated in <u>Ezek. 44:1-3.</u> They have no idea what they are messing with. Therefore, it is extremely critical that you, your family, all your loved ones, friends, and all fellow Israelites take heed to return to the true ways, the ways of the Old Testament, and flee from following this pagan christian babylonian religion, with their pagan jesus christ, and all their pagan saints, virgin mother, etc. Always keep <u>Isa. 42:8,</u> in your mind, when God states, *"I am the Lord God: that is my name: and my glory will I <u>not</u> give to another, <u>neither</u> my praise to graven images".*

God will never answer a prayer you make to him, when you ask for whatsoever, in the name of anyone else, for there is absolutely no other so-called gods with him or besides him. Please understand this; the christian religion is the most paganism religion that has ever existed. Talk about being primitive; one would think that our highly educated society would be able to discern the difference between right and wrong, real from unreal, truth from obvious lies. The above Isaiah scripture it appears is not understood by our society, when God himself tells us in plain English;

*"My glory will I <u>not</u> give* (or share with any other so-called gods); <u>neither</u> *share my praise* (with any graven images of these so-called gods)".

Our christian organizations are loaded with graven/painted images of their pagan christ idol, and all their canonized saint idols, etc., that their followers worship, pray to, and serve as if they were real.

God states in Deut. 32:37 after he brings his wrath upon us, and says to us, *"Where are their gods, their rock* (pagan christ) and (all their pagan canonized saints, virgin mother, etc.) *in whom they trusted, which did eat the fat of their sacrifices, and drank the wine of their drink offerings? Let them rise up and be your protection"*.

Then God confirms his oneness in verse 39, *"See now that I, even I, am he, and there is no other god with me: I kill, and I make alive; I wound, and I heal: neither is there any that can deliver out of my hand"*.

Here again God is using a plain language that even a young individual can understand. There is only one God to worship, pray to, serve, sacrifice to, and fear: for there is no other God with him. To believe what the christian religion has been deceiving us with, over these past centuries, is an insult to our educational system, for we are unable to discern truth from lies, good from evil, right from wrong. All one has to do is compare the so-called christian holy days and events, with that of the Old Testament holy days and events, which we are instructed to observe and keep holy forever. Beginning with the Old Testament holy Sabbath day, which is a sign/mark between God and his people. Individuals observing and keeping this day holy from just before sundown Friday to just after sundown Saturday, by worshipping our ONE GOD and refraining from all our duties, all our pleasurable activities, and all business activities, are God's people, for they are obedient to his 4th commandment. But they must also <u>worship him only, pray to him only, serve him only and truly fear him only for our eternal life is in his hands</u>, without kneeling, standing or facing any image of whatsoever in his stead or of any pagan god. For this action would be breaking the 1st and 2nd commandments. They must observe and keep all the other holy events, that we are instructed to keep forever, which are mentioned in the Old Testament, to the best of their abilities. Then they will be God's full-fledged holy members or saints. In other words, we must live up to the covenant that our forefathers have made with their Lord God of Israel, as referred to below:

2 Kings 17:34-41, *"Unto this day <u>they</u>* (God's Israelite peoples) *do after the former manners: they fear not the Lord God, neither do they after their Statutes, or after their Ordinances, or after the Laws and Commandments which the Lord their God commanded the children of Jacob, whom he named Israel; With whom the Lord God had made a covenant, and charged them, saying, '<u>Ye shall not fear other gods, nor bow yourselves to them, nor serve them, nor sacrifice to them</u>: But <u>only the Lord thy God</u>, who brought you up out of the land of Egypt with great power and*

*a stretched out arm, <u>him shall ye fear</u>, and <u>him shall ye worship</u>, and <u>to him shall ye do sacrifice</u>.*

*And the Statutes, and the Ordinances, and the Laws, and the Commandments, which he wrote for you, ye shall observe to do forevermore; and ye shall not fear other gods. And the Covenant that I made with you, ye shall not forget; neither shall ye fear other gods. But the Lord your God ye shall fear; and he shall deliver you out of the hands of all your enemies".*

This covenant that God made with our ancestors, we have forgotten. We are the most sinful Israelites that have ever walked on the surface of this earth.

*Howbeit they did not hearken, but they did after their former manner. So these* (Israelite) *nations feared not the Lord their God, and served their graven images* (of their other so-called gods), *both their children, and their children's children: as did their fathers, so do they unto this day".*

The christians' so-called holy weekly day is observed on the 1st day of the week, Sunday, midnight to midnight. This is derived from the ancient worshipping of the pagan sun god, and it is the sign/mark of the beast or devil, mentioned in <u>Rev. 19:20</u>. No one has the authority to change God's creation day of rest, as indicated above.

The christians' easter is again an ancient pagan event, worshipping the pagan goddess of fertility, Ishtar/Ester; and is condemned in <u>Jer. 7:17-19</u>, by God himself, when he states, *"Seest thou not what they do in the cities of Judah and in the streets of Jerusalem? The children gather wood, and the fathers kindle the fire, and the women kneed their dough, to make cakes* (today's hot cross buns) *to the queen of heaven* (pagan goddess of fertility), *and to pour out drink offerings unto other gods, that they may provoke me to anger. Do they provoke me to anger? Saith the Lord God: do they not provoke themselves to the confusion* (babylon, which is related to confusion) *of their own faces?*

Also condemned by Jeremiah, in all of chapter 44, where Jeremiah explains to the remnant, of the House of Judah, that survived the Babylonian's invasion of their home land, that God brought his wrath upon them because of their pagan worshipping; and like we of the House of Israel, they vowed to continue worshipping this pagan queen of heaven. This pagan event the christians took and connected it to the rebirth/resurrection of their pagan imaginary jesus christ. They also added the hen and rabbit laying coloured and chocolate eggs to keep the fertility aspect alive.

The christians' christmas is another ancient pagan event of worshipping a tree, and is again condemned in <u>Jer. 10:3-5</u>, which states below:

*"For the customs of the people are vain: for one cuts a tree out of the forest, the work of the hands of the workman, with the axe. They deck it with silver and with gold; they fasten it with nails and with hammers, that it move not. They are*

*upright as the palm tree, but speak not: they must be carried, because they cannot go themselves. Be not afraid of them; for they cannot do evil, neither also is it in them to do good".*

The christians took this event and connected it to the birth of their pagan christ, and added the gifts, taken from the 3 wise men bearing gifts, and progressed to what we have today. Are we that naïve to believe God would bring his Holy Messiah forth, and connect him to these pagan events, that he in fact despises and condemns? If so, you can expect God's great wrath to come upon you in full force and without any mercy. For by chasing after this pagan christ/another god, and all the christians' so-called canonized saints, virgin mother, lady fatima, etc.; you would be, in effect, breaking the covenant the Lord God of Israel made with our forefathers, before they crossed over the river Jordan, to possess all the lands that God had given them.

By breaking this covenant, you can expect the devastating curses, of total desolation, to come upon you, in the very near future. We must stay upon the Lord our God of Israel as stated in the following scriptures to receive success, just as King Asa received because he stayed upon the Lord God.

Isa. 28:12, "*To whom he (Lord God) said,' This is the rest wherewith ye may cause the weary to rest; and this is the refreshing': Yet they would not hear".*

2 Chron. 14:7, "*Therefore he (King Asa) said unto the house of Judah, 'Let us build these cities, and make about them walls, and towers, gates and bars, while the land is yet before us; because we have sought the Lord our God, he has given us rest on every side. So they built and prospered".*

2 Chron. 14:11-12, "*And Asa cried unto the Lord his God, and said, 'Lord, it is nothing with thee to help, whether with many, or with them that have no power: Help us, O Lord our God; for we rest on thee, and in thy name we go against this multitude. O Lord, thou art our God; Let not man prevail against thee. So the Lord God smote the Ethiopians before Asa, and before Judah; and the Ethiopians fled".*

2 Chron. 16:8, "*Were not the Ethiopians and the Lubim a huge host, with very many chariots and horsemen? Yet, because thou* (Asa) *didst rely on the Lord God, He delivered them into thine hand".*

Jer. 6:16-19, "*Thus said the Lord God, 'stand ye in the old paths; where is the good way, and walk therein, and ye shall find rest for your souls'. But they said, 'we will not walk therein'. "Also I (the Lord God) set watchmen over you, saying, 'Hearken to the sound of the trumpet'. But they said, 'We will not hearken'.*

*Therefore hear, ye nations, and know, o congregation, what is among them.*

*Hear, O earth: behold, I will bring evil upon this people* (us modern day Israelites), *even the fruit of their thoughts, because they have not hearkened unto my words, nor to my laws, but rejected it".*

Isa. 8:20-22, "*To the law, and to the testimony: if they speak not according to this word, it is because there is no light in them".* Just as all us modern Israelites.

*"And they shall pass through it* (the coming world war III), *hardly bestead and hungry, they shall fret themselves, and curse their king and their God, and look upward"."*

*And they shall look unto the earth, and behold trouble and darkness, dimness of anguish: and they shall be driven to darkness".*

<u>Jer. 18:15,</u> *"Because my people has forgotten me, they have burned incense to vanity, and they have caused them to stumble in their ways from the ancient paths, to walk in paths, in a way not cast up".*

<u>Mal. 4:4,</u> *"Remember ye the Laws of Moses my servant, which I commanded unto him in Horeb for all Israelites, with the statutes and judgments".*

Oh wicked Israelites of today, that do not search for the ancient path, the ways of the Lord our only true God of this universe, the good ways; but instead continue on stubbornly with all their false and evil ways, the christian ways brought forth by King Saul disguised as this Saul and called Paul in the New Testament days, who is the master builder of the christian religion, and in it, bringing about a pagan imaginary christ, which was/is of himself. He, King Saul, is also the emerging little horn on the 10 horned beast of <u>Dan. 7:20 & 25,</u> that was bigger, taller, more imposing than the other horns, and who has eyes and mouth speaking great arrogant boasting words against the Most High God, and wears out the saints of the Most High God, and thinks to change the laws and statutes of the Most High God; and he returns disguised as Karl the man, Char le magne, via the French; to impose his christian religion upon our ancestors, the Saxons/sons of Isaac, with this pagan imaginary christ as the foundation of this religion. A religion that consists of a different sabbath day, contrary to God's holy Sabbath day, and statutes and judgments that are <u>not good</u> for us and whereby we <u>ought not to live in</u>, as recorded in <u>Ezek. 20:24-26</u> scriptures. It is this Charlemagne, by setting an image of his abominable pagan christ upon the Saxons' Altar of God, that made this altar desolate; and it was this Charlemagne with his forces, that destroyed their place of worship, known today as the Stonehenge ruins, located in England, bringing an end to the sacrifices they were carrying forth, and killing these worshippers who refused to worship his pagan christ. This action is exactly what he, called Saul and later called Paul, performed against the Jewish synagogues in the New Testament times. These 2 actions brought alive <u>Dan. 12:7-13</u> scriptures, where each day represents one biblical year. In historical material Charlemagne is even mistakenly referred to, the New David.

# Chapter 4

# The Ten Commandments Taken from Exodus 20:1-17

God spoke these words, saying, *"I am the Lord God, which have brought thee out of the land of Egypt, out of the house of bondage".*

<u>1st Commandment:</u> *"Thou shall have no other gods besides me".*
<u>2nd Commandment:</u> *"Thou shall not make unto thee any graven images, or any likeness of anything that is in heaven above, or that is in the earth beneath, or that is in the water under the earth. Thou shall not bow down thyself to them, nor serve them: For I the Lord thy God am a jealous God, visiting the iniquities of the fathers upon the children unto the third and fourth generation of them that hate me; And show mercy unto thousands of them that love me, and keep my commandments".*
<u>3rd Commandment:</u> *"Thou shall not take the name of the Lord thy God in vain; For the Lord thy God will not hold them guiltless that takes his name in vain".*
<u>4th Commandment:</u> *"Remember the Sabbath Day, to keep it Holy. Six days shall thou Labor, and do all thy work: But the seventh day is the Sabbath to the Lord thy God: In it thou shall not do any work, thou, nor thy son, nor thy daughter, thy manservant, nor thy maidservant, nor thy cattle, nor thy stranger that is within thy gates: For in six days the Lord thy God made heaven and earth, the sea, and all that in them is, and rested the seventh day: Wherefore the Lord thy God blessed the Sabbath Day and hallowed it".*
<u>5th Commandment:</u> *"Honour thy father and thy mother: That thy days may be long upon the land which the Lord thy God give thee".*
<u>6th Commandment:</u> *"Thou shall not kill".*
<u>7th Commandment:</u> *"Thou shall not commit adultery".*
<u>8th Commandment:</u> *"Thou shall not steal".*
<u>9th Commandment:</u> *"Thou shall not bear false witness against thy neighbour".*

<u>10th Commandment:</u> *"Thou shall not covet thy neighbour's house, wife, nor his manservant, nor his maidservant, nor his ox, ass, nor anything that is thy neighbour's".*

## **How many of the above commandments are your christian establishments violating?**

<u>Commandment #1</u>: *Thou shall have no other gods with me, before me, besides me, or behind me. For I the Lord thy God is the only God.*

They are violating this 1st commandment by worshipping, serving, and praying to Saul/Paul's christ, the virgin mother, and various individuals that are canonized as saints, to many to even mention, and being completely ignorant that a saint is a living obedient one of the tribes of Israel, and are not to be prayed to, served, or worshipped as a god. Not even God's Holy Messiah, King David, for he is only a human being just as you and I are. Even the devil himself is worshipped and served, by observing and participating in the helloween event, for he is the god of this event, there is absolutely nothing hallowed in this event, reason I spelled it as above.

These above christians' so-called other gods are referred to in <u>Deut. 32:37-38,</u> where the Lord our God is referred to in <u>Deut. 32:39,</u> *"See now that I, even I, am he, and there is no god with me: I kill, and make alive; I wound, and I heal: Neither is there any that can deliver out of my hand".*

In this chapter of <u>Deut. 32</u> is a song God told Moses to write and teach it to the tribes of Israel. This song depicts the entire future of these tribes of Israel, and the time towards the coming of the end begins shortly after <u>verse 26,</u> as it states, *"I said, I would scatter them into corners, I would make the remembrance of them to cease from among men".*

We of the House of Israel, the British Commonwealth of Nations (the younger son of Joseph, Ephraim, Jacob's designated 1st born, predicted group of nations), the United States of America (Joseph's 1st born son, Manasseh, Jacob's predicted single great Nation), and all the Northwestern European nations (from France, tribe of Reuben, to Switzerland, Belgium, Netherlands, Norway, Denmark, Sweden, Finland, Iceland, Greenland, all the nations within the British Isles) are the Israelites that the remembrance ceased to be from among men—even from our own selves. For the Jewish peoples are our brethren of the House of Judah, and they are the keepers of God's laws and ordinances, and we ought to be following the same laws and ordinances as the Jewish peoples observe and keep. <u>Minus</u> of course the ritual of drinking the pagan christians' christ's wine/blood and eating his bread/body. They, the House of Judah, are also snared into participating with this abominable christian ritual, and is condemned by King David below:

<u>Psalms 16:4,</u> *"Their sorrows shall be multiplied that hasten after another god: their drink offerings of blood, will I* (David) *not offer, nor take up their names into my lips"*.

This scripture is backed up by <u>Ezek. 23:31-34,</u> *"Thou has walked in the way of thy sister; therefore will I give her cup into thine hand. Thus says the Lord God; Thou shall drink of thy sister's cup deep and large: thou shall be laughed to scorn and had in derision; it contains much. Thou shall be filled with drunkenness and sorrow, with the cup of astonishment and desolation, with the cup of thy sister Samaria"*.

This abominable ritual is the christians' communion cup that the House of Judah adopted and connected it to their Atonement event, by drinking this wine/blood from a shot glass, etc., and accompanied with the eating of a piece of unleavened bread/body. This ritual is condemned in the above David's Psalm, and which is totally against God's blood laws and unclean laws, this is one of the reasons King David, God's true Messiah, rejects this practice in his Psalm. Our ancient Israelites never drank the blood of any sacrificial animal, to receive God's forgiveness for the sins they have committed. It was the sacrificial ritual of shedding the animal's blood, and then placing their multiple sins on the head of a second goat, that they set free into the wilderness. And the blood was sprinkled on the altar and poured around the base of the altar, and also sprinkled towards the worshippers.

<u>Deut. 32:28-29,</u> continues, God stating, *"For they are nations void of counsel, neither is there any understanding in them. O that they were wise, that they understood this, that they would consider their latter end!"*

In <u>verse 35,</u> God is speaking about the calamity that is at hand, and the things that shall come upon us make haste, after he states, *"Their foot shall slide in due time:"*

The calamity that follows is mentioned in <u>Jer. 30:7,</u> *"Alas! For that day is great, so that none is like it: it is even the time of Jacob's trouble* (us Israelites)*"*.

<u>Deut. 32:36-38,</u> *"For the Lord God shall judge his people, and repent himself for his servants, when he sees that their power is gone, and there is none shut up, or left. And He shall say, where are their gods, their rock* (pagan christ and pagan saints) *in whom they trusted? Let them rise up and help you, and be your protection"*.

This pagan christ that Saul/Paul brought about <u>is none other than himself.</u> This may seem to be a bizarre statement to make, until you read in the first two chapters of <u>2 Esdras 2:42-47,</u> where it states, *"In the middle* (of a crowd of Gentile and Heathen peoples) *stood a very tall young man, taller than all the rest, who was setting a crown on the head of each one of them; he stood out above them all"*. Does not this statement match that of 1 Sam. 9:2 and 10:23-24? *"And Kish had a son, whose name was Saul, a choice young man, and a goodly: and there was not among the children of Israel a goodlier person than he: from his shoulders and upward he was higher than any of the people"*.

In verse 47 of 2 Esdras it states, this tall individual is the *"Son of God"*. But in reality this is King Saul posing as the false christ, overriding the true Messiah of God, King David. This false christ is the same christ that the christians are worshipping, praying to, and serving as their another god. These first two chapters of 2 Esdras have definitely been added too, or wholly altered within this book of 2 Esdras, for this tall individual is telling this non Israelite crowd that God has given up on the Israelites and is now choosing other people instead. In essences telling them that God is breaking his promise made with the Israelites; and the unaltered portions continue on with chapter 3.

The true Messiah of God, King David, makes his appearance within the 13th chapter; *"Where he is collecting a different company, a peaceful one. They are the ten tribes which were taken off into exile in the time of King Hosea, whom Shalmaneser king of Assyria took prisoner* (734-721 b. cue.)*"*.

We modern day Israelites of the countries I have mentioned, many times, within this book are the children of these Israelites mentioned in this above 2 Esdras scripture. These gathered Israelites by King David, God's Holy Messiah, and his company are those Israelites who'll survive the coming 30 days, of biblical years, of this 3rd world war, called within the Bible, as the Day of the Lord God, which will begin in our year of 2016.667 from sunset of previous day, and the follow-up period of 45 days, of biblical years, of total desolation. Therefore, I challenge anyone to prove me wrong.

Commandment #2: *Thou shall not make any graven images/painted images of any thing whatsoever, for you to worship, pray to, serve, and fear as a God; even of what you may think the Lord thy God may look like.*

The christians are violating this commandment by making graven/painted images of all the above-mentioned so-called other gods, by worshipping, serving, praying to them, as if they are real living Gods.

Deut. 4:15-16 & 23-24, should set you straight if you use your God given mind to understand what God via Moses is relating to you:

*"Take ye therefore good heed unto yourselves; For ye saw no manner of similitude on the day that the Lord our God spoke unto you in Horeb out of the midst of the fire: Lest ye corrupt yourselves, and make you a graven image, the similitude of any figure, the likeness of male or female."*

*"Take heed unto yourselves; Lest you forget the covenant of the Lord God, which He made with you, and make you a graven image, or the likeness of anything, which the Lord thy God has <u>forbidden</u> thee. For the Lord thy God is a consuming fire, even a jealous God".*

<u>Commandment #3</u>: *Thou shall not take/use the name of the Lord thy God in vain.*

This commandment is being continuously violated by praying to God for favourable outcomes of whatsoever, and then adding at the end of this prayer, *"In the name* (of Saul/Paul's pagan imaginary christ or some canonized saint) *I ask these favours of you".*

In doing so, giving Saul/Paul's pagan christ power over our Lord God Almighty.

Just as in <u>Acts 13:35</u>, where <u>Saul/Paul states</u>, *"He* (God) *said* (to his christ) *also in another psalm, "Thou shall not suffer Thine Holy One to see corruption"".*

In this scripture, with God doing the speaking, would give Saul/Paul's christ power over God. For it would be up to Saul/Paul's christ whether God would see the corrupting powers of the grave; because the Lord our God would be referring to himself, as *'Thine Holy One'*. This scripture is taken from <u>Psalms 16:10</u>, for it doesn't appear anywhere else in the Old Testament. David in this Psalm is speaking to God, not the other way around. David is referring to himself as *'Thine Holy One'*. Giving the power to God whether David would see the corrupting powers of the grave. This is a good example of using God's name in vain, besides using it in an obscene Manner. No wonder very few, if any, of our prayers are answered.

For in <u>Isa. 42:8</u>, God states, *"I am the Lord God: that is my name: and my glory will I <u>not</u> give to another, <u>neither</u> my praise to graven images".*

<u>Commandment #4</u>: *Thou shall keep holy the Sabbath day.*

This commandment is being continuously violated, by observing and keeping, God's holy Sabbath day, on the wrong day of the week. This holy Sabbath day is to be observed and kept on the 7th day of the week, from just before sundown Friday to just after sundown Saturday. Ask your brethren the Jewish peoples of the House of Judah. The christians' so-called holy day of the week is derived from an ancient event of worshipping the pagan sun god. There can only be one, original holy Sabbath day, of the week, and it is definitely not the christians' day, nor even its time of day, midnight to midnight. This holy Sabbath day is very important in the scheme of God's ways, for this day represents the day God rested, after recreating this earth on the first six days of this creation week. But before God rested, he blessed and sanctified this 7th day, making it holy. Therefore, God demands we also observe this day of rest, and keep it holy by refraining from all our duties and all our pleasurable activities, and to bring in remembrance God's creation week, including his day of rest. This is the <u>one day</u> of the week that we are to worship this <u>one great God</u>, who brought us about on day six of this creation week, via Adam and Eve. We are to keep in remembrance, <u>this day was made holy by God himself, it is no ordinary day.</u> This day <u>cannot</u> be changed by anyone, and replaced by another day of the week, as the christian or any other so-called religion or philosophy, contrary to the ways of God, have done.

<u>Isa. 58:2-14,</u> "Yet they seek me daily, and delight to know my ways, as a nation that did righteousness, and forsook not the ordinances of their God: they ask of me the ordinances of justice; they delight in approaching to God. Wherefore have we fasted, say they, and thou see not? Wherefore have we afflicted our soul/body/person, and thou take no knowledge?"

"Behold, in the day of your fast ye find pleasure, and exact all your labours. Behold, ye fast for strife and debate, and to smite with the fist of wickedness: ye shall not fast as ye do this day, to make your voice to be heard on high. Is it such a fast that I have chosen? A day for a man to afflict his soul? Is it to bow down his head as a bulrush, and to spread sackcloth and ashes under him? Wilt thou call this a fast, and an acceptable day to the Lord thy God?"

"<u>Is not this the fast that I have chosen?</u> To loose the bands of wickedness, to undo the heavy burdens, and to let the oppressed go free, and that ye break every yoke? Is it not to deal thy bread to the hungry, and that thou bring the poor that are cast out to thy house? When thou see the naked, that thou cover him; and that thou hide not thyself from thine own flesh?"

"Then shall thy light break forth as the morning, and thine health spring forth speedily: and the Lord thy God shall be thy re-reward. Then shall thou call, and the Lord thy God shall answer; "Here I am". If thou take away from the midst of thee the yoke, the putting forth of the finger, and speaking vanity; and if thou draw out thy soul/body/person to the hungry, and satisfy the afflicted soul/body/person; then shall thy light rise in obscurity, and thy darkness be as the noonday: And the Lord thy God shall guide thee continually, and satisfy the soul/body in drought, and make fat thy bones: and thou shall be like a watered garden, and like a spring of water, whose waters fail not. And they that shall be of thee shall build the old places: thou shall raise up the foundations of many generations; and thou shall be called, The repairer of the breach, The restorer of paths to dwell in".

"If thou turn thy foot on the Sabbath Day, from doing thy pleasure on My Holy Day; and call the Sabbath a delight, the Holy of the Lord, honourable; and shall honour him, not doing thine own ways, nor finding thine own pleasure, nor speaking thine own words":

*"Then shall thou delight thyself in the Lord God; and I will cause thee to ride upon the high places of the earth, and feed thee with the heritage of Jacob thy father: For the mouth of the Lord God has spoken it".*

Jer. 17:21-22, 27, *"Thus says the Lord God; Take heed to yourself, and bear no burden on the Sabbath Day, nor bring it in by the gates of Jerusalem* (nor any city, town, village, etc.). *Neither carry forth a burden out of your houses on the Sabbath Day, neither do any work, but hallow ye the Sabbath Day, as I commanded your fathers".*

*"But if ye will not hearken unto me to hallow the Sabbath Day, and not to bear a burden, even entering in at the gates of Jerusalem* (nor any city, town, village, compound, etc.): *Then will I kindle a fire in the gates thereof, and it shall not be quenched".*

Ex. 31:12-17, *"And the Lord thy God spoke to Moses, saying, Speak thou also unto the children of Israel, and saying <u>Verily my Sabbaths ye shall keep</u>: <u>For it is a sign between me and you throughout all your generations</u>; that ye shall know that I am the Lord God that does sanctify you. Ye shall keep the Sabbath therefore; <u>For it is Holy unto you</u>: Everyone that defiles it shall be put to death: For whosoever does any work therein, that soul/body/person shall be cut off from his people. Six days may work be done; but in the 7th day is the Sabbath of rest; Holy to the Lord God: Whosoever does any work in the Sabbath Day, he shall be put to death. Wherefore the children of Israel shall keep the Sabbath, to observe the Sabbath throughout their generations, for a perpetual covenant. <u>It is a sign between me and the children of Israel forever</u>: For six days the Lord God made heaven and the earth, and on the 7th day he rested, and was refreshed".*

Ezekiel 20:24-26 scripture states, *"Because they* (our ancient ancestors) *had not executed My Judgments, but had despised My Statutes, and had polluted My Sabbaths, and their eyes were after their father's idols. Wherefore I gave them <u>also</u> statutes that were <u>not good</u>, and judgments whereby they should <u>not live</u>; And I polluted them in their own gifts, in that they caused to pass through the fire all that opens the womb* (why?) *that I might make them desolate, to the end that they might know that I am the Lord God* (that has brought all this destruction upon us, because of our continuous evil ways).

In <u>Daniel 7:25</u>, God tells us that he will put <u>them</u> (the <u>remnant</u> of the House of Israel, according to <u>Rev. 12:17</u>) into the emerging little horn's hand of the 10 horned beast, for a time, times, and half a time, or a total of 1,260 days, of biblical years, or 1241.8891 of our Gregorian calendar years.

This all came about in a fall month of the year 774.778 hours from sunset of previous day cue., when Charles the Great began imposing the christian religion upon our ancestors, the Saxon tribes, living in the area that Charlemagne ruled over, on behest of the christians' pope, or more than likely his own initiative. We their children have been in this horn's hand ever since. This is why none of the christians' so-called holy days and events have absolutely nothing to do with God's holy days and events written in the books of Moses. For we are now in the hand of the devil's 1st born son's religion, for the master builder of this christian religion is the so-called Apostle Paul, whose name is actually Saul, and who in turn is none other than King Saul, with the evil spirit still upon him, that God placed upon him, after God rejected him as king over the Israelites in the days of Samuel. This King Saul is that horn of <u>Dan. 7:20-25</u>; he is also Charles the Great, and his exploits are mentioned in <u>Dan. 11:30-39</u>. He will also be the <u>last</u> and <u>next</u> pope of the christian religion. Refer to chapter 5 for details.

This came about as <u>Rev. 12:13-17</u> progressed, *"And when the dragon saw that he was cast unto the earth, he persecuted the woman* (Zion) *which brought forth the man child. And to the woman were given two wings of a great eagle, that she might fly into the wilderness, into her place, where she is nourished for a time, and times, and half a time, from the face of the serpent. And the serpent cast out of his mouth water as a flood after the woman, that he might cause her to be carried away of the flood. And the earth helped the woman, and the earth opened her mouth, and swallowed up the flood, which the dragon cast out of his mouth. And the dragon was wroth with the woman, and went to make war with the <u>remnant of her seed</u>* (the remnant of the House of Israel), *which keep the Commandments of God, and his Testimony"*.

All the above occurred at the same time and at the same place upon the Saxon tribes. These 1241.8891 years expire in 1241.8891 + 774.778 = 2016.667 from sunset of previous day cue., and God will begin to claim us back with a 30-biblical-year world war described in <u>Jer. 30:7</u>, which I quoted above, for it took Charles 30 biblical years to fully impose this christian religion upon them. Is it any wonder we are not observing God's statutes and judgments and keeping the proper holy Sabbath day, which is to be a sign between God and his people, for we have been in the hands of the devil and his disciples, the christian religious leaders, for 1,233 of our calendar years to the fall year 2006 cue., and there is now approx. 10 of our years left until God's reclaiming time springs upon us. Therefore, take great heed upon which gods you are worshipping, praying to, and serving. Flee from this babylonian paganism christian religion before it is too late and worship, pray to, and serve the one and only true living God. The Lord Our God, for there are no other gods with him.

<u>Isa. 43:10-12,</u> *"Ye are my witnesses, saith the Lord God, and my servant* (David) *whom I have chosen: that ye may know and believe me, and understand that I am he: before me there was no God formed, neither shall there be after me. I, even I, am the Lord God; and beside me there is no saviour. I have declared,*

*and have saved, and I have showed, when there was no strange god among you: therefore ye are my witnesses, saith the Lord God, that I am God".*

<u>Psalm 118:17-18,</u> *"I (David) shall not die, but live, and <u>declare the works of the Lord God.</u> The Lord has chastened me sore: but he has not given me over unto death".*

<u>Isa. 55:4,</u> *"Behold, I have given him (David) for a witness to the people, a leader and commander to the people".*

<u>Psalm 89:18-20, 26-27,</u> *"For the Lord God is our defence; and the Holy One of Israel is our king. Then thou spoke in vision to thy holy one, and said, I have laid help upon one that is mighty; I have exalted <u>one chosen out of the people.</u> I have found <u>David my servant;</u> with my holy oil have I anointed him":*

*"He (David) shall cry unto me, Thou art my father, my God, and the rock of my salvation. Also I will make him (David) my firstborn, higher than the kings of the earth".*

Is there any doubt David is God's servant, chosen one, witness, 1st born, human king of kings and Holy Messiah, and not this imaginary pagan christ that Saul/Paul brought about to deceive us?

<u>Commandment #5</u>: *Honour thy father and thy mother.*

All parents should be honoured if they live their lives according to the ways of God. One cannot honour them if they commit heinous crimes that deserve the death penalty. We must not honour a parent, child or loved ones and honoured individuals, so much so, as to light a candle for or beside them, upon their death; in the funeral ceremony or even at the burial site. For this is a sign of worshipping them, and we must only worship God and absolutely no one else.

<u>Deut. 27:16,</u> *"Cursed be he that setteth light by his father or his mother <u>(or anyone else)</u> ".*

The christian establishments have special stands, full of candles, for their followers, to light up candles for the dead or to light up candles in front of their favourite pagan god's images. For this is a sign of worshipping them.

<u>Commandment #6</u>: *Thou shall not kill.*

No one has the right to kill an innocent individual, even an embryo, even upon the initial conception via the morning after pill, this is murder. Our peoples under the influence of the christian religion, which basically ignores God's ways, have been practising this type of murder for decades as of this date.

But there is a killing that we are instructed to carry out: we must kill anyone that has killed an innocent individual. For their guilty blood must be shed to atone for the innocent blood they shed; the curses of the murderer's guilty blood will be upon their own head and upon their children to the third and fourth generations, and <u>not</u> upon the general population of the nation. We must also kill anyone that has committed a heinous crime; the curses associated with the perpetrator's guilty action will be upon their own head and upon their seed's head to the third and fourth generation. These good killings are a way to put evil out of the country/system. Our mercy is to be directed towards the victim and their loved ones, who themselves are victims; and definitely not towards the perpetrator. To ask the victims if they can ever forgive the perpetrator is an insult towards the victim and the heinous crime inflicted upon them. The christian religion has God's laws turned around ass backwards, and has negatively influenced our minds throughout the many centuries, to think as they do. No wonder the heinous crime rate is souring out of control, along with all the lesser crimes that we have totally lost control of, because of our improper enforcement and sentencing. In our society the victim is always left hanging, and the curses attached to these crimes are spreading like wildfire throughout our Israelite countries, I have mentioned earlier.

The drug and gambling scene, the same sex activities, the prostitution scene are all heinous crimes that can lure people within and totally ruin thousands of lives; and the individuals involved in bringing them about and continue to feed these crimes, must be eliminated from the system, according to God's ways; this is how corrupt we have become under the hand of this emerging horn on the 10 horned beast.

<u>Jer. 48:10,</u> *"Cursed be he that does the work of the Lord God deceitfully* (such as our christian religious leaders), *and cursed be he that keeps back his sword from* (shedding guilty*) blood"*. (such as our law makers and judges). Also check out <u>Numbers 35:16-33</u>. Always keep <u>Malachi 3:6</u> in mind. God's ways do not change.

The above scriptures are telling us that we have the right/obligation to take vengeance on anyone that has killed an innocent loved one of ours, not to have mercy on the perpetrator, but to put this perpetrator away for good, after of course he is found guilty of this crime. He or she is not to be kept in jail for a long period of time, where we are then saddled with the expenses of their upkeep, etc., and then set free, after the court's set time expires, amongst the population to perhaps commit even worst crimes; all other heinous crimes are to be handled as if the perpetrator has shed innocent blood. No wonder our crime scene is continuing to reach new heights. When a drug smugglers/growers/makers and dealers, sell drugs to an individual, due to the greed of the almighty dollar, he is in effect destroying/killing that person's mind, in effect making that person a burden on society. This drug smuggler/dealer/grower and maker deserve the death penalty. We must conform to the laws of God written down for us throughout the Old Testament books, in order to get a handle on our crime scene, and quit pussyfooting around with the perpetrators.

Consider the following scriptures: <u>Gen. 9:5-6,</u> *"Surely your blood of your lives will I require; at the hand of every beast will I require it, and at the hand of man; at the hand of every man's brother will I require the life of man.*

*Whoso sheds man's blood, by man shall his blood be shed: for the image of God made he man".*

Consider what <u>2 Esdras 15:8-9, 22-24 states</u>, *"I will hold my tongue no longer as touching their wickedness, which they profanely commit, neither will I suffer them in those things, in which they wickedly exercise themselves: behold, the innocent and righteous blood cries unto me, the souls of the just complain continually. And therefore, says the Lord God, I will surely avenge them, and receive unto me all the innocent blood from among them.*

*My right hand shall not spare the sinners, and my sword shall not cease over them that shed innocent blood upon earth.*

*Woe to them that sin, and keep not my commandments! Saith the Lord God".*

The one grievous sin that we are committing is the fact that we are not avenging the shedding of innocent blood, by putting the perpetrator to death and placing the curses that follow this and other heinous crimes on their own head and their own seed where it ought to be, instead of on the nation as a whole. We are not to show any mercy to the perpetrator of any heinous crime they have committed. We are not following the 6th commandment that God even gave to Noah in <u>Gen. 9:5-6,</u> *"Surely your blood of your lives will I require; at the hand of every beast will I require it, and at the hand of man; at the hand of every man's brother will I require the life of man. Whoso sheds man's blood, by man shall his blood be shed: For in the image of God made he man".*

Please consider <u>1 Kings 2:1-46,</u> when King Solomon took over the reign of David's throne. King David gave Solomon specific instructions of what to do concerning Joab; who killed Abner captain of the host of Israel, and Amasa a captain of the host of Judah, after a truce was made, for Joab shed the blood of war in the time of peace, which was an act of murder. David told Solomon in <u>1 Kings 2:6,</u> *"Do therefore according to thy wisdom, and let not his gray head go down to the grave in peace".* When King Solomon had the chance, he told his executioner, Benaiah, to kill Joab. As <u>1 Kings 2:31-33 states</u>, *"That thou may take the innocent blood, which Joab shed, from me and from the house of my father. And the Lord God shall return their innocent blood upon Joab's own head and his seed".*

King David also told Solomon, to take care of Shimei, a Benjamite, that cursed him with a grievous curse in the day he was fleeing from his own son, Absalom. King Solomon via his wisdom, restricted Shimei from leaving Jerusalem to ever cross over the brook Kidron. For as King Solomon states in 1 Kings 2:37, *"Thou shall know for certain that thou shall surely die. Thy blood shall be upon thine own head"*. The king said moreover to Shimei after he did indeed cross over the Kidron brook, in Vrs. 44-45, *"Thou know all the wickedness which thine heart is privy to, that thou did to David my father: therefore the Lord shall return thy wickedness upon thine own head; And King Solomon shall be blessed, and the throne of David shall be established before the Lord forever"*. King Solomon had his executioner kill him.

It was absolutely necessary for Solomon to carry out David's requests in order to rid his kingdom from the curses of shedding innocent blood, and from the grievous curses placed upon David and his throne by Shimei, the Benjamite. In the eyes of God these killings were a necessity for his peaceful blessings upon David's throne, and upon King Solomon's reign over the tribes of Israel.

The above killings Solomon carried out to rid his kingdom from these curses is a very good example to our Israelite nations of today, that refuse to avenge the shedding of innocent blood with that of the perpetrator's blood; these curses then would be upon our nations as a whole, instead of on the perpetrator's head and his seed to the third and fourth generations. We must shed all guilty blood to rid ourselves from the many curses that plaque our nations. We have our jails jammed with perpetrators that should have been killed years ago; even leaving them out early, amongst the public, for lack of space; to commit even more crimes. We have women killing their own children via the pill, so they can continue on with their lusty activities; and via abortions that they do not want, or to carry to full term, to have a normal birth, and to have a normal life. Even killing their own children via drowning in bath tubes, etc.; and because no one is found guilty enough of shedding this, Oh! So innocent blood; the curses are spreading throughout the general population like wildfire. Instead of showing mercy to the victims; we are showing mercy to the perpetrators, the ones we should put to death for their crimes. As a result the Lord our God will come upon us all with his Great and Terrible Wrath, bringing us all down to our knees begging for forgiveness, which will be in vain. All heinous crimes such as rapes, abductions, drug smugglers/growers, and sellers, and all who refuse to stop these abominable practices, and our many prostitutes, and persons involved in gay activities, financial rip-off artists, including those in our governments, and thievery repeaters, etc., must be eliminated from our system via the death penalty. Anyone who is incarcerated must pay for their upkeep, and all expenses they incurred via legal, police charges, etc. They must be put on a working chain gang, if necessary, to pay for their expenses, so we the public, who has not committed any crime, do not have this burden on our pocket book. The method used for heinous crime committees is to put them to death via the victim, if still alive, and via the victim's family members and close friends, on an open on stage setting, surrounded by a high heavy wire mesh fencing, where the general public can watch the victim's loved ones, kick, punch, club, stone or even hang this nemeses of theirs to death, without putting a hood over the perpetrator's head, so not to hide this <u>ugly putdown</u> from the General public witnessing this putdown. Doing it this way turns the perpetrator's <u>negative action</u> into <u>a huge positive</u> by putting the <u>fear factor</u> into the general public, particularly the criminally minded individuals. We have gone so far away from God's ways; we no longer know what we are doing anymore.

God states in <u>Isa. 44:25</u>, *"It is I, the Lord God, that turns wise men backward, and makes their knowledge foolish"*. God has indeed made our so-called wise leader's knowledge foolish. Even the lowly educated ordinary person on the street, know what must be done to our many heinous perpetrators. Our justice system has created an industry for themselves, at the expense of the good law abiding tax paying citizens; the faster that invisible revolving door spins, the more money our greedy lawyers, judges, and anyone else connected to this justice system of ours, make. Making their jobs securer.

<u>Micah 6:8</u>, *"He has shown thee, O man, what is good; and what does the Lord God require of thee, but to do justly, and to love mercy* (on the victims and on us good taxpayers, <u>not on the perpetrators</u>), *and to walk humbly with thy God"*.

<u>Dan. 7:20-21, 23-25</u>, *"And of the ten horns that were in the beast's head, and of the other which came up, and before whom three fell; even of that horn that had eyes, and a mouth that spoke very great things, whose look was more stout than his fellows. I beheld, and the same horn made war with the saints, and prevailed against them; thus he said: The fourth beast shall be the fourth kingdom upon earth, which shall be diverse from all kingdoms, and shall devour the whole earth, and shall tread it down, and break it in pieces. And the 10 horns out of this kingdom are 10 kings that shall arise: and another shall rise after them; and he shall be diverse from the first, and he shall subdue 3 kings. And he shall speak great words against the most High, and shall wear out the saints of the Most High, and think to change times and laws* (God's times and laws), *and they shall be given into his hand until a time and times and the dividing of time"*. 1,260 days, where each day represents one biblical year, of 360 days.

This little horn is none other than Saul/Paul-King Saul with the evil spirit still upon him. He is also Charles the Great, called Charlemagne by the French people, who believe to this day, that he was one of them. Their belief has some merit to it, for he was an Israelite of the tribe of Benjamin, and the French people are Israelites of the tribe of Reuben; but Charles was a German-speaking individual, representing the Assyrian/German nation and the Roman Empire and, most of all, his christian religion, which he in fact is the master builder of, according to 1 Cor. 3:10-11. Believe it or not, King Saul, Saul/Paul, Charlemagne and Justin Welby are one of the same, and was put in all of these positions by God himself, to carry out God's great master plan, to teach us a lesson we will never forget, for our total disregard of all of God's commandments, judgments, laws, and statutes, which were given to our ancient ancestors, depicting a perfect way to live our lives according to God's perfect ways. God is in total control of whatsoever.

## **Consider the following scriptures:**

Deut. 32:39, "*See now that I, even I, am he, and there is no god with me: I kill, and I make alive; I wound, and I heal: neither is there any that can deliver out of my hands*".

2 Kings 17:35-39, "*With whom the Lord God had made a covenant, and charged them, saying, Ye shall not fear other gods* (who are no gods at all) *nor bow yourselves to them, nor serve them, nor sacrifice to them:*

*But* the Lord God only, *who brought you up out of the land of Egypt with great power and a stretched out arm,* him shall ye fear, *and* him shall ye worship, *and* to him shall ye do sacrifice.

*And the Statutes, and the Ordinances, and the Laws, and the Commandments, which he wrote for you, ye shall observe to do for evermore; and ye shall not fear other* (so-called) *gods.*

*And the Covenant that I made with you ye shall not forget; neither shall ye fear other gods. But only the Lord your God ye shall fear; and he shall deliver you out of the hands of all your enemies*".

Isa. 43:25-28, "*I, even I, am he that blots out thy transgressions for mine own sake, and will not remember thy sins. Put me in remembrance: let us plead together. Declare thou, that thou may be justified.*

*Thy first father has sinned, and thy teachers have transgressed against me. Therefore I have profaned the princes of the sanctuary, and have given Jacob to the curse, and Israel to reproaches*".

Isa. 45:5-7, "*I am the Lord, and there is none else, there is no god beside me: I girded thee, though thou has not known me: That they may know from the rising of the sun, and from the west, that there is none beside me. I make peace, and create evil: I the Lord God do all these things*".

Commandment #7: *Thou shall not commit adultery.*

The death penalty is to be carried out upon all those that commit adultery. As we stand today in our Israelite nations, more than 75% of the adults deserve the death penalty for breaking this commandment. That's how far we have strayed away from God's ways. All I can say at this point of time, God have mercy upon us for our continuous evil ways.

Commandment #8: *Thou shall not steal.*

We have lost complete control of this commandment, because we have failed to execute proper judgments. The perpetrator when caught with the items, must be made to replace the items or their worth in money value, plus any damages that was brought about during the theft, plus pay the victim up to at least 3 times the total cost of the items and the repairs, plus the inconvenience caused in time and money value. This thief must be told, the next time will result in their death, for his blood will now be put upon their own head.

Commandment #9: *Thou shall not bear false witness against thy neighbour* (anyone).

By falsely accusing anyone of a crime is breaking this commandment. One's accusations must be backed up with proof of at least 2 or 3 true witnesses. Even doctoring up the evidence to be of an advantage or a disadvantage, even hiding critical evidence or a failure to bring known vital evidence forward is breaking this commandment. This commandment is continuously being broken within our enforcement agencies, even within the justice system, particularly by the lawyers defending the perpetrator. They must defend them only to bring out the truth, not to hide it; and to make sure the accused is not being railroaded, and definitely not to follow up a claim of an insanity plea. An individual with a sick mind has the devil's mind upon him. For the words spirit and mind are the same, and are used interchangeably within the Bible. God's Holy Mind and God's Holy Spirit is the same. Therefore, a plea of insanity is as being a false witness.

Commandment #10: *Thou shall not covet thy neighbour's whatsoever belongs to him.*

His wife, house, maid and man servants, all animals and material goods, etc. This is similar to the 8th commandment; but also includes abuse and/

or taking control illegally of the neighbours' possessions, even with the misguided help of the justice system.

There are many other laws of God that we must confront, that the christian religion completely ignore, and are the prime reason behind all the reasons of the runaway of our health problems. The population isn't getting healthier as we are made to believe, but are in fact getting unhealthier; and the costs are escalating out of control. And will continue, unless this problem is confronted the proper way.

## God's blood laws and fat laws:

## Thou shall not consume the blood of any flesh and the fat of the flesh

Lev. 3:17, *"It shall be a perpetual statute for your generations throughout all your dwellings, that you eat neither fat nor blood"*.

Lev. 7:23, 26-27, *"Speak unto the children of Israel, saying, you shall eat no manner of fat, of ox or of sheep, or of goat* (of any classified clean animal)*". Moreover you shall eat no manner of blood, whether it be of fowl or of beast, in any of your dwellings* (classified clean fowl, fish, insects, beasts only). *Whatsoever soul* (person) *it be that eats any manner of blood, even that soul* (person) *shall be cut off from his people"*.

It is common knowledge that diseases are spread through the consumption of blood, for the blood is the life of the flesh, and any diseases within this blood is within the flesh. You don't have to be a rocket scientist to understand this.

Lev. 17:12-14 states, *"Therefore I said to the children of Israel: No soul/body/person of you shall eat blood, neither shall any strangers that sojourns among you eat blood. And whatsoever man there be of the children of Israel, of the strangers that sojourn among you, which hunts and catches any beast or fowl that may be eaten; he shall even pour out the blood thereof, and cover it with dust. For it is the life of the flesh; the blood of it is for the life thereof: whosoever eats it shall be cut off"*.

We, who live in a christian society, break this law every time we administer a blood transfusion to a patient, and being completely ignorant that we are breaking God's blood laws, that will cut us off from receiving eternal life. We are trying to save a temporary life, by throwing away an eternal life. How smart is this? Do we not have enough intelligence to realize that by giving a blood transfusion runs the risk of transferring all the donor's <u>detectable</u> and <u>undetectable</u> diseases to the recipient? And do you not realize, by performing this act on the recipient, brings upon the recipient, the curses of perhaps a multitude of diseases that they may be subjected to, for the rest of their temporary life? And do you not realize that the ones ordering, administering, and enforcing this blood transfusion on the recipient are as guilty of this act as the recipient? This is how far removed we have become from the true laws of God; and it's all because the christian religion has completely ignored the true ways of God. This is one of the major reasons we have so many people walking around with various devastating, ugly, crippling, deadly diseases within and upon their bodies, for we are administering blood transfusions by the thousands every day of the year; and the curses for breaking God's blood law is obviously seen upon our diseased population. Many of us modern Israelites, when reading the above blood and fat laws, will probably shrug their shoulders and completely ignore them; being completely ignorant that it will make the difference between receiving God's salvation to a glorious eternal life or receive instead eternal damnation. This chose is up to you, but you should instead be extremely grateful that this book is bringing this knowledge to you; being ignorant of God's ways, will not excuse your faults. Therefore, bite your tongue, pull up your socks, and do the works that we all must do to receive this gift from your Creator; do not be angry at me or this book for pointing this out to you; instead direct your anger towards the christian religion and any other pagan religions and philosophy that has been deceiving you all these years. Please read the following scriptures:

<u>Ezek. 33:24-29,</u> "*Son of man, they that inhabit those wastes of the land of Israel speak, saying, Abraham was one, and he inhabited the land: but we are many; the land is given us for inheritance.*

*Wherefore say unto them, Thus says the Lord God; <u>Ye eat with the blood,</u> and <u>lift up your eyes toward your idols,</u> and <u>shed</u>* (innocent) *<u>blood:</u> and shall ye possess the land? <u>Ye stand</u>* (refuse to shed guilty blood) *<u>upon your sword, ye work abominations,</u> and <u>ye defile every one his neighbour's wife:</u> and shall ye possess the land?*

*Thus says the Lord God; As I live, surely they that are in the wastes shall fall by the sword, and him that is in the open field will I give to the beasts to be devoured, and they that be in the forts and in the caves shall die of the pestilence. For I will lay the land most desolate, and the pomp of her strength shall cease; and the mountains of Israel shall be desolate, that none shall pass through. Then shall they know that I am the Lord God, when I have laid the land most desolate because of all their abominations which they have committed*".

## The clean and unclean laws of God:

## Thou shall eat only classified clean animals, sea creatures, fowl, and insects

Lev. 11:2-3, "Speak unto the children of Israel, saying, These are the beasts which ye shall eat among all the beasts that are on the earth. Whatsoever <u>parts the hoof, and is clovenfooted, and chews the cud,</u> among the beasts, that shall ye eat".

Lev. 11:9, "These shall ye eat of all that are in the waters: Whatsoever <u>has fins and scales in the waters,</u> in the seas, and in the rivers, them shall ye eat".

Deut. 14:11, "Of all clean birds ye shall eat". These birds are <u>only grain-eaters,</u> they must not be fed with any meat mixed into their food; as our so-called know-it-all scientists determined; creating an unclean bird.

Lev. 11:21-22, "Yet these may ye eat of every flying creeping thing that goes upon all four. Which have legs above their feet, to leap withal upon the earth. Even these of them ye may eat; the locust after his kind, and the bald locust after his kind, and the beetle after his kind, and the grasshopper after his kind".

Naturally these insects must be boiled first, and then fried thereafter with your favourite spices.

Lev. 11:46-47, "This is the law of the beasts, and of the fowl, and of every living creature that moves in the waters, and of every creature that creeps upon the earth: To make a difference between the <u>unclean</u> and the <u>clean,</u> and between the beasts that <u>may be eaten,</u> and the beasts that <u>may not be eaten".</u>

All the above clean beasts, fowl, fish and insects; have a proper way to prepare them to be consumed. All the beasts are to be bled upon killing them, but there still remains blood residue within this meat, even after it has been cut up into much smaller pieces. These pieces must be cooked in such a way as to allow the blood residue, fats, and any foreign substance, such as poisons and drugs that may have been injected previously, and diseases within this meat, to seep out during the cooking process. This meat when roasted and baked must not be seared, for this procedure locks in the juices, which is the blood residue, fats and other impurities within this meat. This meat must be elevated off the bottom of the pan to insure proper seepage, and this meat must be cooked very well, and <u>the seepings must not be made into a gravy,</u> as we in our society are accustomed in doing; but must be discarded. For therein lies a host of curses, of our health problems. This meat when boiled, <u>which should also be the preferred method used,</u> before the roasting and baking, must be submerged within the water by at least 2 inches above the meat, and the scum should be periodically scooped off and discarded; give it a good boiling time to insure all blood, fats and foreign substances are omitted. This meat can then be fried, roasted, baked, ground up and reheated with your favourite spices. If you do not cook your meat as prescribed above, you will be subject to the curses of a host of devastating, crippling, ugly, deadly diseases. The chose is yours. When I mention clean beasts, I do not include beasts that have eaten the food that has been so-called protein enriched, with meat produces from whatever animal scrapes. This horrendous practice is making this clean beast into an unclean beast, and we have our so-called highly educated, know-it-all scientists to thank for this screw-up; and this also applies to the clean fowl; <u>they are vegetarians, not meat eaters.</u> Also internal organs are not to be eaten, these, along with the blood, fat, and head, were sacrificed upon the altar only. They were never eaten by the Israelites, for the meat is of a different texture, and may not shed its impurities as readily as the other flesh. The fish, according to the Dead Sea Scrolls, must be cleansed while they are still alive, with their head cut off, and hung up by their tails to allow proper seepage of their blood, and then can be prepared according to your favourite recipes.

## <u>Then there are the unclean beasts, fowl, sea creatures, and insects</u>

<u>Lev. 11:4-8</u> states, *"These shall ye <u>not eat</u> of them that chew the cud, or of them that divide the hoof: The camel, the coney, the hare, because they chew the cud, but divide not the hoof; they are unclean unto you; and the <u>swine,</u> though it divide the hoof, and is cloven-footed, yet it chews not the cud; it is unclean to you; Of their flesh shall you not eat, and <u>their carcasses shall you not even touch</u>; they are unclean to you".*

<u>Lev. 11:12,</u> *"Whatsoever has no fins nor scales in the waters, that shall be an abomination unto you:*

<u>Lev. 11:13,</u> *"All birds that are meat eaters, must not be eaten, they are an abomination unto you:*

The list is very long, and mentioned in <u>vrs. 14-20</u>. Do Not Eat Any Classified Unclean Animals, Birds, Fish, or Insects. For this is the primary source of all our ugly, devastating, crippling, deadly diseases, and the multitude of cancerous diseases are one of these curses. Take a good look at our vast diseased population with a host of these ugly, devastating, crippling, deadly diseases. You will notice that this meat is cheaper than the classified clean meats; which ends up being the snare to encourage us to purchase it more often than the classified clean. In our society pork and products with pork added to it is a very common meal—such as pork and beans, bacon and eggs, pork chops and roasts, pork sausages, baloney with pork mixed with beef, wieners with a mixture of pork with beef, chop suey with pork pieces, pork sweat and sour ribs, pork fried rise, Spam and numerous other canned produces with pork added, and every time these products are eaten, the curses of a host of various diseases will sooner or later affect your health adversely. And our christian leaders don't say a word, knowing full well that we are breaking God's commandments that are within his writings throughout the books of Moses. No amount of drugs can stop this curse, or any other curses, being continually received by breaking these clean and unclean laws of God. The nations of the whole world must be re-educated according to the ways of the Old Testament, which the christian religion has completely ignored over the past centuries. Is it any wonder we have a society riddled with such a large host of the curses of all our ugly, devastating, crippling, deadly, diseases; even too many to mention. If we are sincere in solving the nation's health problems, all the answers are within the Old Testament books.

## The following is another law of God, that the christian religion completely ignore:

To begin with I must quote the whole chapter of Leviticus 15:2-33, which will indicate to you just how far removed we are from God's ways, due to the deceptive and ignored teachings of the christian organizations, and whom the majority of the population was deceived to trust:

Lev. 15:2-33, *"Speak unto the children of Israel, and say unto them, When any man has a running issue out of his flesh, because of his issue he is unclean. And this shall be his uncleanness in his issue: whether his flesh run with his issue, or his flesh be stopped from his issue, it is his uncleanness.*

*Every bed, whereon he lies that has the issue, is unclean: and every thing, whereon he sits, shall be unclean. And whosoever touches his bed shall wash his clothes, and bathe himself in water, and shall be unclean until the evening. And he that sits on anything whereon he sat that has the issue shall wash his clothes, and bathe himself in water, and be unclean until the evening.*

*And he that touches the flesh of him that has the issue shall wash his clothes, and bathe himself in water, and be unclean until the evening.*

*And if he that has the issue spits upon him that is clean; then he shall wash his clothes, and bathe himself in water, and be unclean until the evening.*

*And what saddle so ever he rides upon that has the issue shall be unclean. And whosoever touches any thing that was under him shall be unclean until the evening: and he that carries any of those things shall wash his clothes, and bathe himself in water, and be unclean until the evening. And whomsoever he touches that has the issue, and has not rinsed his hands in water, he shall wash his clothes, and bathe himself in water, and be unclean until the evening.*

*And the vessel of earth, that he touches which has the issue, shall be broken: and every vessel of wood shall be rinsed in water.*

*And when he that has an issue is cleansed of his issue; then he shall number to himself seven days for his cleansing, and wash his clothes, and bathe his flesh in running water, and shall be clean".*

<u>Vrs. 14-15,</u> *"And on the eighth day he shall take to him two turtledoves, or two young pigeons, and come before the Lord God unto the door of the tabernacle of the congregation, and give them unto the priest: And the priest shall offer them, the one for a sin offering, and the other for a burnt offering; and the priest shall make an atonement for him before the Lord God for his issue".* Obviously the sacrifices of these birds cannot be performed today without the presence of God's Holy Tabernacle with God's Holy Altar, let alone the presence of a Levi priest without the presence of uncleanness upon him. However, we now have King David, God's Holy Messiah, shed blood to make atonement for this sin (<u>for the obedient ones only</u>).

*"And if any man's seed of copulation go out from him, then he shall wash all his flesh in water, and be unclean until the evening. And every garment, and every skin, whereon is the seed of copulation, shall be washed with water, and be unclean until the evening.*

*The woman also with whom man shall lie with seed of copulation, they shall both bathe themselves in water, and be unclean until the evening.*

*And if a woman has an issue, and her issue in her flesh be blood, she shall be put apart* (separated from children, family, friends, business associates, etc.) *seven days: and whosoever touches her shall be unclean until the evening. And everything that she lies upon in her separation shall be unclean: everything also that she sits upon shall be unclean. And whosoever touches her bed shall wash his clothes, and bathe himself in water, and be unclean until the evening. And whosoever touches anything that she sat upon shall wash his clothes, and bathe himself in water, and be unclean until the evening. And if it be on her bed, or on anything whereon she sits, when he touches it, he shall be unclean until the evening. And if any man lie with her at all, and her flowers be upon him, he shall be unclean seven days; and all the bed whereon he lies shall be unclean.*

*And if a woman have an issue of her blood many days out of the time of her separation, or if it run beyond the time of her separation; all the days of the issue of her uncleanness shall be as the days of her separation: she shall be unclean. Every bed whereon she lies all the days of her issue shall be unto her as the bed of her separation: and whatsoever she sits upon shall be unclean, as the uncleanness of her separation. And whosoever touches those things shall be unclean, and shall wash his clothes, and bathe himself in water, and be unclean until the evening. But if she be cleansed of her issue, then she shall number to herself seven days, and after that she shall be clean".*

And (as vrs. 14-15 stated above) *"on the eight day she shall take unto her two turtledoves, or two young pigeons, and bring them unto the priest, to the door of the tabernacle of the congregation. And the priest shall offer the one for a sin offering, and the other for a burnt offering; and the priest shall make an atonement for her before the Lord God for the issue of her uncleanness".* The Holy Messiah's blood comes into play, for the obedient ones.

*"Thus shall ye separate the children of Israel from their uncleanness; that they die not in their uncleanness, when they defile my tabernacle that is among them.*

*This is the law of him that has an issue, and of him whose seed goes from him, and is defiled therewith; And of her that is sick of her flowers, and of him that has an issue, of the man, and of the woman, and of him that lies with her that is unclean".*

<u>Lev. 5:2,</u> *"If a person touches any unclean thing, whether it be a carcass of an unclean beast, or a carcass of unclean cattle, or the carcass of unclean creeping things, and if it be hidden from him: he also shall be unclean, and guilty. Or if he touches the uncleanness of man, whatsoever uncleanness it be that a man shall be defiled withal, and it be hid from him; when he knows of it, then he shall be guilty".*

<u>Lev. 12:2-5,</u> *"Speak unto the children of Israel, saying, If a woman have conceived seed, and born a man child: then she shall be unclean seven days; according to the days of the separation for her infirmity shall she be unclean. And in the eighth day the flesh of his foreskin shall be circumcised. And she shall then continue in the blood of her purifying thirty three days; she shall touch no hallowed thing, nor come into the sanctuary, until the days of her purifying be fulfilled. But if she bare a maid child, then she shall be unclean two weeks, as in her separation: and she shall continue in the blood of her purifying sixty six days".*

Upon reading the laws of uncleanness above, one can see that we of the House of Israel are living in a totally unclean state, so much so that our places of residences, places of employment—from the carpets, to all the furnishings and clothing—give me a feeling of total hopelessness and exasperation, that we can ever make it right in the eyes of the Lord our God. I can see why God must bring to an end our present corrupt civilization with a war that will destroy approximately 2/3rd of the Israelite population of this present world, which will begin in our year of 2016 on Aug. 31st from sunset of previous day, approx. 10 years from late summer in our year 2006. This end-time world war is described below, where God tells us how we will react when it comes upon us:

<u>Ezek. 21:7,</u> *"Every heart shall melt, and all hands shall be feeble, and every spirit shall faint, and all knees shall be weak as water: Behold it comes, and shall be brought to pass, saith the Lord God".*

God tells us within this 21st chapter that this sword that is sharpened and furbished will be <u>doubled</u> this 3rd time around, and it will be upon

God's people, us Israelites; and God has set the point of this sword against all our gates, that our hearts may faint and our ruins be multiplied: *"Ah! It is made bright, it is wrapped up for the slaughter* (of us Israelites)*"*. This end-time world war against the revised so-called Holy Roman Empire and their allies, hidden today within the European Union of Nations, will have the Israelite nations that are members of this union defeated and taken over—such as France, Belgium, and the Netherlands. The other Israelite nations that are also members, such as Finland, Ireland, and even, God forbid, England, will hopefully opt out of this union when they recognize the danger; but like before the 2nd world war, they will be totally unprepared for this coming 3rd world war, known within the Bible as *the Day of the Lord God* and is fully explained within the 9th chapter.

Mentioning France above may also include lands that are occupied by the French people, such as French Quebec of Canada and the French areas of Ireland, making the whole country of Canada and Ireland vulnerable to attacks. If this is so, this may also put the whole of the United States of America and the whole of the British Isles vulnerable to a surprise attack. For according to Jacob, Reuben was his initial strength, but Reuben lost his firstborn birthright blessings to Ephraim, the British. He, Reuben, would rather be flirting with our enemies because it is with them he can fulfil that leadership role he so desires; but our enemies turn against him when he refuses to go along with them to take the rest of us Israelites on, for Reuben still has within him the righteousness to save Joseph alive. Therefore, they find it necessary to defeat Reuben, along with Belgium and the Netherlands. This is why in <u>Dan. 7:20</u>, the little emerging horn on the 10 horned beast, it states, *"And before whom three* (Israelite nations) *fell"*. This is exactly what occurred at the start of the 2nd world war. We can expect a similar scenario this 3rd time around, with <u>double</u> the consequences. Of the <u>one-third</u> of all the <u>Israelites</u> that make it through the war, must go through a devastated land of nothingness, just trying to stay alive, for a period of 45 biblical years. A time period that no one in their right mind would ever want to live through, where only <u>one out of ten Israelites</u> will survive. A time when mankind will revert to cannibalism in trying to stay alive, which is reported below:

<u>Ezek. 34:1-31,</u> *"And the word of the Lord God came unto me, saying, Son of man, prophesy against the shepherds of Israel, prophesy, and say unto them, Thus says the Lord God unto the shepherds; Woe be to the shepherds of Israel that do feed themselves! Should not the shepherds feed the flock? Ye eat the fat, and ye cloth you with wool, ye kill them that are fed: but ye feed not the flock. The diseased have ye not strengthened, neither have ye healed that which was sick, neither have ye bound up that which was broken, neither have ye brought again that which was driven away, neither have ye sought that which was lost; but with force and with*

cruelty have ye ruled over them. And they were scattered, because there was no shepherd: and they <u>became meat to all the beasts of the field</u> (non-Israelite peoples are included), *when they were scattered. My sheep wandered through all the mountains, and upon every high hill: yea, my flock, were scattered over all the face of the earth, and none did search and seek after them.*

*Therefore ye shepherds, hear the word of the Lord God; As I live, says the Lord God, surely because my flock became a prey, and my flock <u>became meat to every beast of the field</u>* (non-Israelites are considered with the beasts) *because there was no shepherd, neither did my shepherds search for my flock, but the shepherds fed themselves, and fed not my flock:*

*Therefore, O ye shepherds, hear the word of the Lord God; Thus saith the Lord God; Behold, I am against the shepherds; and I will require my flock at their hand, and cause them to cease from feeding the flocks; neither shall the shepherds feed themselves any more; for I will deliver my flock from <u>their mouth,</u> that they may not be <u>meat for them.</u>*

*For thus says the Lord God; Behold, I, even I, will both search my sheep, and seek them out. As a shepherd seeks out his flock in the day that he is among his sheep that are scattered; So will I seek out my sheep, and will deliver them out of all places where they have been scattered in the cloudy and dark day. And I will bring them out from the people, and gather them from the countries, and will bring them to their own land, and feed them upon the mountains of Israel by the rivers, and in all the inhabited places of the country. I will feed them in a good pasture, and upon the high mountains of Israel shall their fold be: there shall they lie in a good fold, and in a fat pasture shall they feed upon the mountains of Israel. I will feed my flock, and I will cause them to lie down, saith the Lord God. I will seek that which was lost, and bring again that which was driven away, and will bind up that which was broken, and will strengthen that which was sick: But I will destroy the fat and the strong; I will feed them with judgment. And as for you, O my flock, thus says the Lord God; Behold, I judge between cattle and cattle, and between the rams and the he goats. Seemeth it a small thing unto you to have eaten up the good pasture, but ye must tread down with your feet the residue of your pastures? And to have drunk the deep waters, but ye must fowl the residue with your feet? And as for my flock, they eat that which ye have trodden with your feet; and they drink that which ye have fouled with your feet.*

*Therefore thus says the Lord God unto them; Behold, I, even I, will judge between the fat cattle and between the lean cattle. Because ye have thrust with the side and with shoulder, and pushed all the diseased with your horns, till ye have scattered them abroad; Therefore I will save my flock, and they shall no more be a prey; and I will judge between cattle and cattle. And I will set one shepherd over them, and he shall feed them, <u>even my servant David</u>; he shall feed them, and he shall be their shepherd* (not Saul/Paul's pagan christ). *And I the Lord God will* *be their God, and <u>my servant David</u>, shall be a prince among them; I the Lord God have spoken it.*

Thereafter, God will send out his fishers and hunters, as <u>Jer. 16:16</u> states, to gather the <u>remnant</u> together, and lead them back to the promised land, just as <u>Jer. 16:15</u> says, for these will be the blessed ones that survived, as <u>Dan. 12:12</u> states, *"Blessed is he that waits, and comes to the thousand three hundred and thirty fifth days* (of biblical years)*"*. Or as <u>Isa. 6:13</u>, *"But yet in it shall be <u>a tenth</u>, and it shall return, and shall be eaten: as a teil tree, and an oak, whose substance is in them, when they cast their leaves: so the Holy seed shall be the substance thereof"*.

<u>Ezek. 20:33-38</u> states, *"As I live, saith the Lord God, surely with a mighty hand and with a stretched out arm, and fury poured out, will I rule over you. And I will bring you out from the people, and will gather you out of the countries wherein ye are scattered. And I will bring you into the wilderness of the people, and there will I plead with you face to face. Like I pleaded with your fathers in the wilderness of the land of Egypt, so will I plead with you, saith the Lord God. And I will cause you to pass under the rod, and I will bring you into the <u>bond of the covenant</u>: And I will purge out from among you the rebels and them that transgress against me: and ye shall know that I am the Lord God"*.

<u>Ezek. 34:25-31</u>, continues, *"And I will make with them a covenant of peace, and will cause the evil beasts to cease out of the land: and they shall dwell safely in the wilderness, and sleep in the woods. And I will make them and the places round about my hill a blessing; and I will cause the shower to come down in his season; there shall be showers of blessings. And the trees of the field shall yield her fruit, and the earth shall yield her increase, and they shall be safe in their land, and shall know that I am the Lord their God, when I have broken the bands of their yoke, and delivered them out of the hand of those that served themselves of them. And they shall no more be a <u>prey to the heathen</u>, neither shall <u>the beast of the land</u> devour them; but they shall dwell safely, and none shall make them afraid. And I will raise up for them a plant of renown, and they shall be no more consumed with hunger in the land, neither bare the shame of the heathen any more. Thus shall they know that <u>I the Lord their God am with them, and that they, even the house of Israel, are my people, says the Lord God</u>. And ye my flock, the flock of my pasture, are men, and <u>I am your God, says the Lord God</u>"*.

This 1,335 biblical years began counting when "KARL THE MAN", Char le magne, via the French peoples, Saul called Paul in the New Testament times, the emerged little horn on the 10 horned beast of <u>Dan. 7:20-25</u>, that had eyes, and <u>a mouth that spoke very great arrogant boasting words against the most high</u>, matching the same words that came out of Charles'/King Saul's mouth in <u>Dan. 11:36</u>, *"And the king shall do according to his will; and he shall <u>exalt himself</u>, and <u>magnify himself</u> above every god, <u>and shall speak marvelous</u>*

<u>*arrogant things against the God of gods,*</u> *and shall prosper till the indignation be accomplished: for that that is determined shall be done"*. And setting up an image of his imaginary pagan abominable christ upon the Saxons' Altar of God, making it desolate, as stated below:

<u>Dan. 12:11</u>, *"And from the time that the daily sacrifice shall be taken away, and the abomination that makes the altar desolate set up, there shall be a thousand two hundred and ninety days"*.(1,290 days, of biblical years*) "And all shall be finished"* (our civilization will be totally destroyed).

The act that Charles/King Saul brought about, happened on 774.778 cue. by attacking the Saxons' place of worship and set an image of his pagan jesus christ, or even perhaps the shroud, which was in reality an image of <u>himself</u>, upon their Altar of God, making the altar desolate, and then forced the Saxons to worship his pagan christ, killing those who refused: thereafter he destroyed their place of worship, bringing an end to their sacrifices. From this point, it brought <u>Dan. 12:7</u> alive, as stated below:

*"And I heard the man clothed in linen, which was upon the waters of the river, when he held up his right hand and his left hand unto heaven, and sware by him that lives forever that it shall be for <u>a time, times, and an half</u>* (1,260 days of biblical years), *and when he shall have accomplished to scatter the power of the holy people* (30-biblical-year world war against the 4th world so-called Holy Roman Empire and their allies), *all these things shall be finished"*.

No one was able to understand Daniel's scriptures until the time of the end was upon us: but being that we are now in the time of the end, God has given me the keys to unseal Daniel's shut up and sealed scriptures, and it is my job to enlighten my fellow Israelites of the real truth, and warn them of the coming devastation in the very near future; giving them that final chance to flee from this paganism christian religion, that Charles/King Saul/Saul called Paul, Daniel's horn in <u>7:20 and 25</u>, imposed upon our ancient ancestors in the year of 774.778 from sunset of previous day cue., with his pagan christ <u>of himself</u> that he imposed upon them as their another god. And yes! It was the christians' christ that made God's Altar desolate. This is why no one was able to understand Daniel's scriptures. For in the minds of the christian, it would be impossible that it would be '<u>their christ</u>', that they worshipped and prayed to, and served, that could make God's Altar desolate.

<u>Dan. 12:4 & 8-10 tells us.</u> *"But thou, O Daniel, shut up the words, and seal the book, even to the time of the end: many shall run to and fro, and knowledge shall be increased"*.

*"And I heard, but I understood not: then said I, O my Lord, what shall be the end of these things? And he said, go thy way, Daniel: for the words are closed up and sealed <u>till the time of the end</u>. Many shall be purified, and made white, and*

*tried; but the wicked shall do wickedly; and none of the wicked shall understand; but the wise shall"*.

God put our Saxons' ancestors, the <u>remnant</u> of the House of Israel, into the emerged little horn of <u>Dan. 7:25,</u> for 1,260 days (of biblical years) or 1241.8891 of our calendar years. It took Charles 30 days, of biblical years, or 29.5688 of our Gregorian years to fully impose his christian religion upon our ancestors.

Therefore, after 1241.8891 of our years, God must reclaim us, our ancestors' children, back with also a 30 biblical year, world war, which will begin in 774.778 + 1241.8891 = 2016.667 on Aug. 31st from sunset of previous day cue. This war will be for 29.5688 of our years, which will end in 2046.2358 on Mar. 27th. This year also ends all the 12 ages of this present world as we know it, and the 1/3rd remaining <u>remnant</u> will try to survive the 45 days, of biblical years, a period of nothingness, and the very few 1/10th who survive will be the blessed ones, to be gathered up, and lead back to the promised land, where King David (not this pagan christ that Saul called Paul brought forth in the New Testament times), shall be their king, shepherd and prince.

## As stated below:

<u>Jer. 30:9,</u> *"But they shall serve the Lord their God, and <u>David</u> their king, whom I will raise up unto them"*.

<u>Ezek. 34:23-24,</u> *"And I will set up one shepherd over them, and he shall feed them, even my servant <u>David</u>; he shall feed them, and he shall be their shepherd"*.

<u>Ezek. 37:24-25,</u> *"And <u>David</u> my servant shall be king over them; and they all shall have one shepherd: they shall also walk in my judgments, and observe my statutes, and do them. And they shall dwell in the land that I have given unto Jacob my servant, wherein your fathers have dwelt; and they shall dwell therein. Even they, and their children, and their children's children forever: and my servant <u>David</u> shall be their prince forever"*.

<u>Hosea 3:5,</u> *"Afterward shall the children of Israel return, and seek the Lord their God, and <u>David</u> their king; and shall fear the Lord God and his goodness <u>in the latter days</u>"*.

# Chapter 5

# Newly Revealed Workings of Our Current World

<u>2 Esdras 11:1-46, 12:1-3,</u> *"On the second night I Ezra had a vision in a dream; I saw, rising from the sea, an eagle with 12 wings and 3 heads. I saw it spread its wings over the whole earth; and all the winds blew on it, and the clouds gathered. Out of its wings I saw rival wings sprout, which proved to be only small and stunted. Its heads lay still; even the middle head, which was bigger than the others, lay still between them. As I watched, the eagle rose on its wings to set itself up as ruler over the earth and its inhabitants. I saw it bring into subjection everything under heaven; it met with no opposition at all from any creature on earth. I saw the eagle stand erect on its talons, and it spoke aloud to its wings: "Do not all wake at once," it said; "sleep in your places, and each wake up in turn; <u>the heads are to be kept till the last.</u>" I saw that the sound was not coming from its heads, but from the middle of its body. I counted its rival wings, and saw that there were 8 of them. As I watched, one of the wings on its right side rose and became ruler over the whole earth.* (This leader was Justinian 554-565 cue.) *After a time, its reign came to an end, and it disappeared from sight completely. Then the next rose and established its rule, which it held for a long time* (this was Charlemagne, who inherited his father Pepin's throng in 771 cue. and ruled until 836 cue.). *When its reign was coming to an end and it was about to disappear like the first one, a voice could be heard saying to it: "You have ruled the world for so long; now listen to my message before your time comes to disappear. None of your successors will achieve a reign as long as yours, nor even half as long." Then the third wing arose, ruled the world for a time like its predecessors, and like them disappeared. In the same way all the wings came to power in succession, and in turn disappeared from sight. As time went on, I saw the wings on the left side also raise themselves up to seize power. Some of them did so, and passed immediately from sight, while others arose but never came to power. At this point I noticed that 2 of the little*

*wings were, like the 12 big wings, no longer to be seen. Nothing was now left of the eagle's body except the 3 motionless heads and 6 little wings. As I watched, 2 of the 6 little wings separated from the rest and took up a place under the head on the right. The other 4 wings remained where they were; and I saw them planning to rise up and seize power. One rose, but disappeared immediately; so too did the second, vanishing even more quickly than the first. I saw the last 2 small wings* (Mussolini and Hitler) *planning to seize the kingship for themselves. But while they were still plotting, suddenly one of the heads woke from sleep, the one in the middle, the biggest of the three. <u>I saw how it joined with the other 2 heads,</u> and along with them turned and devoured the 2 little wings, which were planning to seize power. <u>This big head got the whole earth into its grasp, establishing an oppressive rule over all its inhabitants and a world-wide kingdom mightier than any of the wings had ruled.</u> But after that I saw the middle head vanish just as suddenly as the wings had done. There were 2 heads left, and they also seized power over the earth and its inhabitants, but as I watched, <u>the head on the right devoured the head on the left.</u> Then I heard a voice, which said to me: "Look carefully at what you see before you." I looked, and saw what seemed to be a lion roused from the forest; it roared as it came, and I heard it address the eagle in a human voice. "Listen to what I tell you", it said. "The Most High says to you: Are you not the only survivor of the 4 beasts to which I gave the rule over my world, intending through them <u>to bring my ages to their end?</u> You are the fourth beast, and you have conquered all who went before, ruling over the whole world and holding it in the grip of fear and harsh oppression. <u>You have lived long in the world,</u> governing it with deceit and with no regard for the truth. You have oppressed the gentle and injured the peaceful, hating the truthful and loving liars; you have destroyed the homes of the prosperous, and razed to the ground the walls of those who had done you no harm. Your insolence is known to the Most High, and your pride to the Mighty One. The Most High has surveyed the periods he has fixed: they are now at an end, and <u>his ages have reached their completion.</u> So you, eagle, must now disappear and be seen no more, you and your terrible great wings, your evil small wings, your cruel heads, your grim talons, and your whole worthless body. Then all the earth will feel relief at its deliverance from your violence, and look forward hopefully to the judgment and mercy of its* Creator". *While the lion was still addressing the eagle, I looked and saw the one remaining head disappear. Then the 2 little wings, which had gone to him arose and set themselves up as rulers. Their reign was short and troubled, and when I looked at them they were already vanishing. Then the eagle's entire body burst into flames, and the earth was struck with terror. So great was my alarm and fear that I awoke".*

## The angel in 2 Esdras 12:10-34 gives Ezra the interpretation of his vision

"*The eagle you saw rising from the sea represents the fourth kingdom in the vision seen by your brother Daniel. But he was not given the interpretation, which I am now giving you or have already given you. The days are coming when the earth will be under an empire more terrible than any before. It will be ruled by 12 kings, one after another. The second to come to the throne* (Charlemagne) *will have the longest reign of all the 12. That is the meaning of the twelve wings you saw. As for the voice which you heard speaking from the middle of the eagle's body, and not from its heads, this is what it means: After this second king's reign, great conflicts will arise, which will bring the empire into danger of falling; and yet it will not fall then, but will be restored to its original strength. As for the 8 lesser wings which you saw growing from the eagle's wings, this is what they mean: The empire will come under 8 kings whose reigns will be trivial and short-lived; 2 of them will come and go just before the middle of the period, 4 will be kept back until shortly before its end, and 2 will be left until the end itself. As for the 3 heads which you saw sleeping, this is what they mean: In the last years of the empire the Most High will bring to the throne 3 kings/popes, who will restore much of its strength, and rule over the earth and its inhabitants more oppressively than anyone before. They are called the eagle's heads, because they will complete and bring to a head its long series of wicked deeds. As for the greatest head, which you saw disappear, it signifies one of the kings* (popes), *who will die in his bed, but in great agony* (this can only be Pope John Paul II, whom the whole world witnessed passing away in great agony). *The 2 that survived will be destroyed by the sword; one of them will fall by the sword of the other, who will himself fall by the sword in the last days*".

This newly elected Benedict XVI, is the head on the left, but he retired and was replaced by pope Frances, he will, while occupying his position, be assassinated by the head on the right, who will be none other than Saul called Paul in the New Testament times, with the evil spirit still upon him, and who was the master builder of this pagan christian religion, this head on the right today is masquerading as Archbishop of the High Anglican Church of England, by the name Justin Welby, and who in turn will be destroyed by the true Messiah of God, King David. These 3 heads were joined together by the false christ that Saul/Paul brought about, as it states in Ezra's vision above, "*I saw how it joined with the other 2 heads*". Just as all the christian religions are also joined together by the pagan christ that Saul/Paul brought forth, which was an imaginary figure of himself.

"*As for the 2 little wings that went over to the head on the right side, this is what they mean: They are the ones whom the Most High has reserved until the last days, and their reign, as you saw was short and troubled*".

"As for the lion which you saw coming from the forest, roused from sleep and roaring, which you heard addressing the eagle, taxing it with its wicked deeds and words, this is the Messiah whom the Most High has kept back until the end. He will address those rulers, taxing them openly with their sins, their crimes, and their defiance. He will bring them alive to judgment; he will convict them and destroy them. But he will be merciful to those of my people that remain, all who have been kept safe in my land; he will set them free and give them gladness, until the final day of judgment comes, about which I told you at the beginning".

## **The following is the vision that Daniel saw concerning this fourth world empire:**

Daniel 7:7-8, 11, 19-21, 23-25, "After this I saw in the night visions, and behold a fourth beast, dreadful and terrible, and strong exceedingly; and it had great iron teeth: it devoured and brake in pieces, and stamped the residue with the feet of it: and it was diverse from all the beasts that were before it; and it had 10 horns. I considered the horns, and, behold, there came up among them another little horn, before who there were three of the first horns plucked up by the roots: and, behold, in this horn were eyes like the eyes of man, and a mouth speaking great things.

I beheld then because of the voice of the great words, which the horn spoke: I beheld even till the beast was slain, and his body destroyed, and given to the burning flame.

Then I would know the truth of the fourth beast, which was diverse from all the others, exceedingly dreadful, whose teeth were of iron, and his nails of brass; which devoured, brake in pieces, and stamped the residue with his feet; And of the 10 horns that were in his head, and of the other which came up, and before whom 3 fell; even of that horn that had eyes, and a mouth that spoke very great things, whose look was more stout than his fellows (Saul/Paul-King Saul). I beheld, and the same horn made war with the saints, and prevailed against them (Charlemagne-King Saul, with the evil spirit still upon him)".

Thus he said, "The fourth beast shall be the fourth kingdom upon earth, which shall be diverse from all kingdoms, and shall devour the whole earth, and shall tread it down, and break it in pieces. And the 10 horns out of this kingdom are 10 kings that shall arise: and another shall rise after them; and he shall be diverse from the first, and he shall subdue 3 kings. And he shall speak great words against the Most High, and shall wear out the saints of the Most High, and think to change times and laws: and they shall be given into his hand until a time, and times, and the dividing of time. But the judgment shall sit, and they shall take away his dominion, to consume and to destroy it unto the end".

As I have been constantly conveying to you, that we are in the last days of this world as we know it, the end of the ages of this world will be after the 30-biblical-year world war, when God has completed the reclaiming period of us Israelites, out of the hand of the little horn of Daniel's 7:25 and Esdras's right head of the eagle, who devours/assassinates the eagle's head on the left, who is the newly elected Pope Frances, and the middle large head representing the deceased Pope John Paul, who like this middle head died in his bed with great agony, and witnessed by the whole world. These 3 kings/popes were to be kept till the last years of the empire, and who will restore much of its strength, and rule over the earth and its inhabitants more oppressively than anyone before. They are called the eagle's heads, because they will complete and bring to a head its long series of wicked deeds. Did not John Paul travel extensively to tighten the christians' grip on their subjects? I believe you will see Pope Frances enforce more control over his subjects, preparing the way for King Saul's return. This King Saul will come on the scene 2046.2358 - 29.5688 = 2016.667 - 3.45 = 2013.3 or Mar. 20th from sunset of previous day, 1,260 days prior to the start of the end-time world war, and be crowned as the christians' Archbishop of England's High Anglican Church, which is a separate part from the Roman Christian churches. According to the Apocrypha books of Esdras, this is King Saul returning to place his atrocities upon us and the whole world, by overriding the authorities of the Roman Church and reign over us all for his 1,260 days, then God's Holy Messiah King David comes on the scene and puts this King Saul to death. God then begins to take us back from the hands of this horn on the beast of Dan. 7:25 for he is the right head of the eagle. King Saul himself, the devil's 1st born son, the christians' christ, with a 30-biblical-year world war, as described in Jer. 30:7.

The difference between Daniel's vision from that of Ezra's vision is that Daniel's vision of the 10 horns mainly represent nations, where in Ezra's visions the wings represent individual leaders of nations. Also in Daniel's vision we do not have any mention of the 2 christian leaders, preceding the last horn, who by now you should be able to understand that he is none other than Saul/Paul/King Saul; and the true Messiah, as I have stated in all of my previous articles, is none other than King David. This battle between the 2 first kings of the Israelites for control over the Israelites and indeed over all the nations of the world to come isn't over as yet. There will be a battle this world has never seen before, nor shall it see the likes of it again. This battle will expire at the end of God's reclaiming period in the year 2046.2358 cue. *"All will be finished"*. Including all 12 ages of our present corrupt world.

If this article does not penetrate your mind, to see the truth, there is nothing more I can say. We must truly prepare ourselves to really meet our maker, by fleeing from this christian paganism religion, and all other false ways that have held our God given minds captive; throw away your proud stubborn ways, for this is one of the first roadblocks of many, that you must defeat, in order to succeed. Keep in your mind that your educational degrees acquired, the position in life you acquired, and your wealth, means absolutely nothing, when God's great judgments comes forth. The only requirement that really matters; is how you have conducted your life according to the ways of God, which are the ways recorded in the Old Testament. All God's statutes, God's judgments, God's laws, and God's commandments (His everlasting covenant with us) are still in force, no matter what your falsely trusted christian leaders state. God's holy Sabbath day is still from just before sundown Friday to just after sundown Saturday. All you individuals that follow the christian faith, whether Catholic or any of the Protestant christian organizations, and participate in any of their so-called holy events, also partake or not in their communion ritual, and pray to God but ask your requests in the name of his (Saul/Paul's) christ, which overrides the power of God, are indeed on the slippery steep slope to hell of eternal damnation, with King Saul, the devil's 1st born son, welcoming you to his abyss. Those of you who don't really believe there is a God, but also partake in the christian' events, your fate is no better than the faithful christian, King Saul will also welcome you into his dark abyss. Then you will truly find out that there is a living God with his Holy Messiah, King David; and a living devil with his cursed son, King Saul. These two kings, you will recall, if you have read the first book of Samuel, are the first two chosen kings of the tribes of Israel. King Saul, because of his disobedience of God's direct command to eradicate all the Amalekite men, women, and even the children, and all their possessions, even all the animals and their valuables. By allowing his forces to take whatsoever they wanted is showing he feared the people he ruled over, more than he feared God. He was thereby rejected by God, and received an evil spirit from God, which troubled him. God then chose David to be king over the Israelites, who received God's Holy Spirit that Saul originally had. David, for the most part, took full advantage of God's Holy Spirit upon him, and conducted his life according to the ways of God, when he too slipped up big time. But God forgave David, but only after extreme repercussions from God. David thereafter never lost his focus of God's greatness. David's backsliding with extreme consequences should give us great hope that no matter how far we have strayed away from God's ways, this avenue to receive God's forgiveness and his salvation to receive our eternal life, after our initial life unto death, is still open to us, if only we will take full advantage of David's shed blood and wholeheartedly make an about face and return to the ways of God, with your whole heart, soul, and mind, before it is too late, for as I stated earlier, we only have approx. 10 years before God's reclaiming period is upon us from this late summer month of year 2006 cue. There is no new covenant as stated in the New Testament. The only true difference that the New Testament brings to us is the fact that we no longer need to sacrifice an animal and use it's blood to make atonement for our sins, for the blood of God's Holy Messiah, King David, shall wash us clean from sins, for this was the ultimate sacrifice brought about by God, shedding the blood of his only begotten firstborn son to make atonement for our sins. But please take note that in order to take advantage of this ultimate sacrifice, we must perform the works to the best of our abilities. Such as worshipping and praying to our one Lord God only and no one else, for there are no other gods with him or besides him. We must keep holy His Sabbath day, not the christians' made-up day. We must observe and keep the holy days that the Jewish peoples keep and not the christians' pagan days. We must cast away all our graven images of whatsoever so-called christians' pagan christ and pagan canonized saints. We must stop observing and participating in any of the christians' pagan events. In other words we must flee from all falsehood. Even the true Messiah, King David, we are not to worship or pray to, for he is a human being just as we are. He is not a God. The abomination that the Jewish people do is they are also trapped into drinking the blood and eating the body of the christians' pagan christ, and they also pray to and serve this pagan christ as a god. Being completely ignorant that King David is God's Holy Messiah. It is David that condemns the drinking of his blood in <u>Psalms 16:4</u>, and obviously the eating of his body, that the christians are performing of their pagan christ. The Jewish people of the House of Judah and us Israelites of the House of Israel should read <u>Jer. 25:15-18</u> and <u>Ezek. 23:31-34</u> and consider what they are doing, for we are so far off track, we don't have a clue of what we are doing. God is about to bring us through the fire of total desolation in the very near future, in an attempt to undeceive our deceived minds. Hopefully this book will give you that head start you will obviously need. I can't emphasize enough just how important the truths within this book will assist you, with all the reproving that you can ever hope for at your fingertips to prove all things, as indicated via the following scriptures.

## **<u>Take note of the following scriptures:</u>**

<u>Proverbs 1:20-33</u>, *"Wisdom cries outside; she utters her voice in the streets: she cries out loud in the chief place of concourse, in the opening of the gates: in the city she utters her words, saying, How long, ye simple ones, will ye love simplicity? And the scorners delight in their scorning, and fools hate knowledge? Turn you at my*

*reproof: Behold, I will pour out my spirit unto you, I will make known my words unto you.*

*Because I have called, and ye refused; I have stretched out my hand, and no man regarded; but ye have set at naught all my counsel, and would none of my reproof:*

*I also will laugh at your calamity; I will mock when your fear comes; when your fear comes as desolation, and your destruction comes as a whirlwind; when distress and anguish comes upon you.*

*Then shall they call upon me, but I will not answer; they shall seek me early, but they shall not find me: for that they hated knowledge, and did not choose the fear of the Lord God: They would none of my counsel: they despised all my reproof.*

*Therefore shall they eat of the fruit of their own way, and be filled with their own devices. For the turning away of the simple shall slay them, and the prosperity of fools shall destroy them.*

*But whoso hearkens unto me shall dwell safely, and shall be quiet from fear of evil".*

# Chapter 6

# Proving New Testament Wrong with That of the Old Testament

Before we begin with this chapter, one must keep in mind that the Old Testament is the source of God's ways; therefore, all scriptures must agree with the Old Testament in order to have any legitimacy. If the legitimacy is missing, one cannot believe its message.

Rev. 1:5, *"And from Jesus Christ, who is the faithful witness, and the first begotten of the dead, and the prince of the kings of the earth. Unto him that loved us, and washed us from our sins in his own blood"*.

Ps. 89:18-20, 26-27, *"For the Lord God is our defence; and the Holy One of Israel is our king. Then thou spakest in vision to thy holy one, and said, I have laid help upon one that is mighty; I have exalted one chosen out of the people. I have found David my servant; with my holy oil have I anointed him"*.

*"He* (David) *shall cry unto me, Thou art my father, my God, and the rock of my salvation. Also I will make him* (David) *my firstborn, higher than the kings of the earth"*.

This scripture of Rev. 1:5, does not agree with the Old Testament scripture of Psalms 89, there can only be one firstborn and one King of kings, definitely not two, and seeing David's name is in fact being used; proves Rev. 1:5 is wrong. This is also verified in Ps. 2:7 and Ps. 118:17-18 as indicated below.

Ps. 2:7, *"I* (David) *will declare the decree: the Lord God has said unto me* (David), *Thou art my Son; this day have I begotten thee"*.

Notice David is using the 1st person pronouns "I" and "me", indicating that he is speaking of himself.

Ps. 118:17-18, *"I* (David) *shall not die, but live, and declare the works of the Lord God. The Lord has chastened me sore: but he has not given me over unto death"*.

David, again is using 1st person pronouns, and is telling us that he is the faithful witness to declare the works of God, which is also disproving above New Testament Rev. 1:5 scripture.

This Rev. 1:5 scripture should read as follows: *"And from King David, God's Holy Messiah, who is our faithful witness, and the first begotten of the dead, and prince of the kings of the earth; being a willing participant unto him* (the Lord God) *that loved us, and washed us from our sins in the shedding of his first begotten son's blood".*

Check Ps. 89:18-20, 26-27, above.

\* \* \*

Rev. 22:16, *"I Jesus have sent mine angel to testify unto you these things in the churches. I am the root and the offspring of David, and the bright and morning star".*

Isa. 11:1, *"And there shall come forth a rod out of the stem of Jesse, and a Branch shall grow out of his roots".* The rod that grew out of Jesse, was David. David will be the root that brings forth his branches. David's branches are his offspring. Therefore, Jesus can't be the root, for he has no reported children.

This Rev. 22:16 should read: *I, King David, God's Holy Messiah, have sent mine angel to testify unto you these things in the churches, I am the offspring of Jesse, and the root of my offspring, and the bright and morning star".*

\* \* \*

Acts 13:33-37, "God has *fulfilled the same unto us their children, in that he has raised up Jesus again; as it is also written in the second psalm, Thou art my Son, this day have I begotten thee".*

Vr. 34, *"And as concerning that he raised him up from the dead, now no more to return to corruption, he said on this wise, I will give you the sure mercies of David".*

Vr. 35, *"Wherefore he said also in another psalm, Thou shall not suffer thine Holy One to see corruption".*

Vr. 36, *"For David, after he had served his own generation by the will of God, fell on sleep, and was laid unto his fathers, and saw corruption".*

Vr. 37, *"But he, whom God raised again, saw no corruption".*

In Vrs. 33 & 37 Saul/Paul states that God raised up Jesus again. This would mean that this Jesus had a previous birth, life, death and redemption. You can search the entire Old Testament Bible, and you will not find any scripture to prove the above claim. The only person that had a previous birth, life, death, and redemption is none other than King David. For he had a previous birth, life, and was redeemed before his death from the corrupting powers of the grave, reported firstly in the books of Samuel, and in many of the other books within the Old Testaments, and reported by David himself in his Psalms of 16:10, 30:3, 49:15, 118:17-18, which state as follows:

Ps. 16:10, *"For thou will not leave my soul in hell; neither will thou suffer thine Holy One to see corruption"*.

Ps. 30:3, *"O Lord, thou has brought up my soul from the grave: thou has kept me alive, that I should not go down to the pit"*.

Ps. 49:15, *"But God will redeem my soul from the power of the grave: for he shall receive me"*.

Ps. 118:17-18, *"I shall not die, but live, and declare the works of the Lord God". The Lord has chastened me sore: but he has not given me over unto death"*.

This statement, "raised again," can only refer to David, and absolutely no one else. These above Psalms also prove Acts 13:36 above as being false, for David did not see the corrupting powers of the grave.

You will also notice that in Acts 13:35 above, that Saul/Paul is saying that he (God) is speaking to his christ and saying *"thou shall not suffer thine Holy One to see corruption"*.

With God doing the speaking, it would give Saul/Paul's christ power over God, for it would be up to Saul/Paul's christ whether God would see the corrupting powers of the grave, for this is precisely what this statement is implying, and we all know God cannot die. You will notice Saul/Paul took this scripture from Ps. 16:10, for this scripture does not exist anywhere else in the Old Testament. In this scripture of David's, it is David speaking to God, not the other way around. Here this scripture is giving the power to God, whether David would receive the corrupting powers of the grave.

This same scenario is played out when we pray to our Lord God for certain favourable outcomes, and ask God for these favourable outcomes in the name of Saul/Paul's imaginary pagan christ; this is the same as giving Saul/Paul's imaginary christ power over God. No wonder very few, if any, of our prayers are ever answered.

For God states in Isa. 42:8, *"I am the Lord God: that is my name: and my glory will I not give to another, neither my praise to graven images"*.

Again I emphasize that this prayer of yours is exactly the same as if you are taking the glory away from God and giving it to another pagan god or its graven image.

Saul/Paul pulls somewhat the same stunt in Acts 13:34, where Saul/Paul states God said to his (Paul's) christ, *"I will give you the sure mercies of David"*.

This scripture is taken from Isaiah 55:3, which states, *"Incline your ear, and come unto me; hear, and your soul shall live; and I will make an everlasting covenant with you, even the sure mercies of David"*.

This scripture, as noticed refers to you, me, Joe blow, or whoever else submits their life to the ways of God. There is absolutely no way Saul/Paul can legitimize his christ with a scripture that refers to anyone.

You will also notice in the above stated Psalms, David is using first person pronouns; which is telling us that David is referring only to himself. How in the world can Saul-Paul pull his deceptive veil over so many individual's eyes, throughout all these years, and as a result, deceiving all his followers to believe his christ is the true Messiah of God? It is absolutely unbelievable, what Saul/Paul is doing in these scriptures of Acts, he is actually overriding the true Messiah of God, King David, with his imaginary individual he names jesus christ; proving he is that "anti-Messiah" mentioned below:

1 John 2:18, *"Little children, it is the last time: and as ye have heard that antichrist/Messiah shall come, even now are there many antichrists/Messiahs; whereby we know that it is the last time"*.

These "many anti-Messiahs" are being referred to the priests, ministers and clergy persons, preaching the gospel of Saul/Paul's imaginary pagan christ, which is today the christians' other pagan entity, and all their pagan entities such as the canonized saints, virgin mother, etc.

This above scripture is referring to our present day priests, ministers, clergy-persons, and all the way up to the pope as the 'many anti-Messiahs' within this christian religion. Which would also agree with the scriptures of Ezek. 22:25-27 and Zeph. 3:3-4, that they are also referred to as the wolves in sheep's clothing, devouring the mind/spirit of whomever they come in contact with.

For God states in Isa. 42:8, *"I am the Lord God: that is my name: and my glory will I not give to another, neither my praise to graven images"*.

The christian establishments have standing/painted images of all their canonized saints, virgin mother, etc., along with graven, standing/painted images of their pagan christ, which is totally breaking God's first 3 commandments. These commandments from Exodus 20:1-17 are as below:

*"I am the Lord thy God which have brought thee out of the land of Egypt, out of the house of bondage. Thou shalt have no other gods before me. Thou shalt not make unto thee any graven images, or any likeness of anything that is in heaven above, or that is in the earth beneath, or that is in the water under the earth: Thou shalt not bow down thyself to them, nor serve them: for I the Lord thy God am a jealous God, visiting the iniquity of the fathers upon the children unto the third and fourth generation of them that hate me; and showing mercy unto thousands of them that love me, and keep my commandments. Thou shalt not take the name of the Lord thy God in vain; for the Lord will not hold him guiltless that takes his name in vain"*.

Even God's true Messiah, King David, is not to be prayed to, served, and worshipped as a God, nor any graven, painted images made of him, that the followers can pray to, serve, or worship in his stead.

This is also verified in <u>Deut. 4:14-19, 23-24,</u> *"And the Lord God commanded me at that time to teach you statutes and judgments, that ye might do them in the land whither ye go over to possess it.*

*Take ye therefore good heed unto yourselves; for ye saw no manner of similitude on the day that the Lord God spoke unto you in Horeb out of the midst of the fire: lest ye corrupt yourselves, and make you a graven image, the similitude of <u>any figure,</u> the likeness of male or female, the likeness of any beast that is on the earth, the likeness of any winged fowl that flies in the air, the likeness of any thing that creeps on the ground, the likeness of any fish that is in the waters beneath the earth: and lest thou lift up thine eyes unto heaven, and when thou seest the sun, and the moon, and the stars, even all the host of heaven, shouldest thou be driven to worship them, and serve them, which the Lord thy God has divided unto all nations under the whole heaven. Take heed unto yourselves, lest ye forget the covenant of the Lord your God, which he made with you, and make you a graven image, or the likeness of <u>any thing,</u> which the Lord thy God has <u>forbidden</u> thee. For the Lord thy God is a consuming fire, even a jealous God".*

The anti-christ/<u>Messiah</u> scriptures of <u>1 John 2:22, 4:2-3, 2 John 1:7,</u> must be changed to comply with the truth. The proper terminology should be anti-Messiah, for King David is God's Holy Messiah, not Saul/Paul's imaginary pagan christ; as proven in the following end-time related scriptures. One must remember that Charlemagne/King Saul/Saul called Paul spent a whole winter in the Vatican working on the scriptures, naturally according to his way of thinking.

<u>Jer. 30:9,</u> *"But they shall serve the Lord their God, and David their king, whom I will raise up unto them".*

<u>Ezek. 34:23-24,</u> *"And I will set up one shepherd over them, and he shall feed them, even my servant David; he shall feed them, and he shall be their shepherd".*

<u>Ezek. 37:24-25,</u> *"And David my servant shall be king over them; and they all shall have one shepherd: they shall also walk in my judgments, and observe my statutes, and do them. And they shall dwell in the land that I have given unto Jacob my servant, wherein your fathers have dwelt; and they shall dwell therein, even they, and their children, and their children's children forever: and my servant David shall be their prince forever".*

<u>Hosea 3:5,</u> *afterward shall the children of Israel return, and seek the Lord their God, and David their king; and shall fear the Lord and his goodness <u>in the latter days</u>".*

As a matter of fact the entire New Testament must be changed by replacing the name jesus christ, with "King David, God's Messiah", to get as far as you can from the name of Saul/Paul's pagan imaginary christ, within your mind. Even than there will be corruption within the New Testament, because many of the scriptures have been altered to corrupt the truth, as indicated above and below within the scriptures of 1 and 2 John, with the replacement of the name jesus christ, should read as follows:

1 John 2:22, "*Who is a liar but he that denies that* (King David is the Messiah)? *He is antichrist* (anti-Messiah) *that denies the Father and the Son*".

1 John 4:2-3, "*Hereby know ye the Spirit of God: Every spirit that confesses that* (King David, God's Holy Messiah) *is come in the flesh is of God: And every spirit that confesses not that* (King David, God's Holy Messiah) *is come in the flesh is not of God: and this is that spirit of antichrist* (anti-Messiah), *whereof ye have heard that it should come; and even now already it is in the world*".

2 John 1:7, "*For many deceivers are entered into the world, who confess not that* (King David, God's Messiah) *is come in the flesh. This is a deceiver and an antichrist* (anti-Messiah)"

The underlined statement "*it is the last time*" in the above 1 John 2:18 is referring to the end of the 10th age or division of this world, for 2 Esdras 14:10-13 states, "*The world has lost its youth, and time is growing old. For the whole of time is in twelve divisions; nine divisions and half the tenth have already passed, and only two and a half still remain*".

This was the end of the 10th division and the beginning of the 11th age John is referring, which occurred in 74.9834 on Dec. 24th, 180 days after the switching from year 73 to 74. When the temple was completely destroyed, and the war against the Roman forces ended.

One division or age of time is one of God's day, or 1,000 biblical years to us human's, as referred to in 2 Peter 3:8, "*But, beloved, be not ignorant of this one thing, that one day is with the Lord God as a thousand years, and a thousand years as one day*". Which is the same as $1000 * 360/365.25 = 985.62628$ of our Gregorian calendar. This tells us that the angel was speaking to Ezra after $985.62628/2 = 492.81314 - 74.9834 = \underline{417.82974}$ b. cue. being that the end of all 12 divisions came about at the end of 2046.2358 cue., which is using the calculations from the time Charlemagne began imposing the christian religion upon the Saxon tribes living in the area that he ruled over, in the year 774.778 cue., and according to Dan. 7:25, God put these Saxons, our ancestors, the remnant (Rev. 12:17), of the House of Israel, into his hand for 1,260 biblical years or 1241.889 of our years. According to Dan. 12:7 & 7:25, this is the same time, times, and half a time recorded in Dan. 12:11, which also has God's reclaiming period of 30 biblical years attached to it, with the portion of Dan. 12:7, that states, "*And when he shall have accomplished to scatter the power of the holy people* (us Israelites that are living in all the dispersed areas that God has scattered us), *all these things shall be finished* (end of all 12 divisions/ages and our civilization)". Each creation day is equal to 985.62628 Gregorian years; therefore, 12 creation days equal to 12 * 985.62628 = 11827.515, and with Charlemagne planning to impose his christian religion upon the Saxons at an assembly in an early summer month indicates with a bit of calculations that the year 2046 would be the final Gregorian year. Therefore, we can match the ending of 2046 to that of the end of 12,000 biblical years after converting the 12,000 years to Gregorian years as follows (12000 * 360)/365.25 = 11827.515 Gregorian years. Therefore, 2046.2358 with the denominator is the number to use in all our calculations. However, according to Charlemagne he began imposing the christian religion upon the Saxon tribes living in the area that he ruled over, in the year 2046.2358 - 1271.4579 = 774.778 or Oct. 10th. Therefore, the date Charlemagne attacked the Saxons' place of worship was on Oct. 10Th in year 774.778 and because a day begins and ends at sunset all times are from the previous sunset.

According to the above-mentioned Dan. 7:25, God put these Saxons, the remnant (Rev. 12:17), of the House of Israel, into his hand for 1,260 biblical years, or 1241.8891 of our Gregorian years.

According to Dan. 12:7 & 7:25, this is the same (time, times, and an half a time) recorded also in Dan. 12:7 and 11, which also has God's reclaiming period of 30 biblical years attached to it, with the portion of Dan. 12:7, that states, *"And when he shall have accomplished to scatter the power of the holy people, all these things shall be finished"*. For whoever is interested, the 11th age ended and the 12th age began in the year 1060.6096 on Aug. 10th from sunset of previous day cue.; the time when the christian leaders came together and signed a document with the idea of giving themselves the power to elect their own pope, and had it ratified by the military leader of the empire, rather than being appointed by the Roman emperor.

Here again this underlined statement is referring to the finishing of, not only God's pursuing reclaiming war, but also of all the 12 divisions of this world. In this year of, 1290 b. or 1271.4579 G. yrs +774.778 = 2046.2358 cue. It most likely will interest the readers of this revealed information, that God's reclaiming period will begin on Aug. 31st in year 2016 cue. from sunset of previous day, and end on Mar. 27th in 2046.2358 cue., which will be the expiry time of the "time, times, and half a time", that God put our ancestors into the hands of the little horn recorded in Dan. 7:25, which began in a fall month of 774.778 on Oct. 10th from sunset of previous day, by Charlemagne imposing the christian religion upon the Saxon tribes, who were at the time, stated in Rev. 12:17, keeping the commandments of God and his testimonies. *"And the dragon was wroth with the woman, and went to make war with the remnant of her seed, which keep the commandments of God and his Testimonies"*.

This place of worship is in fact known today as the Stonehenge ruins, located in England, but all times will be from Jerusalem's time zone. This site is now being excavated by these ignorant archaeologists, that have absolutely no idea what they are getting themselves into, even the east doorway opening lining up with the summer solstice sunrise should have caused them to take note that this opening was of major importance. This opening was used only by God and the King/Prince of the people of Israel to enter and exit as indicated in Ezek. 44:2-3 scripture, and where the King/Prince of the people sat and ate his meals. I am of an understanding that most of these archaeologist sites are funded via the taxpayers' hard-earned dollars. No wonder we are paying such an exorbitantly amount of taxes when our governments throw away our dollars so carelessly. Even the buried bones aren't safe from this corrupt world. The west entrance that lines up with the winter solstice sunset indicates this entrance of secondary importance, and was used only by the Levi priestly family tribe, where outside they slaughtered the animals and strung them up on a hanging tree a short distance away, to skin, and extracted the animal parts they sacrificed upon the Altar of God within this place of worship. The rest of the carcase was cut up to place in the boiling pots located outside this west entrance, for the worshippers to eat. The north and south entrances were used by the worshippers, the ones who entered via the north entrance had to exit via the south entrance and the ones entering via the south entrance had to exit via the north entrance, such as passing through. This place of worship is referred to in Daniel's 12:7 and 11 scriptures. Our highly educated christian religious leaders and scholars are completely ignorant that this Altar of God has already been made desolate by Charlemagne/King Saul/Saul called Paul/the next and last pope of the christian religion, due to show up and take hold of his christian throne by March 20th of 2013 from sunset of previous day, and will occupy this throne for 1,260 days, and bring his atrocities upon us Israelites and upon the rest of the population who resist his ways within this pagan christian religion, a religion he initially brought about in the New Testament times. After the 1,260 days, King David, God's true Holy Messiah, will show up and put him to his final death, which is then followed by God's reclaiming period of us Israelites from this hand that He, God put us into as indicated via <u>Daniel's 7:25</u> scripture. God will then begin to reclaim us back with a 30-biblical-year world war, matching the same number of years it took Charlemagne to fully impose this pagan christian religion upon our Saxon ancestors in the years 774.778 Oct. 10th to 804.3468 May 5Th. God's reclaiming period will be in the form of what we shall call, world war III, against the revival of the fourth world empire, the so-called Holy Roman Empire, which is being formed and <u>hidden</u> today within the European Union of Nations. This empire with their allies will be greatly influenced by the last pope of the christian religion, King Saul/Saul/Paul/Charlemagne in person, who should be coming on the scene, 1,260 days prior to the beginning of this end-time world war 2016.667 - 3.45 = 2013.217 on Mar. 20th from sunset of previous day. This war will last for 30 biblical years or 29.5688 of our Gregorian years, matching the same amount of time it took Charlemagne to fully impose the christian religion upon our ancestors; and will end on Mar. 27th in year 2046.2358 cue., the same time the 12th division ends. Our world as we see it today, will be totally desolated; saying that this world will continue, but our civilization as we now know it, will be utterly destroyed, and will be followed by 45 biblical years of nothingness, as Daniel states below.

Dan. 12:12 states, *"Blessed is he that waits, and comes to the thousand three hundred, and five and thirty days* (1,335 biblical years). And 45 biblical years beyond Daniel's 12:11's and 12:7's 1,290 (of biblical years), *"all these things shall be finished"*. This time as stated above began when Charlemagne attacked the Saxons' place of worship and set up a graven/painted image or even the shroud with the image of the face of his imaginary christian pagan jesus christ (of himself), upon their Altar of God, making this altar desolate, and he thereafter destroyed this place of worship, bringing an end to any sacrifices they previously performed.

Read Jer. 16:14-21, in this new arrangement: 17-18, 16, 14-15, 19-21, which is from the beginning of this coming desolation 2016.667 cue., to the end of the age in 2046.2358 cue. to its conclusion in 2090.5888 when the 1/10th survivors will be gathered together and led back to the promised land and rebuild the temple by the year (-166.266) + 2266.9404 G. yrs. = 2100.6744 on Sept. 30 Gregorian year. This rebuilt temple will be cleansed and the sacrifices resumed upon God's new Altar within the temple in Jerusalem in 2100 in the month and date of Sept. 30 @ 3:45, obviously from sunset of previous day, according to Daniel's 8:13-14 scriptures. *"For mine eyes are upon all their ways: they are not hid from my face, neither is their iniquity hid from mine eyes. And <u>first I will recompense their iniquity and their sin double</u>; because they have defiled my land, they have filled mine inheritance with the carcasses of their detestable and abominable things. Behold, I will send for many fishers, saith the Lord God, and they shall fish them; and after will I send for many hunters, and they shall hunt them from every mountain, and from every hill, and out of the holes of the rocks. Therefore, behold, the days come, saith the Lord God, that it shall no more be said, The Lord God lives, that brought up the children of Israel out of the land of Egypt; But, The Lord God lives, that brought up the children of Israel from the land of the north, and from all the lands whether he had* driven them: and I will bring them again into their land that I gave unto their fathers.

O Lord God, my strength, and my fortress, and my refuge in the day of affliction, the Gentiles shall come unto thee from the ends of the earth, and shall say, Surely our fathers have inherited lies, vanity, and things wherein there is no profit. Shall a man make gods unto himself, and they are no gods? Therefore, behold, I will this once cause them to know, I will cause them to know mine hand and my might; and they shall know that my name is THE LORD GOD.

The scripture that agrees with a portion of the above set of scripture, namely, when it states, *"And first I will recompense their iniquity and their sin double"*, is Ezek. 21:14, when it states, *"And let the sword be doubled the third time, the sword of the slain"*. This is stating that a third world war will come upon us, that will be doubled in intensity. This third world war, as I have stated in my writings, will begin on Aug. 31st from sunset of previous day in the year of 2016 cue., Approx. 10 Greg. years in the future from this late summer month of 2006 cue.

\* \* \*

Matt. 24:22 states, *"And except those days should be shortened, there should no flesh be saved: but for the elect's sake those days shall be shortened"*.

Mark 13:20 states, *"And except that the Lord had shortened those days, no flesh should be saved: but for the elect's sake, whom he has chosen, he has shortened the days"*.

These two scriptures are telling us that if God doesn't cut the days short, there would be no one saved. This is the same as telling us that God hasn't the power to save his elect if he doesn't cut it short. These two above scriptures do not agree with Daniel's set of scriptures, where the angel states to the day that this desolation will be full-filled. For Dan. 12:12 states, *"Blessed is he that waits, and comes to the 1335 days"*. They have also completely ignored Daniel's 8:13-14 scriptures, where the temple must be rebuilt 2,300 biblical years after Antioch decimated it on the 15th day of the 9th month of year -166.707 and -166.734. Therefore, this desolation must be cleansed with the blood of a 3-year-old red heifer, without spot and without yoke placed upon it in the year 2300 * 360/365.25 = 2266.9404 - 166.266 = 2100.6744 or Sept. 3rd @ 3:45 cue.

Therefore, the set of scriptures of Matt. and Mark are false, for they are limiting God's power. This 1,335 days, of biblical years, are even 45 biblical years beyond the end of the 12th age of this present world that we live in, which is the end of this civilization as we know it. The remnant's children of our corrupt civilization may enter into the following incorruptible world. For further information read the Apocrypha books of Esdras 1 and 2.

\* \* \*

Matt. 26:26-28 states, *"And as they were eating, Jesus took bread, and blessed it, and brake it, and gave it to the disciples, and said, Take, eat; this is my body. And he took the cup, and gave thanks, and gave it to them, saying, Drink ye all of it; For this is my blood of the new testament, which is shed for many for the remission of sins".*

Mark 14:22-24 states, *"And as they did eat, Jesus took bread, and blessed, and brake it, and gave to them, and said, Take, eat: this is my body. And he took the cup, and when he had given thanks, he gave it to them: and they all drank of it. And he said unto them, This is my blood of the new testament, which is shed for many".*

Luke 22:19-20 states, *"And he took bread, and gave thanks, and brake it, and gave unto them, saying, This is my body which is given for you: this do in remembrance of me. Likewise also the cup after supper, saying, This cup is the new testament in my blood, which is shed for you".*

John 6:54-56, *"Whoso eats my flesh, and drinks my blood, has eternal life; and I will raise him up at the last day. For my flesh is meat indeed, and my blood is drink indeed. He that eats my flesh, and drinks my blood, dwells in me, and I in him".*

1 Peter 1:2 & 19 states, *"Elect according to the foreknowledge of God the Father, through sanctification of the Spirit, unto obedience and sprinkling of the blood of* (David, God's Messiah): *Grace unto you, and peace, be multiplied. But with the precious blood of* (David), *as of a lamb without blemish and without spot".*

1 John 1:7 states, *"But if we walk in the light, as he is in the light, we have fellowship one with another, and the blood of* (King David) *his Son cleanses us from all sin".*

You will notice that the 4 gospel books of Matt., Mark, Luke, and John tell us that Saul/Paul's christ demands his followers to eat of his body and drink of his sacrificial blood. But the apostles in 1 Peter and 1 John tell us that the sprinkling of God's Holy Messiah's blood and unto obedience by walking according to God's ways, we will receive sanctification of our spirit to acquire eternal life.

James states, in his book, works with our faith and the sprinkled blood of David, God's Holy Messiah, will wash us clean from all our sins. But only if we flee from following this paganism christian teachings and from participating in any of their events that glorify their pagan imaginary christ, which is their another god, that David mentions in Psalms 16:4, and all their other so-called pagan canonized saints, pagan virgin mother, etc. And make an about face, to return back to the ways of the Old Testaments, which is God's true ways. There is absolutely no place in the Old Testament where the blood of the sacrificial lamb or goat was a drink offering. It was sprinkled on

God's Altar and toward the worshippers and poured around the base of the altar. King David, God's true Messiah, states below:

Psalms 16:4, *"Their sorrows shall be multiplied that hasten after <u>another god</u>* (christians' pagan jesus christ): *their drink offerings of blood, <u>will I (David) not offer</u>, nor take up their names into my lips".*

David, whose words are God inspired, is very aware that consuming the blood of the flesh is against God's blood laws, without any exceptions, as stated in:

Lev. 7:26-27, *"Moreover ye shall consume <u>no manner of blood</u>, whether it be of fowl or of beast, in any of your dwellings. Whatsoever person it be that consumes <u>any manner of blood, even that person shall be cut off from his people</u>".*

This scripture is referring to being cut off from his (God's) people, not in our present temporary life, but in our permanent eternal life. Do you really believe God would allow his Holy Messiah to bring about a ritual that contradicts his laws? In this ritual is the same wine cup that God gave to Jeremiah, to make all the nations to whom God sent him, to drink of this cup of the fury of God, and the last one to drink of this wine cup was Babylon, as Jer. 25:15-26 states.

In Jer. 51:5-7, it states, *"For Israel has not been forsaken, nor Judah of his God, of the Lord God of hosts; though their land was filled with sin against the Holy One of Israel. Flee out of the midst of Babylon, and deliver every man his soul: be not cut off in her iniquity; for this is the time of the Lord's vengeance; he will render unto her a recompense. Babylon has been a golden cup in the Lord's hand, that made all the earth drunken: the nations have drunken of her wine; therefore the nations are mad* (upon their idols)*".*

The name Israel in the above scripture is referring to the House of Israel, and the name Judah is referring to the House of Judah, and which is telling us that we are drinking out of this wine cup full of the wrath of God, for we of the British Commonwealth of Nations (Ephraim), the United States of America (Manasseh), France (Ruben), Switzerland, Belgium, Netherlands, Denmark, Norway, Sweden, Finland, Scotland, Ireland, Wales, Iceland, Greenland, and whatsoever other lands that they have possession of are of the House of Israel. We are all trapped within this Babylonian (confused) paganism religion—namely, via the Roman Catholic religion and all her daughters, the breakaway protestant christian religions. A good description of this confused christian paganism religion is in Rev. 17:1-18. Is not this the same religion that emerged on the 10 horned beast, via Saul/Paul in Daniel's 7:20-25? Where it states, *"And of the ten horns that were in his head, and of the other which came up, and before whom three fell; even of that horn that had eyes, and a mouth that <u>spoke very great things, whose look was more stout than his fellows</u>. I beheld, and the same horn made war with the saints, and prevailed* *against them; Thus he said, The fourth beast shall be the fourth kingdom upon earth, which shall be diverse from all kingdoms, and shall devour the whole earth, and shall tread it down, and break it in pieces. And the ten horns out of this kingdom are ten kings that shall arise: and another shall rise after them; and he shall be diverse from the first, and he shall subdue three kings. And he shall <u>speak very great words, against the most High</u>, and shall wear out the saints of the most High, and think to change times and laws* (of God): *and they* (the remnant of the House of Israel, reported in <u>Rev. 12:13-17</u>) *shall be given into his hand until a time, and times, and the dividing of time* (1,260 days of biblical years, or 1241.89 years of our Gregorian calendar)".

What makes this 4th kingdom diverse from all the previous kingdoms was the fact that it consisted of a political body and a religious body working in unison. Namely, the Roman Empire and the Roman Catholic Religion.

Please notice the phrase, *"Speak very great things/words"*, matches the same phrase in <u>James 3:5-6.</u> James is talking about the tongue among our members that *<u>boasts great things.</u>*

James states in <u>4:16,</u> *"But now ye rejoice in your <u>boastings:</u> all such rejoicing is evil"*. Who do you think James is referring to?

In <u>2 Cor. 7:14; 9:2-4; 10:8, 13, 15; 11:16-17,</u> Saul/Paul admits to being a boaster, which also tells us that he has the evil spirit upon him, which is verified via James's scripture. It is also telling us that he is none other than the devil's son, which is the reappearance of King Saul with the evil spirit still upon him, which God placed upon him after rejecting him as the first king of the Israelites, and replaced him with David to be king over the ancient Israelites.

## The following 2 Cor. scriptures state

<u>2 Cor. 7:14,</u> *"For if <u>I have boasted</u> any thing to him of you, I am not ashamed; but as we spoke all things to you in truth, even so <u>our boastings</u>, which I made before Titus, is found a truth".*

<u>2 Cor. 9:2-4,</u> *"For I know the forwardness of your mind, for which <u>I boast</u> of you to them of Macedonia, that Achaia was ready a year ago; and your zeal provoked very many. Yet have I sent the brethren, lest <u>our boasting</u> of you should be in vain in this behalf; that, as I said, ye may be ready: Lest haply if they of Macedonia come with me, and find you unprepared, we* (that we say not, ye) *should be ashamed in this same <u>confident boasting</u>".*

<u>2 Cor. 10:8, 13, 15,</u> *"For though <u>I should boast</u> somewhat more of our authority, which the Lord God has given us for edification, and not for your destruction, I should not be ashamed":*

"But we will not *boast of things* without our measure, but according to the measure of the rule which God has distributed to us, a measure to reach even unto you".

"Not *boasting of things* without our measure, that is, of other men's labours; but having hope, when your faith is increased, that we shall be enlarged by you according to our rule abundantly".

2 Cor. 11:16-17, "I say again, Let no man think me a fool; if otherwise, yet as a fool receive me, that *I may boast myself a little*. That which I speak, I speak it not after the Lord God, but as it were foolishly, in this *confidence of boasting*".

This statement that James in 4:16 makes, "*boasting is evil*", in the above scripture, proves Saul/Paul has an evil spirit upon him. This Saul/Paul can be none other than the reappearance of King Saul, the very first king of the Israelites. And we all know that it was this Saul called Paul, who is the master builder of this christian religion, as stated below:

1 Cor. 3:10-11, "According to the grace of God which is given unto me, as a wise masterbuilder, I have laid the foundation, and another builds thereon. But let every man take heed how he builds thereupon. For other foundation can no man lay than that is laid, which is jesus christ".

By comparing the scripture of Dan's. 7:25, "*He* (the horn) *shall speak great words against the Most High*", to that of James 3:5-6, "*The tongue among our members that boasts great things*", with that of the boasting of Saul called Paul in the above 2 Cor. scriptures; and the scripture of the leader in Daniel's 11:36, "*And speaks marvelous things against the God of gods*", point to the fact that Saul called Paul is none other than King Saul with the evil spirit still upon him, and he is also the little horn or pope of his pagan christian religion, which he is the master builder of, he is also the leader in Dan's. 11:36, known as 'Karl-the-Man/Char-le-magne', who imposed his pagan christian religion upon the Saxons (Isaac's sons, or sons of Isaac) our ancient ancestors of the House of Israel. His religion is not of God, but is of the devil; and he has deceived us Israelites of the House of Israel for almost the past 1,251 biblical years and counting, when he as Charles, imposed his pagan christian religion upon our ancient ancestors, the Saxons, beginning in a late autumn month of year 774 cue. We have approximately 10 Gregorian years left and counting, as of mid-2006 cue., before God begins to claim us back from his (King Saul's) hand, with a 30-biblical-year world war; the same amount of time it took Charlemagne to fully impose his pagan christian religion upon our ancestors. Therefore, be prepared to meet your creator, the Lord Our God, in the very near future. In the time of Charles the Great, it was the leader or emperor of the fourth world empire who chose the pope of the pagan christian religion. Therefore, Charles/King Saul was in effect, even in control of the christian religion.

\* \* \*

<u>Eph. 2:8-9,</u> *"For by grace are ye saved through faith; and that not of yourselves: it is the gift of God: <u>not of works</u>, lest any man should boast"*.

<u>Gal. 2:16,</u> *"Knowing that a man is not justified by the works of the Law, but by the faith of Jesus Christ, even we have believed in Jesus Christ, that we might be justified by the faith of Christ, and not by the works of the Law: for by the works of the Law shall no flesh be justified"*.

<u>Ro. 4:2-3,</u> *"For if Abraham were justified by works, he has whereof to glory; but not before God. For what says the scripture? Abraham believed God, and it was counted unto him for righteousness"*.

<u>James,</u> the leader of the true apostles, states in <u>2:14-26,</u> *"What doth it profit, my brethren, though a man says he has faith, and have not works? Can faith save him? If a brother or sister be naked, and destitute of daily food, and one of you say unto them, Depart in peace, be ye warmed and filled; notwithstanding ye give them not those things which are needful to the body; what doth it profit? Even so faith, if it has not works, is dead, being alone"*.

*"Yea, a man may say, Thou has faith, and I have works: Show me thy faith without thy works, and I will show thee my faith <u>by my works</u>"*.

*"Thou believe that there is one God; thou do well: the devils also believes, and tremble. But will thou know, <u>O vain man,</u> that faith without works is dead?"*

*"Was not Abraham our father justified by works, when he had offered Isaac his son upon the altar? Seest thou how faith wrought with his works, and by works was faith made perfect? And the scripture was fulfilled which says, Abraham believed God, and it was imputed unto him for righteousness: and he was called the Friend of God. Ye see then how that by works a man is justified, and not by faith only"*.

*"Likewise also was not Rahab the harlot justified by works, when she had received the messengers, and had sent them out another way?"*

*"For as the body without the spirit* (mind) *is dead, so faith without works is dead also"*.

This vain man that James is referring to, can be none other than Saul called Paul, for what this Saul/Paul is in fact telling us is that we can go ahead and perform all sorts of atrocities continuously, as long as we believe in his christ, all will be okay. Is this not the actions and statements one can expect from the devil himself, for Saul/Paul with the evil spirit still upon him is in fact the devil himself, or at least the devil's firstborn son.

\* \* \*

<u>Eph. 2:20,</u> *"And are built upon the foundation of the apostles, and prophets, jesus christ himself being the chief corner stone"*.

<u>Matt. 21:42</u>, *"Jesus said unto them, Did ye never read in the scriptures, The stone which the builders rejected, the same is become the head of the corner"*.

<u>Mark 12:10</u>, *"And have ye not read this scripture, The stone which the builders rejected is become the head of the corner"*.

<u>Luke 20:17-18</u>, *"And he beheld them, and said, What is this then that is written, The stone which the builders rejected, the same is become the head of the corner?"*

<u>Acts 4:11</u>, *"This is the stone which was set at nought of you builders, which is become the head of the corner"*.

<u>Ps. 118:22</u>, *"The stone which the builders refused is become the head stone of the corner"*.

Eph.'s scripture tells us that their christ is the chief corner stone of their religion, which is built upon the foundations of the apostles and prophets. Where Matt., Mark, and Luke scriptures tell us that the builders rejected their christ, who became the head of the corner (stone), and Acts is also referring to the christ as the head of the corner (stone), but Saul/Paul is calling his audience the builders. One must remember that Saul/Paul is building the christian religion, and he is referring to his audience as fellow builders of his pagan christian religion. These New Testament scriptures when lumped together spells 'confusion', just as the word 'babylon' spells 'confusion'. For this is the pagan babylon christian religion mentioned in <u>Rev. 17:1-18</u>.

But the truth emerges in <u>Ps. 118:22</u> Scripture, where the builders (sons of Jacob, the builders of their own tribes) refused their brother Joseph, and sold him to a caravan heading towards Egypt. This same Joseph attained great stature in Egypt, and via his two mentioned sons, received the firstborn status and blessings, plus even Jacob's God given name Israel. The tribes of Joseph are the chief corner stone of all the houses of Israel. And God's true Messiah, King David, will be the head of this chief corner stone.

<u>Gen. 49:22-26</u> are the blessings Israel placed upon the tribes of Joseph, and in <u>verse 24</u>, it states, *"But his bow abode in strength, and the arms of his hands were made strong by the hands of the mighty God of Jacob; (from thence is the shepherd, the stone of Israel)"*.

God's true Messiah will emerge out of the tribe of Joseph, the chief corner stone, to be their end-time leader or head of this chief corner stone.

<u>Isa. 28:16</u>, *"Therefore, thus says the Lord God, Behold, I lay in Zion for a foundation a stone, a tried stone, a precious corner stone, a sure foundation: he that believes shall not make haste"*.

<u>Zech. 3:9</u>, *"For behold the stone that I have laid before Joshua; upon one stone shall be seven eyes: behold, I will engrave the graving thereof, saith the Lord, and I will remove the iniquity of that land in one day"*.

## Mysterious Secrets from Behind the Veil

These two scriptures are related to one another, for this tried precious corner stone that has seven eyes are the two tribes of Joseph, where each eye represents a major nation, such as the British Commonwealth of Nations, being 5 eyes, namely, England, Canada, Australia, New Zealand, and (South Africa?). The United States of America, being another eye, even portraying this '<u>one eye</u>' as the capstone on the Great Pyramid, on the back of their seal, and the tribe of Judah being an eye, being that the Holy Messiah, King David, is of the tribe of Judah and will be the head of this tried precious cornerstone.

\* \* \*

2 Cor. 6:16, *"And what agreement has the temple of God with idols? For ye are the temple of the living God; as God has said, I will dwell in them, and walk in them; and I will be their God, and they shall be my people"*. Here Saul/Paul is implying that we shall be separate parts of the temple, as a building is set together, and God will live in us.

Ezek. 37:27-28, *"My tabernacle also shall be with them: Ye, I will be their God, and they shall be my people. And the heathen shall know that I the Lord God do sanctify Israel, when my sanctuary shall be in the midst of them for evermore"*.

Lev. 26:11-12, *"And I will set my tabernacle among you: and my soul shall not abhor you. And I will walk among you, and will be your God, and ye shall be my people"*.

It is quite plain that we will be all separate individuals, living in the Land of Israel, with the Lord our God living amongst us, and we will be his people; not any part of the temple or tabernacle as a building is set together, but individuals.

2 Cor. 3:13-16, *"And not as Moses, which put a veil over his face, that the children of Israel could not steadfastly look to the end of that which is abolished: But their minds were blinded: for until this day remains the same veil untaken away in the reading of the Old Testament; which veil is done away in christ, But even unto this day, when Moses is read, the veil is upon their heart. Nevertheless when it shall turn to the Lord* (his pagan christ), *the veil shall be taken away"*.

Ex. 34:29-34, *"And it came to pass, when Moses came down from mount Sinai with the two tables of testimony in Moses hand, when he came down from the mount, that Moses <u>knew</u> not that the skin of his face shone while he talked with God. And when Aaron and all the children of Israel saw Moses, behold, the skin of his face shone; and they were afraid to come nigh him. And Moses called unto them; and Aaron and all the rulers of the congregation returned unto him: and Moses talked with them. And afterwards all the children of Israel came nigh: and he gave them in commandment all that the Lord God had spoken with him in Sinai:*

*And till Moses had done speaking with them, he put a veil on his face. But when Moses went in before the Lord God to speak with him, he took off the veil, until he came out. And he came out, and spoke unto the children of Israel that which he was commanded: And the children of Israel saw the face of Moses, that the skin of Moses' face shone: and Moses put the veil upon his face again, until he went to speak with God".*

In Saul/Paul's scripture in <u>2 Cor.</u> above, he is using this veil to do away with the laws of God, and tells us that if we then turn to his christ all will be okay. But in Exodus Scripture, the veil is used to cover the face of Moses, because after talking with God face to face, even through the cloud of God's covering, Moses's face radiated a shine on his face so bright that the people were afraid of him. The similarity would be if you or I would sun our face on an enormously hot day, without putting any sun blocking cream to protect our skin, our face would shine also with a burn. There is nothing mysterious about covering his face with a veil, as Saul/Paul is attempting to create.

<u>James 2:10,</u> *"For whosoever shall keep the whole law, and yet offend in one point, he is guilty of all".* James is not doing away with the laws of God; as Saul/Paul is doing in his scripture of <u>2 Cor.</u> above. The only veil that is in effect is the deceptive veil that Saul/Paul put over the eyes, ears, and minds of his followers, from seeing, hearing, and understanding the truth, even when presented to them.

<u>Isa. 8:16, 20</u> states, *"Bind up the testimony, seal the law among my disciples. To the law and to the testimony: if they speak not according to this word* (God's laws and testimonies), *it is because there is no light in them".*

There is a warning for those who do not speak and live their lives according to God's laws and testimonies in <u>Isa. 8:21-22,</u> *"And they shall pass through it* (the coming desolation of 2016.667 to 2046.2358 plus the 45 biblical years of nothingness), *hardly bestead and hungry: and it shall come to pass, that when they shall be hungry, they shall fret themselves, and curse their king and their God, and look upward. And they shall look unto the earth; and behold trouble and darkness, dimness of anguish; and they shall be driven to darkness".*

<u>Pro. 1:23</u> states, *"Turn you at my reproofs: behold, I will pour out my spirit unto you, I will make known my words unto you".*

There is a warning from God, to all those who will not listen to him, and refuse to prove all sayings with his scriptures; this warning is below:

<u>Pro. 1:24-32,</u> *"Because I have called, and ye refused; I have stretched out my hand, and no man regarded; But ye have set at naught all my counsel, and would none of my reproofs; I also will laugh at your calamity; I will mock when your fear comes; When your fear comes as desolation, and your destruction comes as a whirlwind; when distress and anguish comes upon you. Then shall they call upon me, but I will not answer; they shall seek me early, but they shall not find me: For*

*that they hated knowledge, and did not choose the fear of the Lord God: They would none of my counsel: they despised all my reproofs. Therefore shall they eat of the fruit of their own way, and be filled with their own devices. For the turning away of the simple shall slay them, and the prosperity of fools shall destroy them".*

Only a fool will ignore the above knowledge, and not turn and begin to prove this knowledge, for how much easier can I make it for you, by supplying you with all the reproofs one can hope for.

Pro. 1:33 states, *"But whoso hearkens unto me shall dwell safely, and shall be quiet from fear of evil".*

After the 45-biblical-year period of nothingness. God will gather up the remnant of his people, and they shall be brought back to the Land of Israel, where God shall remove the face of the covering cast over all people, the deceptive veil that Saul had spread over all nations of this world, as indicated in the following scripture below:

Isa. 25:7, *"And he* (the Lord God) *will destroy in this holy mountain the face of the covering cast over all people, and the veil* (Saul/Paul's deceptive veil) *that is spread over all nations".*

Then we have the obvious signs, such as the holy Sabbath day of the Lord God Almighty, which according to the books of Moses is the seventh day of the week, and because a biblical day ends and begins with the setting of the sun, this holy Sabbath day begins Friday just before sunset, and ends Saturday just after sunset. This holy Sabbath day is a sign between God and his people and must be observed and kept holy. Our Jewish brethren still observe and keep this holy day on the proper day and time. Where the christians' so-called holy day of the week is observed and kept on the first day of the week, and even into the second day of the week, being their time of a day ends and begins at a set time of midnight to midnight. There is absolutely no place in the Old or New Testaments that this christian day was observed and held on the above-mentioned days and time of a day. No one has the authority to change this day or time of a day, God has instructed the ancient Israelites to observe and keep this day holy, for this special day is connected to the last or seventh day of the creation week, where God rested on this seventh day, and blessed it, and sanctified it for future observances and keeping of this holy day by mankind. This is that holy Sabbath day that mankind are to refrain from their duties and their business activities and their pleasurable activities. This is a day we are to worship the Lord Our God Almighty, our sole Creator, the only God of this whole world. All other so-called gods are nothing more than pagan made up gods—such as the christians' pagan christ, and all their canonized, so-called saints that they pray to, serve, and worship as if they are real Gods that can answer their prayers. We have the impression that our ancients were primitive in whatever they did or worshipped.

Well, the news is that we so-called sophisticated modern generations are worshipping more pagan gods than any other past generations, that we call primitive. The veil can be, and indeed is, pulled over our eyes more than any generations previously. For Saul/Paul has indeed pulled the veil over, not only our eyes, but also over our ears and minds, preventing us from seeing, hearing and understanding the real truth, so much so, that we are now at his mercy via his christian paganism religion that he is the master builder of; and when he comes again on the scene, Mar. 20th from sunset of previous day, 1,260 days prior to Aug. 31st in year 2016, as the last pope of the christian religion, as he came on the scene as Saul called Paul in the New Testament times, and as "Karl-the-Man", Char-le-magne by the French peoples, who with his forces, mainly of French and German descendants, imposed this paganism christian religion upon the remnant of our ancient Israelite ancestors, in the years 774.778 cue. to 804.3468 cue., the Saxon tribes living in the area he ruled over. One of his first target was the Saxons' place of worship, who were at that time keeping God's commandments and His testimonies as indicated in Rev. 12:17.

In Dan. 11:30-39 is the actions taken by Charles the Great, the "devil's firstborn son", who is none other than King Saul with the evil spirit still upon him. *"For the ships of Chittim shall come against him: therefore he shall be grieved, and return, and have indignation against the Holy Covenant: so shall he do; he shall even return, and have intelligence with them that forsake the Holy Covenant* (French leaders, who are of the tribe of Reuben). *And arms shall stand on his part, and they shall pollute the sanctuary of strength* (Saxons' place of worship), *and shall take away the daily sacrifice, and they shall place the abomination that maketh desolate* (a statue/painted image of the christians' christ, or even the image on the shroud of the face of the pagan christ), which was of King Saul, Saul called Paul, Charlemagne, was erected on their Altar of God, which made it desolate). *And such as do wickedly against the covenant shall be corrupted by flatteries: but the people that do know their God shall be strong, and do exploits. And they that understand among the people shall instruct many: yet they shall fall by the sword, and by flame, by captivity, and by spoil, many days* (30 biblical years, even the whole 1,260 biblical years that we will be in the horn's hand of Daniel's 7:25 scripture). *Now when they shall fall, they shall be helped with a little help: but many shall cleave to them with flatteries. And some of them of understanding shall fall, to try them and to purge, and to make them white, even to the time of the end: because it is yet for a time appointed. And the king shall do according to his will; and he shall exalt himself, and magnify himself above every god, and shall speak marvellous things against the God of gods, and shall prosper till the indignation be accomplished: for that that is determined shall be done. Neither shall he regard the God of his fathers* (who are the ancient Israelites), *nor the* *desire of women, nor regard any god: for <u>he shall magnify himself above all</u>. But in his estate shall he honour the god of forces: and a god whom his fathers knew not* (his pagan christ) <u>*shall he honour with gold, and silver, and with precious stones, and pleasant things.*</u> *Thus shall he do in the most strong holds <u>with a strange god, whom he shall acknowledge and increase with glory:</u> and he shall cause them to rule over many, and shall divide the land for gain*". How much stranger can his god be, seeing it is of himself?

Please notice the phrase, "*Speak marvellous things against the God of gods*". Is this not the same phrase used in <u>Dan. 7:25</u>? Where it states, *"And he shall speak great words against the most High God"*, or even the phrase used in <u>James 3:5-6</u>, *"Where the tongue among our members, <u>boasting great things</u>, that it defiles the whole body, and sets on fire the course of nature; and it is set on fire of hell"*. James in his statement is definitely referring to Saul/Paul and his close associations. Also notice the phrase, *"Shall he honour with gold, silver, with precious stones, and pleasant things"*. This phrase to a certain degree is recorded in <u>Rev. 17:4</u>, *"And the woman* (christian religion) *was arrayed in purple and scarlet colour, and decked with gold and precious stones and pearls, having a golden cup in her hand full of abominations and filthiness of her fornication"*. This scripture is definitely making the connection between the 'god' whom the above leader's fathers knew not, and the christians' pagan christ, and it is quite safe to say that the above leader, speaking marvellous things, is none other than Saul/Paul/King Saul, the very first king of our ancestors, the ancient Israelites in the days of Samuel. This mentioned cup is the communion cup, filled with the wrath of God; because it is the same cup that is used in the ritual, of drinking the blood of Saul/Paul's imaginary christ and eating his body, which is totally against God's blood and unclean laws. Which is also condemned by God's true Messiah, King David in <u>Psalm 16:4</u>, when he states, *"Their sorrows shall be multiplied that hasten after another god: their drink offerings of blood will I* (David) *not offer, nor take up their names into my lips"*.

The true Messiah of God, will not demand his followers to perform a ritual that contradicts God's blood laws and unclean laws, and will not even suggest his followers should pray to him, worship him, and serve him as they would a God. For David knew that there is, and always will be, just one God to pray to, serve, fear, and sacrifice too. All other so-called gods are all of falsehood.

Then we have all the christians' so-called holy events. Such as christmas, easter, saint day events, even the helloween event. Not one of these events are even mentioned in the Old Testament as legitimate, but are actually condemned. Nor do they have any connection whatsoever to any of God's holy events mentioned in the Old Testament, events that we are instructed to observe and keep forever.

The christians' christmas is derived from a pagan event condemned in Jer. 10:3-5, *"For the customs of the people are vain: for one cuts a tree out of the forest, the work of the hands of the workman, with an axe. They deck it with silver and with gold; they fasten it with nails and with hammers, that it move not. They are upright as the palm tree, but speak not: they must be moved by someone, because they cannot move themselves. Be not afraid of them; for they cannot do evil, neither also is it in them to do good".*

This was taken by the christians and connected to the birth of their pagan christ, with the gifts added, which is taken from the wise men baring gifts, and progressed to what we have today.

The christians' easter is derived from another pagan event condemned by God in Jer. 7:17-19, *"Seest thou not what they do in the cities of Judah and in the streets of Jerusalem? The children gather wood, and the fathers kindle the fire, and the women knead their dough, to make cakes* (christians' hot cross buns) *to the queen of heaven, and to pour out drink offerings unto other gods, that they may provoke me to anger. Do they provoke me to anger? Saith the Lord God: do they not provoke themselves to the confusion* (Babylon) *of their own faces?"*

And condemned by God and Jeremiah throughout the whole of chapter 44, where Jeremiah is explaining to them why God has brought this great destruction upon them and their home land; but even then the survivors vowed to continue in these evil practices. This event was the worshipping of the goddess of fertility, Ishtar, called Ester, where they baked little cakes for her, which are now the hot cross buns, and the rabbit and hen laying chocolate and coloured eggs, which is keeping the fertility aspect alive within this event. This event is now connected to the resurrection (rebirth) of their pagan christ. Notice the similarity between her name, and the name of the event. Also notice God's quoted scripture above: *"Do they not provoke themselves to the confusion of their own faces"*. The word babylon is associated with the word 'confusion':

In Rev. 17:5, it states, *"And upon her forehead was a name written, MYSTERY, BABYLON THE GREAT, THE MOTHER OF HARLOTS AND ABOMINATIONS OF THE EARTH"*. This is none other than the religion that Saul/Paul brought about, and which should be called the Paganism Babylon Roman Catholic and Greek Christian Religion, and her daughters are all the Protestant Christian Religions. They all worship, pray to, and serve Saul/Paul's pagan christ/another god, and all their pagan canonized saints; more than our one and true living God Almighty, our sole creator. Saul/Paul-King Saul has indeed pulled the veil over our eyes, ears and mind; preventing us from seeing, hearing and understanding the truth. This all began when God gave to us statutes, and judgments that are not good for us, and whereby we ought not to live by, as stated below:

<u>Ezek. 20:24-26,</u> *"Because they had not executed My Judgments, but had despised My Statutes, and had polluted My Sabbaths, and their eyes were after their father's idols. Wherefore I gave them <u>also</u> statutes that were <u>not good</u>, and judgments whereby they <u>should not</u> live; And I polluted them in their own gifts, in that they caused to pass through the fire* (via our incinerators) *all that opens the womb, that I might make them desolate, to the end that they might know* (come to realize) *that I am the Lord God* (who has brought all this upon you, because of your continuous evil ways).

These statutes and judgments where brought upon us when God put us into the little horn's hand of <u>Dan. 7:25;</u> and this little horn is none other than Saul called Paul in the New Testament, who in turn is none other than King Saul, reported in the first book of Samuel, and who was also, believe it or not, "Karl the Man" called <u>Char</u> <u>le</u> <u>magne</u> via the French. Whose actions against our ancestors, the Saxon tribes, living within the area he ruled over, and the destruction of their place of worship after setting the abomination that made their Altar of God desolate, which actions started the countdown of <u>Dan. 12:7-11</u> scriptures, as described in <u>Dan. 11:30-39.</u>

By comparing statements from <u>Dan. 7:20 & 25,</u> to that of <u>Dan. 11:30-39,</u> to that of <u>Rev. 17:3-6,</u> and add to that <u>James's scriptures of 3:5-6 & 4:16,</u> plus the scriptures that proves Saul/Paul is a <u>boaster</u> throughout <u>2 Cor. 7-11</u> verses and displayed on the 1st page of chapter 3 in this book and an earlier page of this chapter.

One cannot omit the fact that all these above-mentioned scriptures are tied together into one huge truth, that King Saul is the individual referred to. Therefore, flee from this paganism christian babylon religion, and return to the ways of the Old Testament, God's ways, and save yourselves alive in your eternal life, the life after this present temporary life. May God take Saul's veil from your eyes, ears and mind; and allow you to see, hear and understand his words. And give you the courage to reverse course and get back to the true ways of God; that are instructed to us throughout the books of Moses.

# CHAPTER 7

# God's Overall Master Plan

The summary of God's overall plan in separating the good and wicked persons, via the struggles between King Saul (the people's choice) and King David (God's choice) over control of the Israelites and eventually over the Gentile nations of this world. This struggle has been going on since the days of their original generation.

## Old Testament Times

King Saul = people's choice = false ways = eternal death. King Saul, tall, good build, rich family, Samuel anoints Saul king of Israel. God puts his Holy Spirit upon him. Saul seen prophesying. King Saul given command to eradicate the Amalekites, by killing men, women, children, and all animals, plus destroy all material belongings. King Saul breaks God's direct command, for he caved in to the desires of his forces to keep the best of the stock, material belongings, gold, silver, etc., for he feared the people more than he feared God. He also kept their king alive. God rejects Saul as king and removes his Holy Spirit from him and places an evil spirit upon him, which troubles Saul. He's now a false prophet. Saul attempts several times to kill David, without success.

King David = God's choice = true ways = eternal life. King David's appearance nothing to be desired, from a poor family, a very good shepherd, even proving he was willing to give his life, protecting them.

David anointed future king of Israel, God places his Holy Spirit upon him; he thereafter becomes the Psalmist of Israel. David becomes a great leader, having great success against his enemies. Although David had the chances, he refused to kill Saul, because he was God's anointed previously.

# New Testament Times

King Saul reappears as Saul and is an officer in the Roman forces, leading a band of Roman soldiers persecuting the true Messiah's followers and ruining their places of worship. Saul and his forces put David, God's true Messiah, to death, shedding his blood, as a lamb brought to the slaughter. Saul and his associates later penetrated into the ranks of the true apostles, claiming he was a changed man after supposedly receiving a vision from heaven, condemning his actions. Saul, who is now called Paul, begins preaching, not the gospel of God, but the gospel of his imaginary pagan christ, called Jesus Christ, taking the true <u>Messiah's</u> title, meaning "holy anointed one", interpreted from the Greek language into the English language as <u>Christ</u>, and with the name <u>Jesus</u>, coming from the Greek language into English meaning <u>salvation</u>, for it is through the blood we can receive atonement for our sins. However, the apostles found out that Paul was preaching a different gospel, not of God, but about his pagan christ, and vowed to kill him. But he received protection from the Roman authorities. He thereafter preached his false gospel to the Gentiles, where he brought about the pagan christian religion, named after his pagan christ, the devil's religion, seeing that he still has the evil spirit upon him. King Saul also returns again as Charlemagne, the military leader and emperor of the Roman Empire. He imposes the pagan christian religion upon the Saxon tribes, the <u>remnant</u> of the 10 lost tribes of the House of Israel. Proven by <u>Rev. 12:13-17</u>.

David, born again as God's Holy Messiah, gathers his apostles together and teaches them of God's ways, such as the gospel of God (<u>Dan. 9:23-27</u>). God allows David's blood to be shed as a sacrificial lamb offering brought to the slaughter, cleansing us obedient ones of our past, present, and even future sins. Opening the way for us to receive God's salvation to an eternal life. But we are still required to live our lives according to God's statutes, judgments, commandments, and laws as best we can to attain eternal life, as indicated in <u>Ezek. 18:1-32 and 33:7-20</u>. David being God's end-time Holy Messiah is proven in the scriptures of <u>Jer. 30:9; Ho. 3:5; Ezek. 34:23-24, 37:24-25</u>; and in the following <u>2 Sam. 22:1-51</u> is a song written by David, where he states in verse 44-45, *"Thou also has delivered me from the striving's of my people, <u>Thou God has kept me to be head of the heathen: a people which I knew not shall serve me. Strangers which I knew not shall submit themselves unto me: as soon as they hear my voice, they shall be obedient unto me"</u>*.

David is definitely speaking about a time, as it now turns out, in the very near future, a lot sooner than we of today can imagine. When he will be King of kings and Lord of lords, under our Creator, the Lord our great God Almighty. Read the above underlined scriptures and take them to heart, for they are coming directly out of the mouth of God's servant, the world's future King of kings and Lord of lords. (I have them written out at the end of this chapter.)

Also scriptures such as <u>Ps. 16:10, 30:3, 49:15; Ps. 118:17-18; Ps. 89:18-22, 25-28</u>. Where in verse 29 his seed is mentioned separately thereafter.

## *End Times*

Saul/Paul-King Saul reappears as the last pope of the Christian religion, the religion that he is the builder of. He is also the false prophet of Rev. 19:20, and taken by King David, God's Holy Messiah, with the beast, and all his followers that worshipped the beast and the false prophet's imaginary pagan christ, which was/is an image of himself (2 Esdras 2:43), and cast them all into the lake of fire.

King David reappears, man sitting on the horse with a sword in his mouth, with his forces. David defeats Saul/false prophet and the beast power, and casts them into the lake of fire, burning with brimstone. Also all their followers that are worshipping Saul's pagan imaginary christ/another god, indicated in Rev. 19:19 & 21.

The struggle between King Saul and King David is a struggle for control of the Israelites and also for control of the Gentile peoples of the whole world. It is also a struggle between the bad and the good—such as separating the righteous from the unrighteous, and only the righteous will have that final chance for eternal life with King David and company, and God Almighty. But God left the choice with us. If we continue to chase after Saul's christ, and ignore all of God's ways, we will lose this opportunity. Therefore, we must flee from this paganism christian religion and all other falsehood, and save our eternal lives, by receiving God's Salvation. The only way is in the Old Testament, which is God's ways.

## Read Deut. 4:1-40, 5:1-33; these scriptures read as follows:

*"Now therefore hearken, O Israel, unto the Statutes and unto the Judgments, which I teach you, for to do them, that ye may live, and go in and possess the land which the Lord God of your fathers gives you. Ye shall not add unto the word which I command you, neither shall you diminish ought from it, that ye may keep the commandments of the Lord your God which I command you. Your eyes have seen what the Lord did because of Baal-peor: for all the men that followed Baal-peor* (or any other pagan god you have conjugated as your christian gods to follow), *the Lord thy God has destroyed them from among you. But ye that did cleave unto the Lord your God are alive every one of you this day.* (God didn't only destroy the wicked from their temporary life here on earth, but will no doubt destroy their permanent life upon the judgment day event; this is why we must fear the Lord our God, for our permanent life rests within his hands. Therefore, we must pursue this goal.) *Behold, I have taught you statutes and judgments,*

*even as the Lord my God has commanded me, that ye shall do so in the land whither ye go to possess it. Keep therefore and do them; for this is your wisdom and your understanding in the sight of the nations, which shall hear all these statutes, and say, Surely this great nation is a wise and understanding people. For what nation is there so great, who has God so near unto them, as the Lord our God is in all things we call upon him for? And what nation is there so great, that has statutes and judgments so righteous as all this Law, which I set before you this day? Only take heed to thyself, and keep thy soul/body/person diligently, lest thou forget the things which thine eyes have seen, and lest they depart from thy heart all the days of thy life: but teach them to thy sons, and thy son's sons; Specially the day that thou stood before the Lord thy God in Horeb, when the Lord said unto me, Gather the people together, and I will make them hear my words, that they may learn to fear me all the days that they shall live upon the earth, and that they may teach their children. And ye came near and stood under the mountain; and the mountain burned with fire unto the midst of heaven, with darkness, clouds, and thick darkness. And the Lord God spoke to you out of the midst of the fire: ye heard the voice of the words, but ye saw no similitude; only ye heard a voice. And he declared unto you his covenant, which he commanded you to perform, even ten commandments; and he wrote them upon two tables of stone. And the Lord God commanded me at that time to teach you statutes and judgments, that you might do them in the land whither ye go over to possess it. Take ye therefore good heed unto yourselves; for ye saw no manner of similitude on the day that the Lord thy God spoke unto you in Horeb out of the midst of the fire: lest ye corrupt yourselves, and make you a graven image, the similitude of any figure, the likeness of male or female, the likeness of any beast that is on the earth, the likeness of any winged fowl that flies in the air, the likeness of anything that creeps on the ground, the likeness of any fish in the waters beneath the earth: And lest thou lift up thine eyes unto heaven, and when thou see the sun, and the moon, and the stars, even all the hosts of heaven, should you be driven to worship them, and serve them, which the Lord thy God has divided unto all the nations under the whole heaven. But the Lord has taken you, and brought you forth out of the iron furnace, even out of Egypt, to be unto him a people of inheritance, as ye are this day. Furthermore the Lord was angry with me for your sakes, and sware that I should not go over Jordan, and that I should not go in unto that good land, which the Lord thy God gives thee for an inheritance: But I must die in this land, I must not go over Jordan: but ye shall go over, and possess that good land. Take heed unto yourselves, lest ye forget the covenant of the Lord your God, and make you a graven image, or the likeness of any thing, which <u>the Lord thy God has forbidden thee</u>. For the Lord thy God is a consuming fire, even a jealous God. When thou shall beget children, and children's children, and ye have remained long in the land, and shall corrupt yourselves, and make a graven image, or the likeness of anything, and shall do evil in the sight of the Lord thy God, to provoke him to anger: I call heaven* and earth to witness against you this day, that ye shall soon utterly perish from off the land whereunto ye go over Jordan to possess it; ye shall not prolong your days upon it, but shall utterly be destroyed. And the Lord shall scatter you among the nations, and ye shall be left few in number among the heathen, whither the Lord shall lead you. And there ye shall serve gods, the work of men's hands, wood and stone, which neither see, nor hear, nor eat, nor smell. But if from thence thou shall seek the Lord thy God, thou shall find him, if thou seek him with all thy heart and with all thy soul/body/person. When thou art in tribulation, and all these things are come upon thee, even in the latter days, if thou turn to the Lord thy God, and shall be obedient unto his voice; (For the Lord thy God is a merciful God;) he will not forsake thee, neither destroy thee, nor forget the covenant of thy fathers which he sware unto them. For ask now of the days that are past, which were before thee, since the day God created man upon the earth, and ask from the one side of heaven unto the other side, whither there has been any such thing as this great thing is, or has been heard like it? Did ever people hear the voice of God speaking out of the midst of the fire, as thou has heard, and lived? Or has God assayed to go and take him a nation from the midst of another nation, by temptations, by signs, and by wonders, and by war, and by a mighty hand, and by a stretched out arm, and by great terrors, according to all that the Lord your God did for you in Egypt before your eyes? Unto thee it was shown, that thou might know that the Lord he is God; <u>there is none else beside him.</u> Out of heaven he made thee to hear his voice, that he might instruct thee; and upon earth he showed thee his great fire; and thou heard his words out of the midst of the fire. And because he loved thy fathers, therefore he chose their seed after them, and brought thee out in his sight with his mighty power out of Egypt; To drive out nations from before thee greater and mightier than thou art, to bring thee in, to give thee their land for an inheritance, as it is this day. Know therefore this day, and consider it in thine heart, that the Lord he is God in heaven above, and upon the earth beneath: <u>there is none else</u>".

<u>Deut. 5:1-33,</u> "And Moses called all Israel, and said unto them, Hear, O Israel, the statutes and judgments which I speak in your ears this day, that ye may learn them, and keep, and do them. The Lord our God made a covenant with us in Horeb. The Lord made not this covenant with our fathers, but with us, who are all of us here alive this day. The Lord talked with you face to face in the mount out of the midst of the fire, (I stood between the Lord and you at that time, to show you the word of the Lord: for ye were afraid by reason of the fire, and went not up to the mount;) saying, I am the Lord thy God, which brought thee out of the land of Egypt, from the house of bondage.

Thou shall have none other gods before me.

Thou shall not make thee any graven images, or any likeness of anything that is in heaven above, or that is in the earth beneath, or that is in the waters beneath the earth: Thou shall not bow down thyself unto them, nor serve them: for I the

*Lord thy God am a jealous God, visiting the iniquity unto the third and fourth generation of them that hate me, and showing mercy unto thousands of them that love me and keep my commandments.*

*Thou shall not take the name of the Lord thy God in vain: for the Lord will not hold him guiltless that takes his name in vain.*

*Keep the Sabbath day to sanctify it, as the Lord thy God has commanded thee: six days thou shall labour, and do all thy work: but the seventh day is the Sabbath of the Lord thy God: in it thou shall not do any work, thou, nor thy son, nor thy daughter, nor thy manservant, nor thy maidservant, nor thine ox, nor thine ass, nor any of thy cattle, nor thy stranger that is within thy gates; that thy manservant and thy maidservant may rest as well as thou. And remember that thou was a servant in the land of Egypt, and that the Lord thy God brought thee out thence through a mighty hand and by a stretched out arm; therefore the Lord thy God commanded thee to keep the Sabbath day.*

*Honor thy father and thy mother, as the Lord thy God has commanded thee; that thy days may be prolonged, and that it may go well with thee, in the land which the Lord thy God gives thee.*

*Thou shall not kill.*

*Neither shall thou commit adultery.*

*Neither shall thou steel.*

*Neither shall thou bear false witness against thy neighbour.*

*Neither shall thou desire thy neighbour's wife, neither shall thou covet thy neighbour's house, his fields, or his manservant, or his maidservant, his ox, or his ass, or anything that is thy neighbour's.*

THESE WORDS *the Lord spoke unto all your assembly in the mount out of the midst of the fire, of the cloud, and of the thick darkness, with a great voice: and he added no more. And he wrote them in two tables of stone, and delivered them unto me".*

## The following scriptures prove King David is the true Messiah of God:

Ps. 2:7, "*I (David) will declare the decree: the Lord God has said unto me* (David), *Thou art my Son: this day have I begotten thee* (David)".

Ps. 16:10, "*For thou will not leave my* (David's) *soul in hell; neither will thou suffer thine Holy One* (David) *to see corruption* (of the grave)".

Ps. 30:3, "*O Lord God, thou has brought up my* (David's) *soul from the grave: thou has kept me* (David) *alive, that I* (David) *should not go down to the pit*".

Ps. 49:15, "*But God will redeem my* (David's) *soul from the power of the grave: for he shall receive me*".

Ps. 89:18-20, 26-27, 29, *"For the Lord God is our defence; and the Holy One of Israel is our king.*

*Then thou spoke in vision to thy Holy One, and said, I have laid help upon one that is mighty; I have exalted one chosen out of the people.*

*I have found* David *my servant; with my holy oil have I anointed him* (David). *He* (David) *shall cry unto me, Thou art my father, my God, and the rock of my salvation. Also I will make him* (David) *my firstborn, higher than the kings of the earth. His seed also will I make to endure forever, and his throne as the days of heaven"*.

Ps. 118:17-18, *"I* (David) *shall not die, but live, and declare the works of the Lord God* (our witness). *The Lord God has chastened me* (David) *sore; but he has not given me over unto death"*.

Jer. 30:9, *"But they shall serve the LORD their GOD, and DAVID their KING, whom I will raise up unto them"*.

Ezek. 34:23-24, *"And I will set up one shepherd over them, and he shall feed them, even my servant DAVID, he shall feed them, and he shall be their SHEPHERD. And I the LORD will be their GOD, and my servant DAVID a PRINCE among them; I the LORD GOD have spoken it"*.

Ezek. 37:24-25, *"And DAVID my servant shall be KING over them; and they shall have one SHEPHERD: they shall also walk in my Judgments and observe my Statutes, and do them. And they shall dwell in the land that I have given unto Jacob my servant, wherein your fathers have dwelt; and they shall dwell therein, even they, and their children, and their children's children* forever*; and my servant DAVID shall be their PRINCE* forever*"*.

Hosea 3:5, *"Afterward shall the children of Israel return, and seek the LORD their GOD, and DAVID their KING; and shall fear the LORD GOD and his goodness* in the latter days*"*.

If the above scriptures do not convince you that King David is God's Holy Messiah, then you are not of God's people. May God open your eyes and your mind to understand his knowledge, and have the courage to do what is necessary to follow his ways. For we MUST perform the WORKS.

# CHAPTER 8

## Calculations to Pinpoint Certain Occurrences of Events

The following are calculations I used, to arrive at the most logical dates and times, to bring about a realistic picture of when stated facts occurred and are yet to occur. The first date I was sure of, comes from the historical sheets of "The Saxons Wars", where Charlemagne's first campaign attack on the Saxons' place of worship, was decided on, at the assembly of the empire, at Worms, in an early summer month of 772 cue. After having many small encounters against the Saxons within the main-land, he then headed north and crossed over the English Channel. After many calculations, particularly with the ages of this world, such as when King Jeroboam uncovered the golden calves for the House of Israel to worship, instead of the Lord their only God, was in the <u>year 911 b. cue. on the 15th of the 8th month</u>, 180 days after the 9th age switched to the beginning of the 10th age, and stated in <u>1 Kings 12:32-33</u>, "*And Jeroboam ordained a feast in the eighth month, like unto the feast that is in Judah, and he offered upon the Altar. So did he in Bethel, sacrificing unto the calves that he had made: and he placed in Bethel the priest of the high places which he had made. So he offered upon the altar which he had made in Bethel the <u>fifteenth day of the eighth month,</u> even in the month which he had devised of his own heart; and ordained a feast unto the children of Israel: and burnt incense*".

With this significant date of 985.62628 - 74.9834 = 910.643 on Aug. 22nd from sunset of previous day, the 10th age began. 116 days later on Dec. 9th, King Jeroboam uncovered the two pagan graven golden calves for the worshippers of the House of Israel to worship in place of the Lord their only God, causing the worshippers to commit a grievous sin against the Lord God. Therefore, being the length of each age is 1,000 biblical years or 985.62628 Gregorian years, the end of the 10th age would be year 985.62628 - 910.643 = <u>74.9834 cue. on Dec. 24th</u> from sunset of previous day, and the end of the 11th age would be 985.62628 + 74.9834 = <u>1060.6096 on Aug. 10th</u> from sunset of previous day, when the leaders of the christian religion had an assembly and wrote a decree giving them the right to select their own pope, which previously was selected by the military leader of the Roman Empire. The end of the 12th age would then be 1060.6096 + 985.62628 = 2046.2358 on Mar. 27th from sunset of previous day.

Daniel 12:11 scripture states, *"And from the time that the daily sacrifice shall be taken away, and the abomination that makes desolate set up, there shall be a thousand two hundred and ninety days".* Obviously each day represents one biblical year; therefore, 1290 * 360/365.25 = 1271.4579 Gregorian years. Therefore, in the year 2046.2358 - 1271.4579 = I finally ended up with 774.778 on Oct. 10th from sunset of previous day. Obviously before this day was over Charlemagne set upon their Altar of God an image of the christians' pagan christ, which was and still is, an image of himself, making this Altar of God desolated, as stated in the above Daniel 12:11 scripture. Charlemagne and his forces later destroyed this place of worship, bringing an end to any further sacrifices. These two abominable actions were completed at the above-mentioned day and time, before sundown. From this point onward it took Charlemagne 30 biblical years to fully impose his pagan christian religion upon the rest of the Saxons, our ancestors of the houses/tribes of Israel. This doesn't include the Jewish population, who also in subsequent future years adopted most of the pagan christian religious ways, even drinking the wine/blood and eating the bread/body of this pagan christians' christ within their Atonement event. In Ezekiel 23:31-34 is referring to the House of Judah drinking from this same wine cup that the christians are drinking from to their own destruction. For there is absolutely no scripture within the Old Testament that has anything good to say about this ritual. This place of worship was/is located in England and is now known as Stonehenge ruins and is not some prehistoric site that the archeologists are claiming. The real giveaway is the east summer solstice sun rises directly in line with the east entrance.

In Ezekiel 44:1-3 it states, *"Then he brought me back the way of the gate of the outward sanctuary which looked toward the east; and it was shut. Then said the Lord unto me; This gate shall be shut, it shall not be opened, and no man shall enter in by it; because the Lord, the God of Israel, has entered in by it; therefore it shall be shut. It is for the Prince/King; the prince shall sit in it to eat bread before the Lord God; he shall enter by the way of the porch of that gate, and shall go out by the way of the same".*

Therefore, with the solstice summer sun rising directly in line with this east entrance indicates the importance of this entrance. Where in Ezekiel 44:1-3 it tells us that this door way is to be used only by God and the Prince/King of the people, and where the Prince/King was to eat his meals. With the west entrance lining up with the winter solstice sunset makes this gate of secondary importance, for it is the entrance where the priestly Levis prepared and carried into the sanctuary the sacrificial parts of the animals. The north and south entrances were for the rest of the people to enter and leave the sanctuary. The ones entering the north entrance exited via the south entrance, and the ones entering the south entrance exited via the north entrance, as like passing through. The end of the 10th age 74.9834 on Dec. 24th from sunset of previous day is also a very important date, for it signifies the end of the war against the Romans and the complete destruction of the temple. From this date one <u>may</u> be able to calculate when the Holy Messiah King David's blood was shed, as in a sacrificial lamb brought to slaughter. For the midst of the week is 3 ½ biblical years or 1,260 days from a set day prior to the end of the war, <u>perhaps</u> from when the switching from year 74 to year 75, which is 116 days before the turn of the ages from 10th to 11th, minus 3.5 b. or 3.45 G. years or 1,260 days, which comes to year 70. Therefore, the Holy Messiah King David was put in the tomb just before sundown Friday, God's end of the 6st day of the week and the beginning of the 7th, holy Sabbath day. This is the end of the midst of the week mentioned in <u>Daniel's 9:27</u> scripture, *"And he* (the Holy Messiah) *shall confirm the covenant with many for one week* (7 biblical years): *and in the midst of the week* (3 ½ biblical years or 1,260 days) *he shall cause the sacrifice and the oblation to cease* (via his blood being shed as a sacrificial lamb brought to the slaughter), *even until the consummation, and that determined shall be poured upon the desolate"* (via a war against the Roman authorities), which ended on 74.9834 Dec. 24th from sunset of previous day, according to God's set times when a day ends and begins.

We have now acquired when the 9th, 10th, and 11th ages have expired and the 12th age will expire in the year and time 2046.2358 Mar. 27th from sunset of previous day, after a 30-biblical-year world war against our arch-enemy, the so-called Holy Roman Empire, now hidden within the European Union conglomerate of nations. But before this war begins, King Saul, the devil's 1st born son, the builder of the christian pagan religion will make his 3rd reappearance as the next and last pope of this christian religion for 1,260 days (3 1/2 b. yrs). This reappearance and crowning as pope will occur 2016.667 - 3.45 = 2013.217 on March 20th and will be crowned from sunset of previous day, and in Revelations 19:20 states, he is that false prophet with miraculous powers, with which he deceived them that had received the mark of the beast, and them that worshipped <u>his image</u>. His image is of the christians' pagan christ that they have been worshipping ever since he as Carl-the-man/Char-le-magne via the French and German forces attacked and destroyed and made the Altar of God desolate in the Saxons' place of worship in the year 774.778 on Oct. 10th from sunset of previous day, and continued thereon until 804.3468 on May 5th from sunset of previous day, imposing his pagan christ, of himself, via his pagan christian religion upon our ancestors, the Saxons of the House of Israel and we have been within this pagan christian religious hand ever since and will continue to be within this hand for 1,260 biblical years or 1241.8891 of our Gregorian years, just as <u>Dan. 7:25</u> states. After this time expires in the year 2016.667, God will reclaim us back with also a 30-biblical-year world war against this same 4th world empire, matching the same number of years it took Charlemagne-King Saul, and the next and last pope of this pagan christian religion that he built in the New Testament times when he was this Saul called Paul, and the false prophet with miraculous powers as stated in <u>Rev. 19:20</u>. This is why in <u>Dan. 12:11</u> scripture, Daniel adds this 30 biblical years to 1,260 biblical years and arrives at the 1,290 figure, which takes into the consideration <u>the order of imposing</u> by Charlemagne and <u>the order of reclaiming</u> by God. The 1st lot of the Saxons that the christian religion was imposed upon, will be the 1st lot of us, their children, will be reclaimed. As it took Charles 30 biblical years to <u>fully impose</u> this pagan christian religion upon our ancestors; therefore, it will take God 30 biblical years to <u>fully reclaim</u> us, their children, back. Making it necessary for Daniel to add 30 to 1,260, total number of years each and every one of us will be within King Saul's Hand. Don't be fooled by the greatness he is allowed to display for 1,260 days, when he arrives as the last pope of this christian pagan religion on March 20th of 2013 cue.

<u>Proverbs 1:26-32</u>, *"I also will laugh at your calamity; I will mock when your fear comes; when your fear comes as desolation, and your destruction comes as a whirlwind; when distress and anguish comes upon you. Then shall they* (you) *call upon me, but I will not answer; they* (you) *shall seek me early, but they* (you) *shall not find me: for that they* (you) *hated knowledge, and did not choose the fear of the Lord God: They* (you) *would none of my council: they* (you) *despised all my reproofs. Therefore shall they* (you) *eat of the fruit of their* (your) *own way, and be filled with their* (your) *own vices. For the turning away of the simple shall slay them* (you), *and the prosperity of fools shall destroy them (you).*

<u>Isaiah 8:21-22</u>, *"And they* (you) *shall pass through it* (the coming world war III and/or even the 45-biblical-year period following the end of this end-time war) *hardly bestead and hungry: and it shall come to pass, that when they* (you) *shall be hungry, they* (you) *shall fret themselves* (yourselves), *and curse their* (your) *king and their* (your) *God, and look upward. And they* (you) *shall look unto the earth; and behold trouble and darkness, dimness of anguish; and they* (you) *shall be driven to darkness".*

But the silver lining of hope is in <u>Proverbs 1:33</u>, *"But whoso hearkens unto me shall dwell safely, and shall be quiet from fear of evil".*

## **Calculations are as below:**

If Charles attacked the Saxon's place of worship on.

.778 * 365 = 283.97 days = Oct. 10th from sunset Oct. 9th

| 774.778 | 2016.667 | 2046.2358 | 985.62628 |
| 1241.889 | 29.569 | 1971.2525 | 74.9833 |
| 2016.667 | 2046.236 | 74.9833 | 910.64298 |
| Start of reclaiming WWIII .667*365 = Aug.31st @ 10:55 WWIII begins. 2016.667 -3.45 = 2013.217 Mar.20th @ 4:55 from sunset of Mar. 19th. King Saul returns and chosen as last pope of christian pagan religion. Also is the false prophet of Rev.19:20. | End of war .236 * 365 = Mar. 27 @ 3:22 End of 12th age | .9833*365 = Dec. 24th @ 21:42 sunset of Dec.23rd Temple destroyed in the days before 10th age ends and 11 age begins. | .64298*365 = Aug.22nd @ 16:30 from sunset Aug. 21st. End of 9th age and beginning of the 10th age .116 days before Jeroboam un-covers the two golden calves for the people to worship. |

    This day was basically an hour within the Sabbath day, our Saturday, when Charles committed his atrocities according to our equivalent calendar of 2006. This assured everyone may have been present when his atrocities began. But as we have it they were also performing the daily evening and morning sacrifices. Therefore, they were at least present to perform the evening sacrifices of this day Charlemagne showed up, he didn't have to summon the people together, for they were indeed present and performing their Sabbath duties. He and his forces proceeded to bring upon this place of worship and the people his 2 atrocities to set an image of his pagan christ upon their Altar of God, which was actually of himself, making this altar desolate, and forced the worshippers to worship his image, which was really an image of himself, killing anyone who refused. After this gruesome atrocity, he destroyed this place of worship, bringing an end to any further morning and evening daily sacrifices to the Lord their only God, and after performing these 2 atrocities he brought Daniel's 7:25 and 12:7 and 12:11 scriptures alive, and the countdown of the 1,290 biblical years began. Our christian leaders and religious scholars of today are still waiting for these 2 atrocities to come about in some future happening, being completely ignorant this has already happened approximately 1,251 biblical years as of May of year 2006 cue.

We have approx. 10 of our years remaining as of the summer of year 2006 until God will proceed to bring us back to him and his ways with a 30-biblical-year world war against this same so-called Holy Roman Empire and their allies, beginning in Aug. 31th @ 2:56 of year 2016 cue. But before this King Saul/Saul called Paul/the last and next pope (false prophet mentioned in Rev. 20:19) of the christian religion/Charlemagne will make his reappearance, for 1,260 days or 3.5 biblical years or 3.45 Gregorian years on Mar. 20th of year 2013 to Aug. 31st in year 2016 cue. and rule directly over us for the entire 1,260 days as the christians' pope.

These two atrocities that Charles performed matched that of what Antiochus Epiphanies did when he entered the temple in Jerusalem and set his pagan god Jupiter Olympius upon the Altar of God, which made the altar desolate in the year -166.707 and 166.734, and via <u>Dan. 8:13-14</u> this sanctuary will not be completely rebuilt and cleansed until 2,300 biblical years expires. Therefore, in year 2266.9404 - (-166.266) = 2100.6744 God's Altar and Sanctuary will be completely rebuilt and cleansed. Please note that this is before our current century ends, and by taking off <u>Dan. 12:12's</u> allotted time of 1335 b. years or 1315.811 Gregorian years leaves us with year 774.778 to 804.3468 (within Charlemagne's exploits against the Saxons' place of worship, which brought <u>Daniel's 12:11</u> scripture alive) = 9.747 years to gather up the remnant and lead them back to the land of Israel to rebuild the above-mentioned temple, with God's Altar. All these actions carried out by Charlemagne against the Saxons and their place of worship fulfilled <u>Daniel's 12:11</u> scripture, which states, *"And from the time that the daily sacrifice shall be taken away, and the abomination that makes it desolate is set up, there shall be a thousand two hundred and ninety days* (biblical years)". These above calculations prove without any doubt the 30 b. year end-time world war is due to come about as stated throughout this book, in the year 2016.667, against our nemeses, the so-called Holy Roman Empire nations and their allies, led by the next and last pope of the christian religion, King Saul himself, with the evil spirit still upon him, matching the same number of biblical years it took Charlemagne/King Saul to fully impose his pagan christian religion upon our Israelite ancestors. The name <u>Saxons</u> actually is a short version or slang for <u>Isaac's sons (or sons of Isaac)</u>, of the House of Israel, the 10 lost tribes. The Franks (French), who were a vital part of Charlemagne's force that attacked these Saxons, are of the tribe of Reuben, also of the House of Israel. The animosity that the Reubenites have against the leaders of these Saxons, who are of the tribes of Joseph, is because they lost their very important firstborn birthright blessings and status to Ephraim of the tribe of Joseph, upon Reuben sexually messing around with his father's mistress. Instead of blaming their own father for their shortcomings of losing this firstborn blessings and status, they find it easier to stubbornly continue on to try and win these blessings and status back. They themselves have absolutely no idea why they behave as they do, for there is within them that craving for the leadership role, being the actual firstborn. Charlemagne knew all about this desire within the franks, and put it to good use, to accomplish his goal, which was to impose his christian paganism religion upon firstly, the leaders of the Saxons, and secondly the remaining tribes of the House of Israel. This Charlemagne is the disguise of King Saul with the evil spirit still upon him, who in turn is the horn of <u>Daniel's 7:20 and 25</u> scriptures, where God in <u>verse 25</u> states that he will put <u>them</u> (the remnant mentioned in <u>Rev. 12:17</u>) into this horn's hand. This horn is also Saul called Paul, so-called Apostle Paul, in the New Testament, the master builder of this christian paganism religion. Is it any wonder why he is so adamant in imposing this religion upon us and our ancestors. This Charlemagne, being King Saul, is of the tribe of Benjamin, also an Israelite. This Charlemagne was of an unusual height, for his height measured 7 times the length of his foot, making him more than likely a 6.4 footer or so; just as King Saul was higher than his country folks from his shoulders upward and both were also well-proportioned. God is using him to give us <u>statutes that are not good for us</u>, and <u>judgments we ought not to live by</u>; and because our ancient ancestors polluted God's holy Sabbath days, as we modern Israelites of today are doing, God tells us that he will pollute us in our own gifts, that will bring us to total desolation as <u>Ezekiel 20:24-26</u> states. These gifts and goodies are coming via our christian events, which hold us fast to this pagan religion, and in turn pollute us via all the pagan gods that we worship, pray to, and serve, as if they are real living Gods; being ignorant that there is only one true living God and none other. We have been totally deceived by our religious leaders. King Saul/Saul-Paul/Charlemagne's veil is indeed preventing us from seeing, hearing, and understanding the truth; and this veil must be removed as <u>Isa. 25:7</u> states, *"He* (God) *will destroy in this mountain the face of the covering cast over all people, and the veil that is spread over all nations".*

Read <u>Ezekiel 20:24-26,</u> *"Because they had not executed my judgments, but had despised my statutes, and had polluted my Sabbaths, and their eyes were after their father's idols. Wherefore I gave them <u>also</u> statutes that were <u>not</u> good* (via all the christians' so-called holy events) *and judgments whereby they should <u>not</u> live* (via all the outlandish judgments handed down upon our heinous and repeat crime committees, such as ignoring the death penalties and charging us good abiding taxpayers the total expenses of keeping them in jails, years without end, instead of putting the heinous crime committees to death and their immediate family members paying the whole bill for their loved ones huge or minor mistakes). *And I polluted them in their own <u>gifts</u>* (via all the gifts and goodies received in all the christian events) *in that they caused to pass through the fire all that opens the womb* (these are all the aborted first born of our very young girls, being burnt within our incinerators) *that I might make them desolate, to the end that they might know* (come to realize) *that I am the Lord God*. God is in complete control of whatsoever comes upon us, so don't lost faith. To arrive at the above calculations I needed to work with all the fixed numbers, such as when King Jeroboam uncovered the two graven golden calves on the 15th day of the 8th month after the sunset of the 14th day or actually on the beginning of Aug. 15th, in the year -910 and according to our equivalent Gregorian calendar 2003 is not a leap year; therefore, the 8th month is August and the beginning of the 15th day (Friday) of the month is .62628 and the time of day calculates out to be at 20:27 upon sunset of previous day, which would be God's holy Sabbath day (Saturday). One also must remember that God's days end and start at sunset and all calculated dates must take this into consideration. This 910.64288 was found by using the number of years in an age (1000 * 360/365.25 = 985.62628) and subtracting 74.9834 which is the end of the 10th age, and it came to 910.64288 which is the end of the 9th age and the beginning of the 10th age and King Jeroboam uncovered the two graven golden calves 116 days into the 10th age, for the tribes of the House of Israel to worship as their gods, as is reported in 1 Kings 12:32-33. This is a very grave date indeed, for it represents the future pagan worshipping the House of Israel will partake in, even our present day with the worshipping of all the many pagan saints and pagan christians' christ. The end of the 8th age and the beginning of the 9th age would be -910.64288 plus 985.62628 = -1896.2691 when Esau and Jacob were born. When these twins were born Jacob's hand was grasping Esau's heel. Esau's heel represented the end of the 8th age and Jacob's hand represented the beginning of the 9th age. The 74.9834 + 985.62628 = 1060.6096 end of 11th age and beginning of 12th age, when the christian leaders wrote a decree giving them the power to select their own pope. Before this the military leader of the 4th world Roman Empire selected the pope. This 12th age that we are now living within, will end in 1060.6096 + 985.62628 = 2046.2358 or Mar. 27th from sunset of previous day, and the 13th age begins with whomever made it into Daniel's extra 45 biblical years of nothingness. The 10 percent that survive will be gathered up by King David and his faithful soldiers mentioned in 2 Samuel 23:8-39, and will be gathered up and lead back to the promised land and begin to rebuild the temple and complete it before 2100.3358 cue. to full-fill Daniel's 8:13-14 scriptures, for this is the date for the temple to be completely rebuilt, cleansed, and rededicated. Please note this temple must be as stated within the last year of this current century in order to full-fill Daniel's 8:14 scripture. This time, times, and half a time (1,260 biblical years) plus the 30-biblical-year reclaiming war, matches this same time in Dan. 12:11, where it states, *"And from the time that the daily sacrifice shall be taken away, and the abomination that makes the Altar desolate is set up, there shall be 1290 days* (of biblical years)". This is telling us, from the time Charlemagne sets up a graven image/statue of his pagan imaginary christians' christ upon the Saxons' Altar of God, that makes this altar desolate, and the sacrifices are brought to an end, there shall be 1,290 days, of biblical years, until God fully reclaims his people back from the hand of this little horn. Charlemagne's actions against this place of worship is the starting point of our counting of these 1,290 biblical years or 1271.458 of our years, *"all these things shall be finished"*. The end of the 30-biblical-year reclaiming world war; the end of all 12 ages of this world; and definitely the end of our civilization as we now know it. The small remnant that lives through this world war, will try to stay alive for a period of 45 biblical years, when mankind will revert to cannibalism in trying to stay alive; of the one-third of all the Israelites, that make it through this third world war, only one out of ten, make it through this 45 days (biblical years) of nothingness, and are gathered up and led back to the promised land.

As it states in Ezek. 34:2-10, *"Son of man, prophesy against the shepherds of Israel, Thus saith the Lord God unto the shepherds of Israel that do feed themselves! Should not the shepherds feed the flocks? Ye eat the fat, and ye clothe you with the wool, ye kill them that are fed: but ye feed not the flock. The diseased have ye not strengthened, neither have ye healed that which was sick, neither have ye bound up that which was broken, neither have ye brought again that which was driven away, neither have ye sought that which was lost; but with force and with cruelty have ye ruled over them. And they were scattered, because there is no shepherd: and they became meat to all the beasts of the field* (non-Israelite peoples or strangers that live amongst us), *when they were scattered. My sheep wandered through all the mountains, and upon every high hill: yea, my flock was scattered upon all the face of the earth, and none did search or seek after them.*

*Therefore, ye shepherds, hear the word of the Lord God; As I live, saith the Lord God, surely because my flock became a prey, and my flock became meat to every beast of the field, because there was no shepherd, neither did my shepherds search for my flock, but the shepherds fed themselves, and fed not my flock: Therefore, O ye shepherds, hear the word of the Lord God; Thus saith the Lord God; Behold, I am against the shepherds; and I will require my flock at their hand, and cause them to cease from feeding the flock; neither shall the shepherds feed themselves any more; for I will deliver my flock from their mouth, that they may not be meat for them"*.

Dan. 12:12, *"Blessed is he that waits, and comes to the 1335 days* (of biblical years)".

2 Esdras 6:7-10 states, "*Tell me, Ezra went on, 'about the interval that divides the ages. When will the first age end and the next age begins?' The angel said, 'The interval will be no bigger than that between Abraham and Abraham; for Jacob and Esau were his descendants, and Jacob's hand was grasping Esau's heel at the moment of their birth. Esau represents the end of the first age, and Jacob the beginning of the next age. The beginning of a man is his hand, and the end of a man is his heel. Between the heel and the hand, Ezra, do not look for any interval*".

The angel also tells Ezra in 14:10-13, "*The world has lost its youth, and the time is growing old. For the whole of time is in twelve divisions; nine divisions and half the tenth have already passed, and only two and a half still remain*". After a few calculations, it turns out that the angel was talking to Ezra in the 420 b. cue. to approximately 415 b. cue. period, and John in 1 John 2:18, was referring to the end of this 10th age, which we know ended with the complete destruction of the temple in Jerusalem and the end of the pursuing war, in the year 74.9834 cue., on Dec. 24th from sunset of previous day. These divisional dates are the ones that must be used to put everything into proper order—such as the divisional date of 910.64288 b. cue., to determine that King Jeroboam unveiled the two golden calves 116 days after the beginning of the 10th divisional date; the division date of 74.9834 cue., with the destruction of the temple in Jerusalem and the end of the war; and the date of the end of the 12th division in the year of 2046.2358 cue., when our civilization is at an end. With these 3 dates and our number of 774.778 cue. when Charlemagne attacked the Saxons' place of worship and set the abomination, a graven/image of his pagan christians' christ or even the shroud with the image of his face upon it, that made their Altar of God desolate; and the time, times, and half a time, the length of time God put them into this horn's hand; and the 1,000 biblical years in each division; plus the fact, according to our calendar, the shedding of the Messiah's blood, in the mid days of April and placing the body in a tomb before the coming sunset that brought in the rest of April in year 69 cue and then onward to continue our current calendar. We have now completed the entire picture and found necessary dates and times.

One would think that our ancient ancestors must have been really naïve to worship these 2 golden calves that King Jeroboam brought forth, which made them sin against the Lord their only God. But in comparing them to the christian followers, who are worshipping not one or two, but perhaps a hundred or more, when you count all their canonized saints, their pagan christ, virgin mother, lady fatima, etc. This is why I made the statement that the christian religion is the most paganism religion that has ever existed. Talk about being naïve, to the stage that the blind are leading the blind, we have regressed to the stage that we don't even know who we are as a people; we definitely do not know the true ways of our Lord God, even though his ways are written down in the books of the Old Testament. There is absolutely no excuse for our ignorance. We are told in the Old Testament, particularly in Proverbs 1:23-25, to prove all things pertaining to the ways of the Lord our God, and if we continue to ignore him and his ways, and chase after all your pagan useless gods, be prepare to receive his great and terrible wrath upon you, your loved ones, our whole nations, and even this whole world in the very near future. Read Proverbs 1:26-32, and Isa. 8:21-22, to get a good picture of what lies ahead for you, if you continue along your present path, I have them quoted below at the end of this chapter.

Ezek. 21:14 states, *"Let the sword be doubled the third time"* (doubled in intensity). Beginning 2016.667 or Aug. 31st from sunset of previous day, Jerusalem time zone. The Billy Grahams of this world of all our christian leaders won't know what hit them when God's wrath comes upon them in full force, for these are the wolves dressed up in sheep's clothing, devouring the Spirit/Mind of whomever comes in contact with them, with their deceptive instructions and evil ways related to their many pagan so-called gods; reported in various scriptures such as Ezek. 22:25-27, Zeph. 3:3-4, from the Old Testament.

You may not like what I am disclosing to you, but the fact remains this is the absolute truth, as long as one can depend on the dates received from any other historical source.

There is one scripture that I would like to quote for you, which the angel is quoting to Ezra, but really applies to all of us today, for we are indeed living in the time of the end:

2 Esdras 14:13-18, *"Set your house in order, therefore; give warnings to your nations, and comfort to those in need of it; and take your leave of mortal life. Put away your earthly cares, and lay down your human burdens; strip off your weak nature, set aside the anxieties that vex you, and be ready to depart quickly from this life. However great the evils you have witnessed, there are worse to come. As this ageing world grows weaker and weaker, so will evils increase for its inhabitants. Truth will move farther away, and falsehood comes nearer. The eagle that you saw in your vision is already on the wing".*

This eagle that the angel is referring to is the 4th world empire, the so-called Holy Roman Empire, which came into existence as an empire approximately 300-400 years after the angel spoke with Ezra. The revival of this empire is coming about again for the last time, with the forming of the European Union countries, and when the christians' next and last pope, King Saul in person, with the evil spirit still upon him, and who is in fact the master builder of this christian religion (1 Cor. 3:10-11) comes on the scene again for his third reappearance, after killing the present Pope

Frances (<u>2 Esdras 12:26-28</u>, refer to chapter 5), will direct this union into the powerhouse it used to be, when he brought all the European countries back together from a broken down Roman Empire when he reappeared for the second time as Charlemagne, but this third reappearance as pope, with <u>miraculous powers</u> (<u>Rev. 13:11-17</u> as one of the two horns on a beast) which states, *"And I beheld another beast coming up out of the earth; and he had two horns like a lamb* (King Saul/pope of the christian religion), *and he speaks as a dragon. And he exercised all the power of the first beast before him, and causes the earth and them which dwell therein to worship the first beast* (so-called Holy Roman Empire), *whose deadly wound was healed. And deceives them that dwell on the earth by the means of those miracles which he has power to do in the sight of the beast; saying to them that dwell on the earth, that they should make an image to the beast, which had the wound by a sword* (via 1st and 2nd world wars), *and did live. And he had power to give life unto the image of the beast, that the image of the beast should both speak, and cause that as many as would not worship the image of the beast should be killed. And he caused all, both small and great, rich and poor, free and bond, to receive a mark in their right hand, or in their foreheads: And that no man might buy or sell, save he that has the mark, or the name of the beast, or the number* (666) *of his name"*. (<u>Rev. 19:20</u> as the false prophet) and the forces equipped with modern weapons.

<u>Ezek. 21:9-12,</u> *"Son of man, prophesy, and say, Thus says the Lord God; A sword, a sword is sharpened, and also furbished: It is sharpened to make a great slaughter; it is furbished that it may glitter: should we Israelites make mirth? It contemns the rod of my son, as every tree. And he has given it to be furbished, that it may be handled: this sword is sharpened, and it is furbished, to give it into the hand of the slayer. Cry and howl, son of man: for it shall be upon my people, it shall be upon all the princes of Israel: terrors by reason of the sword shall be upon my people: smite therefore upon thy thigh. Because it is a trial, and what if the sword contemns even our rod? It shall be no more, says the Lord God"*.

The scripture of <u>2 Esdras 12:26-28</u> states as follows: *"As for the greatest head of this eagle, which you saw disappear, it signifies one of the three kings/popes, who will die in his bed, but in great agony.* (Did not Pope John Paul II die in his bed in great agony? Even the whole world was a witness.) *The two that remained will be destroyed by the sword; one of them will fall by the sword of the other, who will himself fall by the sword in the last days"*. This last Archbishop of the Church of Englsnd is definitely the return of King Saul, with the evil spirit still upon him. And the sword of the Holy Messiah, King David, will finally put him to his final death.

In the above <u>2 Esdras 14:13-18</u> scriptures in the previous page; is this not what we are beginning to experience today with all the evils throughout this world coming to a head? This is only the beginning, and there are approx. 10

years to go, as of late summer of this year of 2006 cue., before the 3rd world war comes about, and all hell will break loose. Even our weather patterns are increasing in intensity.

Proverbs 1:26-32, *"I also will laugh at your calamity; I will mock when your fear comes; when your fear comes as desolation, and your destruction comes as a whirlwind; when distress and anguish comes upon you. Then shall they* (you) *call upon me, but I will not answer; they* (you) *shall seek me early, but they* (you) *shall not find me: for that they* (you) *hated knowledge, and did not choose the fear of the Lord God: They* (you) *would none of my council: they* (you) *despised all my reproofs. Therefore shall they* (you) *eat of the fruit of their* (your) *own way, and be filled with their* (your) *own devices. For the turning away of the simple shall slay them* (you), *and the prosperity of fools shall destroy them.*

Isaiah 8:21-22, *"And they* (you) *shall pass through it* (the coming world war III and/or even the 45-biblical-year period following the end of this end-time war) *hardly bestead and hungry: and it shall come to pass, that when they* (you) *shall be hungry, they* (you) *shall fret themselves* (yourself), *and curse their* (your) *king and their* (your) *God, and look upward. And they* (you) *shall look unto the earth; and behold trouble and darkness, dimness of anguish; and they* (you) *shall be driven to darkness"*. But the silver lining of hope is in Proverbs 1:33, *"But whoso hearkens unto me shall dwell safely, and shall be quiet from fear of evil"*.

In other words we must flee from this christian religion and all her activities, as her so-called holy events, which are as pagan as you can get. Do not pray to, serve, or worship any of her pagan so-called imaginary christ, and pagan saints, virgin mother, etc. We are to pray to, serve, worship and fear only the Lord our one God, the same God as our ancestors Abraham, Isaac, and Jacob/Israel prayed to and worshipped. You are responsible for your children's eternal life to a certain age, and obviously your own. Do not sit in the dark and ignore the chance to know the truth, prove all things.

# Chapter 9

# The Day of the Lord Our God

This Day of the Lord our God is in reality a period of 30 biblical years, which is the time God will take to reclaim us Israelites from the horn's hand of <u>Dan. 7:25</u>; after the expiry period of 1,260 days (of biblical years) or 1241.8891 years of our Gregorian calendar. These 1,260 days, of biblical years, began shortly after Charlemagne and his cronies began planning to impose his pagan christian religion upon our ancestors in a late fall month of year 774 cue. There must be two requirements performed to start the countdown of these 1,260 days, of biblical years. The <u>1st requirement</u> was to set the abomination upon the Saxons' Altar of God that made this altar desolate. This Charlemagne did when he set up a statue/image of the christians' pagan imaginary christ, or even the shroud with the image of his face upon it, upon the Saxons' Altar of God, making this altar desolate. He thereafter forced the Saxons, in attendance, to worship this, another god, killing those who refused. The <u>second requirement</u> was to bring the sacrifices these Saxons performed upon this Altar of God to an end; these sacrifices were brought to an end when he and his forces destroyed their place of worship. These two required actions brought alive <u>Dan. 12:11</u> scripture, which states: *"And from the time that the daily sacrifices shall be taken away, and the abomination that makes the Altar desolate is set up, there shall be a 1290 days* (of biblical years)". This 1,290 biblical years consists of the 1,260 biblical years these Saxons and their future children will be in the horn's hand, who in reality is none other than King Saul with the evil spirit still upon him; who reappeared the 1st time as Saul called Paul in the New Testament days. Did he not go on a rampage destroying many of the Jewish synagogues and maiming many of their followers? Many of these people were of his own tribe of Benjamin of the House of Judah. Only a person with the evil spirit upon them would perform these atrocities. He later penetrated the ranks of the true apostles, led by James, and from this position launched his new gospel of his imaginary pagan christ, instead of the true Gospel of God.

God's true Messiah, King David, was put to death by Saul/Paul and his forces, afterwards he supposedly claims to have received a vision from heaven condemning his actions, and which he now claims, has made him a new and different man. When the true apostles found out he was preaching a new gospel, not the gospel of God, but a gospel of his pagan imaginary christ, they made a vow that they will not eat nor drink until they have killed him. However, he received protection from Agrippa via the Roman soldiers ruling over the Jewish nation. He thereafter only preached to the Gentile peoples. These 1,290 biblical years also consists of the 30 biblical years of God's reclaiming period of us Israelites from this horn's hand, matching the same number of years it took Charlemagne to fully impose his pagan christian religion upon our ancestors, the tribes of Saxons living in the area he ruled over; these 30 biblical years is also known as <u>the Day of the Lord our God</u>; when God will bring his full and terrible wrath, firstly upon us Israelites and then upon the Gentile and heathen nations that hate us Israelites. Just as it was upon the start of the second world war, where the British were pulverized by the flying rockets sent over the English Channel, and the blood bath our soldiers took on the shores of France, upon trying to liberate them from the enemies. One cannot forget the German's oversized battleship, the Bismarck, that devastated the British fleet before we found a way to destroy it, with the help of God himself, when a torpedo rocket dropped from a plane, hit the Achilles' heel, the steering mechanism, making it vulnerable thereafter. God's help even prevailed, when God changed the mind of Hitler; instead of finishing off the British from the devastating flying rockets, he stopped the attack and went to take on the Russians, where again they were very successful until they reached the outskirts of their largest Cities, where God again intervened by bringing on the coldest weather imaginable, bringing the German's machinery to a standstill, and a lot of them literally froze to death out in the opened fields, and while they were trying to make it back to Germany. God's intervention was also prevalent when he calmed the seas and gave the rescue boats the covering of a thick fog upon rescuing our soldiers from the massacre they were receiving on the French shorelines. Just as he gave the ancient Israelites the covering of the cloud in the day light hours to conceal them from the Egyptian forces, and led them through the wilderness at night with a column of fire. The major intervention by God shortly after the assault from the flying rockets, was to give his servant Mr. Winston Churchill the reins of the British government. It was Mr. Churchill that warned the British government about the German's intentions to attack them, and that they were not to be trusted. As we all know today, that his warnings were ignored. Just as my warnings in this book will, more than likely, also be ignored by the readers. A few years after the British assault, somewhat the same occurred in the Pacific Ocean, when the Americans were severely attacked at Pearl Harbour by the Japanese forces, devastating a major part of their Pacific fleet, and because of this and many other major losses, they were impelled to use the big ATOMIC BOMB to bring a halt to this very powerful Japanese force, otherwise this conflict was destined to continue for many more years. One can certainly say that God's intervention in this battle, was allowing the Americans, who are Israelites of the oldest son of Joseph, the first to invent this atomic bomb and the first to use it to scare the hell out of the Japanese government to cause their surrender. This act also brought the American's power to the forefront, and has been in the forefront ever since, which mainly kept the Russians at bay during their hay days. Without the multitudes of God's interventions, this world would be very different, especially for us Israelites.

But THE DAY OF THE LORD OUR GOD will again be upon us in the very near future, when the expiry date of the 1,260 days, of biblical years, comes to an end. Which will begin in the month of Aug. 31st from sunset of previous day, in the year 2016 cue.

Isa. 2:12 & 17 states, *"For the day of the Lord God of Hosts shall be upon every one that is proud and lofty, and upon everyone that is lifted up; and he* (they) *shall be brought low.*

*And the Lord God of Hosts alone shall be exalted in that day".*

One must understand that the word <u>day</u> could mean an actual day, or a biblical year for each day, or a given number of days representing a given number of biblical years, such as the 30 days of the Day of the Lord God, representing the 30 biblical years of God's reclaiming period of us Israelites from the hands of the horn of <u>Dan. 7:25</u>, matching the same number of biblical years it took Charlemagne to fully impose his pagan christian religion upon our ancestors, the Saxons of the House of Israel; or even 1,000 biblical years for each day, such as each creation day represents 1,000 biblical years or one age of this world, as <u>2 Esdras 14:10-13</u> states, *"The world has lost its youth, and time is growing old. For the whole of time is in twelve ages* (divisions); *nine divisions and half the tenth have already passed, and only two and a half still remain".* Ezra the prophet had this talk with the angel approx. 420 to 415 b. cue., which would then make the destruction of the temple in Jerusalem and the end of the war against the Roman forces completed at the end of this 10th division in the year 74:9834 on Dec. 24th from sunset of previous day. Therefore, the end of our civilization will come at an end 2,000 biblical years from this date, which will be (2000 * 360/365.25) + 74.9834 = 2046.2358 on Mar. 27th from sunset of Mar. 26st. By taking God's reclaiming period of 30 biblical years or 29.5688 years of our calendar off this date when our civilization expires, gives us the year 2016.667 on Aug. 31st from sunset of previous day. This date is the beginning of the Day of the Lord our God, and will last for 30 biblical years or 29.5688 of our years. This is again when God's great and terrible wrath will come upon us in the form of what we will call world war III. <u>Ezek. 21:9-17,</u> has a very clear picture of what will come upon us Israelites for our evil ways of chasing after all the falsehood that the christian religious organizations have deceived us with. For we have to remember that it was King Saul as Saul called Paul with the evil spirit still upon him, that built this christian religion. And this is the horn of <u>Dan. 7:25</u> that God put us into his hand, to teach us, whoever survives this 3rd world war, a lesson we will never forget. For the christian religion is the devil's religion, and King Saul is the devil's 1st born and cursed son, as King David is God's 1st born and Holy Messiah. All the christians' priests, ministers, clergy-persons, even all the way up to and including the popes are anti-Messiahs, overriding the true Messiah of God, King David, with their pagan imaginary christ and pagan canonized saints and virgin mother, etc., as their other so-called gods. They are also the wolves dressed up in sheep's clothing, devouring the spirit/minds of their followers. Is it any wonder none of the christians' so-called holy events have absolutely nothing in common with the events God gave to our ancestors, which are recorded in the books of Moses and instructed to keep forever.

<u>Ezek. 21:9-17</u> states," *Son of man, prophesy, and say, Thus says the Lord God; Say, A sword, a sword is sharpened, and also furbished: It is sharpened to make a sore slaughter; it is furbished that it may glitter: should we make mirth? It contemns the rod of my son, as every tree. And he has given it to be furbished, that it may be handled: this sword is sharpened, and it is furbished, to give it into the hand of the slayer.*

*Cry and howl, son of man: for <u>it shall be upon my people</u>, it shall be upon <u>all the princes of Israel</u>; terrors by reason of the sword shall be upon <u>my people</u>: smite therefore upon thy thigh, because it is a trail, and what if the sword contemn even the rod? It shall be no more, says the Lord God.*

*Thou therefore, son of man, prophesy, and smite thine hands together, and let the sword be <u>doubled the third time</u>* (the third world war doubled in intensity) *the sword of the slain: it is the sword of the great men that are slain, which enters into their privy chambers.*

*<u>I have set the point of the sword against all their gates</u>, that their hearts may faint, and their ruins be multiplied: ah! It is made bright, it is wrapped up for the slaughter. Go thee one way or other, either on the right hand, or on the left, whither-soever thy face is set.*

*I will also smite mine hands together and I will cause my fury to rest: I the Lord God have said it".*

There are other scriptures that use the word <u>double</u>. Such as <u>Jer. 16:18,</u> *"And first I will recompense their iniquity and their sin <u>double;</u> because they have defiled my land, they have filled mine inheritance with the carcasses of their detestable and abominable things"*. And <u>Zech. 9:12,</u> *"Turn you to the stronghold, ye prisoners of hope: even today do I declare that I will render <u>double</u> unto thee"*.

These scriptures are referring to the 30 biblical years of world war III that will be doubled in intensity in comparison to any other world war in history. Therefore, I urge you to flee as quickly as you can from this christian paganism religion, while you still can, and return back to the proper Old Testament ways as best you can; cast away all your graven, painted and standing images of whatsoever; all your christmas and easter decorations, etc., or any other religious decorations and goodies for all saint day events, etc., even your <u>hell</u>oween costumes, etc., for the devil is the so-called god of this event, there is absolutely nothing hallowed in this event, reason I spelled it as above. We must keep holy God's Sabbath day on the 7th day of the week, from Friday just before sundown, to just after sundown Saturday, the proper time of a day, this is a good time to study your Bible and prove all things, use my book to help you understand what the Bible is actually relating to you; do not observe the christians' 1st day of the week, as your weekly holy day, which is the wrong day, with even the wrong time of a day from midnight to midnight.

Following the 30 days, of biblical years, the day of the Lord God is a time period that the survivors of this world war must live through for a time period of 45 biblical years. It is a time when all the lands, buildings, and whatsoever will be totally devastated; mankind will revert to cannibalism to stay alive. One-third of all the Israelites will survive God's 30-biblical-year reclaiming world war III, but only <u>one out of ten</u> of this 1/3rd will survive <u>Dan. 12:12</u>'s extra 45 biblical years of nothingness, as stated in <u>Isa. 6:13,</u> *"But yet in it shall be a tenth, and it shall return, and shall be eaten: as a teil tree, and as an oak, whose substance is in them, when they cast their leaves: so the holy seed shall be the substance thereof"*. This one-tenth will be gathered up together again and led back to the promised land. <u>Jer. 16:10-21</u> tells the whole story from our ancestors' defeat at the hands of the Assyrians in the years 734-721 b. cue., leading up to today, through the coming 30 days, of biblical years, of the Day of the Lord our God to back again into the promised land, as <u>Dan. 12:12</u> states, *"Blessed is he that waits and comes to the 1335 days* (of biblical years)".

<u>Jer. 16:10-21,</u> *"And it shall come to pass, when thou shall show this people all these words, and they shall say unto thee, Wherefore has the Lord our God pronounced all this great evil against us? Or what is our iniquity? Or what is our sin that we have committed against the Lord our God?*

*Then shall thou say unto them, Because your fathers have forsaken me, says the Lord God, and have walked after other gods, and have served them, and have worshipped them, and have forsaken me, and have not kept my law; And ye have done worse than your fathers; for, behold, ye walk every one after the imagination of his evil heart, that they may not hearken unto me:*

*Therefore will I cast you out of this land into a land that ye know not, neither ye nor your fathers; and <u>there shall ye serve other gods day and night</u>* (the christian pagan gods); *where I will not show you favour.*

*Therefore, behold, the days come, says the Lord God, that it shall no more be said, The Lord God lives, that brought up the children of Israel out of the land of Egypt; But the Lord God lives, that brought up the children of Israel from the land of the north, and from all the lands whither he had driven them: and I will bring them again into their land that I gave unto their fathers.*

*And first I will recompense their iniquity and their sin <u>double</u>; because they have defiled my land, they have filled mine inheritance with the carcasses of their detestable and abominable things. For mine eyes are upon all their ways: they are not hid from my face, neither is their iniquity hid from mine eyes.*

*Behold, I will send for many fishers, says the Lord God, and they shall fish them; and after will I send for many hunters, and they shall hunt them from every mountain, and from every hill, and out of the holes of the rocks.*

*O Lord God, my strength, and my fortress, and my refuge in the day of affliction, the Gentiles shall come unto thee from the ends of the earth, and shall say, Surely, our fathers have inherited lies, vanity, and things wherein there is no profit. Shall a man make gods unto himself, and they are no gods?*

*Therefore, behold, I will this once cause them to know mine hand and my might; and they shall know that my name is The Lord God".*

The survivors of the Day of the Lord God's great vengeance against us sinful evil Israelites will finally come to their senses and realize that our creator rules the roost, and the quicker they learn this lesson, the better off they will be. We so-called highly educated and sophisticated peoples have a total shock waiting for us in the very near future, that will bring every one of us down to our knees, begging for forgiveness. Wake up, people! We have been led astray by our christian leaders, the disciples of the devil, the many anti-Messiahs, the wolves dressed up in sheep's clothing, devouring the minds/spirits of their followers with all their falsehood. For all one has to read to prove King David is God's Holy Messiah are <u>Jer. 30:9; Ezek. 34:23-24, 37:24-25;</u> and <u>Hosea 3:5</u> scriptures—which even use David's name. These scriptures are backed up via scriptures from the book of Psalms, where in the Psalms David wrote, he is using 1st person pronouns—such as <u>Ps. 2:7, 16:10, 30:3, 49:15,</u> and <u>118:17-18,</u> and definitely reinforced with <u>Psalms 18:43-50,</u> and in 2 Sam. 22:44-45, also in <u>Ps. 89:18-21, 26-27,</u> which is written by

Maschil of Ethan the Ezrahite, where he uses David's name, who shall cry unto God, *"Thou art my father, my God, and the rock of my salvation"*. Where in the New Testament they are stating Saul/Paul's pagan imaginary christ making these same sayings. And where Maschil has God saying, concerning David; *"Also I will make him my firstborn, higher than the kings of the earth"*. These statements again are used in the New Testament, particularly in <u>Rev. 1:5</u>. There can only be one firstborn from the dead, and only one king of kings. There is absolutely no place in the Old Testament that proves this Saul/Paul's pagan christ ever had any existence as a real person; but he is referred to in <u>Deut. 32:37-38,</u> *"And he* (God*) shall say, Where are their gods, their rock* (christians' pagan christ) *in whom they trusted, which did eat the fat of their sacrifices, and drank the wine of their drink offerings* (christians' communion)? *Let them rise up and help you, and be your protection"*.

The christians will be utterly shocked when they find out that they have been worshipping, praying to, and serving all their pagan so-called other gods; particularly their pagan imaginary christ. All the above-mentioned scriptures are written on the last page of chapter 7; read them again and prove the above.

Then God brings forth his greatness in <u>Deut. 32:39-40,</u> *"See now that I, even I, am he* (the only God of this universe), *and there is no god with me: I kill, and I make alive; I wound, and I heal: neither is there any that can deliver out of my hand. For I lift up my hand to heaven, and say, I live for ever"*.

Only a totally deceived individual will argue against these above scriptures to save face, particularly our christian leaders, the many wolves/anti-Messiahs amongst us, dressed up in sheep's clothing devouring our minds/spirits with all their falsehood; referred to in <u>1 John 2:18.</u>

After reading this book; the phrase, <u>"The truth will set you free"</u> will have a new meaning to you. For the truth will set you free from the clutches of the devil's firstborn cursed son, King Saul and his disciples, the many anti-Messiahs/wolves of the pagan christian religion. But only if you flee from this pagan christian religion and all other false beliefs, and return to God's ways, reported in the books of the Old Testament, the only way to receive God's salvation to an eternal life. God bless all those that read this book, and may the truth really set them free, to return back to you Lord God of Israel and all your good ways, instructed to us via the books of Moses and noted books of God's true servants.

Yours sincerely,<br>R.A. Mueller

# The Closing Prayer

*Lord God of Israel, I pray to you and thank you for giving me the courage and knowledge and skills to bring forth this writing with all your truths, even your secret truths that you have revealed to me. And may this writing be the catalyst that leads your people back to you and your ways, laid down for us via the books of your servant Moses and other notable prophets.*

*Now let it please thee, O Lord God Almighty to bless this work within this book, and let it have the power to penetrate the minds of your people Israel, and remove the veil covering from the face of your people Israel, and allow them to see the truth, and hopefully find the courage and strength to return to you and your ways, by praying on their knees with stretched out open arms toward you, Lord God only, and worship you, Lord God only, and serve you as our only God, as their one and only true living God, for there are no other gods with you or besides you. All other so-called gods are of total falsehood.*

*Even making graven, painted and standing images of these false gods is in vain, for this is breaking your second commandment, and the worshipping of these so-called other gods with their graven, painted, and standing images is the breaking of your very first commandment, and when they pray to you Lord God, and ask of you certain favours in the name of these so-called gods, they are breaking your third commandment, for they will be using your name in vain, and when they do not keep your holy Sabbath day, Friday sunset to Saturday sunset, and refrain from all their laborious activities, and all their pleasurable activities, they end up violating your first four commandments, and only you Lord God of Israel, know how they are violating the remainder of your 10 Commandments.*

*We deserve everything whatsoever you bring upon us, for we have completely violated all your good ways, of how we ought to live our lives. May this book cause your people to flee from this paganism babylonian christian religion, that has held them/us captive, ever since king Saul, disguised as Charlemagne, still with the evil spirit upon him, imposed this great false christian religion of his upon our ancestors, the Saxons, which is a short or slang word for Isaac's sons of the House of Israel, with his pagan imaginary christ of himself, and with all their glorified pagan events, loaded with their own gifts and goodies, all being the snares that held us fast, from seeing the truth, and being corrupted with all their pagan so-called other* gods. Even worshipping the devil himself, by participating in the helloween, of which he is the so-called god of.

Hopefully, O Lord God, this book that you have allowed me to bring forth, will be the catalyst to set them free from not only this pagan christian religion, but also from all other false ways that they have been held captive too.

And now, O Lord God Almighty, I thank you again for giving me all this great knowledge, and the understanding of this great knowledge that is written within this book. Grant unto me Lord God all the skills that I will require to accomplish this task of bringing it to your people, the children of Jacob/Israel. Amen.

*Your servant*
*R.A. Mueller*

# Important Calculations Determining Past and Future Events

All the history material mentions is of an assembly was held in an early summer month in year 772, to begin imposing Charlemagne/King Saul's pagan christian religion upon the Saxons. When this attack happened on their place of worship, history doesn't mention a word. This action is important because it brings alive <u>Daniel's 12:7 and 11</u> scriptures. Prior to this I was basically using my most likely scenario dates and as you are aware of turned up false.

However, this last time I decided to go all the way back to the first day of creation, through to the 12th day/age and converting the year 2046 to match the end of the 12th age. Each age or God's day in this world is 1,000 biblical years in duration, as <u>Peter 3:8</u> states, *"But, beloved, be not ignorant of this one thing, that one day is with the Lord God as a thousand years, and a thousand years as one day".*

Therefore, one age = 1000 * 360/365.25 = 985.62628 Gregorian years. <u>12,000 biblical years</u> = 12000 * 360/365.25 = <u>11827.65 Gregorian years,</u> or end of our civilization. Therefore, <u>2046.2358</u> corresponding to end of 12th age with almost the same remainder. This is the number we will use with our calculations.

Therefore, <u>beginning with the end-time 30 biblical years or 29.56879 Gregorian years world war III</u> will begin 2046.2358 - 29.5688 = <u>2016.667 or Aug. 24th</u> against the revised Roman Empire and their allies, hidden today within the EURO conglomerate of nations.

<u>King Saul as the last pope will be crowned</u> 3.5 biblical years or 3.45 Gregorian years before the end-time war begins at 2016.667 - 3.45 = <u>2013.217 or Mar. 20th</u> He is also the false prophet in <u>Rev. 19:20</u> with miraculous powers. He, King Saul/Charles, imposed his christian pagan religion upon our Saxon ancestors, a religion he began building in the New Testament times as Saul called Paul.

<u>Charlemagne attacked the Saxons' place of worship</u>. In <u>Oct. 10th in year 774</u> from sunset of previous day. Please be aware that a day begins at sundown of the previous day. Who could have guessed that this attack happened in an early winter month. Therefore, it sometimes doesn't pay to follow too closely to historical material. Charlemagne must have travelled in the fall months to get all the way to the British Isles, where this place of worship was located, and is known today as the Stonehenge ruins. Why this site was the Saxons' place of worship speaks volumes with the east entrance lining up with the summer solstice sunrise, indicating the importance of this entrance, and it's mentioned in <u>Ezekiel 44:1-3</u> that only God and the Prince/King of the people used this entrance, and where the King/Prince ate his meal. With the west entrance lining up with the winter solstice sun setting makes this entrance of secondary importance, and it was used by the Levi priestly tribe to prepare and bring in the sacrificial parts of the animal to place upon the Altar of God, and to prepare and cook the meat that wasn't sacrificed on the altar but for the worshippers to eat. Outside this west entrance at some distance was the hanging tree where the animals were killed, skinned, and extracted the sacrificial parts to place upon the altar, and the rest of the meat for the cooking pots to feed the worshippers. According to our erroneous history books, this tree was used to sacrifice humans. This is absolutely false, for this is another historian shooting off at the mouth without knowing the real truth. According to the Old Testament, there was absolutely no human sacrifices performed by the Israelites. These Saxons, which is a short version of <u>Isaac's sons</u> (or sons of Isaac) of the House of Israel were Israelites, Anglo-Saxons means <u>English-speaking sons of Isaac</u>, who as we know are the British people, the designated 1st born birthright recipient of Jacob's blessings, that Reuben, the French people, lost, because he sexually assaulted Jacob's mistress, reason why the French despise being under the thumb of the British. The word <u>British</u> is a Hebrew word meaning <u>covenant people</u>. One must also keep in mind that Ezekiel was a prophet of the House of Israel and taken there by the locks of his hair by God himself.

However, in the year 774.778 Oct. 10 from sunset of the previous day, Charlemagne completed his atrocities by placing an image of the christians' pagan christ, which was an image of himself, upon their Altar of God, making this altar desolate. He proceeded to force the worshippers to worship his pagan image, killing any who refused. After these atrocities, he proceeded to destroy this place of worship, bringing an end to any future sacrifices. This is when <u>Daniel's 12:7 and 11</u> countdown began of the 1271.4579 Gregorian years or 1,290 biblical years, consisting of the 30-biblical-year war against Charlemagne imposing his christian religion upon these Saxons, being included within the 1,260 biblical years each of our ancestor's children will be within his hands, and the 30 biblical years it will take God to fully reclaim his people back with the coming 30 b. yr. end-time world war beginning Aug. 31st. The 1st ones this christian religion was imposed upon will be the 1st ones to be reclaimed, and the last ones this christian religion was imposed upon will be the last ones to be reclaimed. Everyone will be within this christian religious hand no longer than 1,260 biblical years. This is why Daniel's 12:11 scripture states the number of years as 1,290 biblical years. Taking God 30 biblical years to reclaim us.

Just as Daniel's 7:25 states, *"They* (the remnant of the House of Israel [Rev. 12:13-17]) *shall be given into his hands for 1260 biblical years"*. Daniel's 7:25 and 12:7 & 11 states, *"That it shall be for a time, times, and a half* (1,260 biblical years). *And when he shall have accomplished to scatter the power of the Holy people* (30-biblical-year war) *all these things shall be finished"* (end of our civilization). This last part of the scripture is referring to the coming 30-biblical-year world war III against the resurrected Roman Empire. This war will begin in 2046.2358 - 29.5688 = 2016.667 on Aug. 31st counting from sunset of previous day, Jerusalem time zone. Therefore, no matter how far-fetched this may sound to you, wait it out and see what happens. This I hope will correct previous predictions, even though I had the wrong years but most months, days, and times. I should have relied on the creation days and biblical information only, rather than historical data as much as I did.

At the beginning of Jan. 6-8, in year 2011, Jessica (my niece) and I were talking about my parents' last names. I told her the name Mueller is really a slave name, meaning grinder of grain via the German language. My male Israelite ancestor when defeated in the years 734-721 b. cue. and the survivors were taken into a German-controlled area and put to work grinding grain and was called Mueller. I told her I tried but failed to connect my mother's maiden name Degelman to any type of work. She immediately got on the computer and found out that it was a Hebrew name meaning flagman. I immediately stated that the only Israelites that carried the flag was of the Levi priestly family. All of a sudden I understood why my family members were so screwed up via the name changes, the vegetarian eating, and only God know what other silly beliefs they were trapped within. Without knowing it, they were searching for the truth, for the Bible tells us to receive his words via the lips of the priestly Levis. All God's prophets, to my knowledge, were of the priestly family. I remember at the beginning of the studying of the Bible I came across the following scripture.

Proverbs 1:20-33, *"Wisdom cries outside; she utters her voice in the streets: She cries in the chief place of concourse* (business), *in the openings of the gates: in the city she utters her words, saying, How long, ye simple ones, will ye love simplicity? And the scorners delight in their scorning, and fools hate knowledge?*

*Turn you at my reproof: behold, I will pour out my spirit unto you, I will make known my words unto you.*

Because I called, and ye refused; I have stretched out my hand, and no man regarded;

But ye have set at naught all my counsel, and would none of my reproof:

I also will laugh at your calamity; I will mock when your fear comes;

When your fear comes as desolation, and your destruction comes as a whirlwind; when distress and anguish comes upon you. Then shall they call upon me, but I will not answer; they shall seek me early, but they shall not find me: For that they hated knowledge, and did not choose the fear of the Lord God:

They would none of my counsel: they despised all my reproof.

Therefore shall they eat of the fruit of their own way, and be filled with their own devices.

For the turning away of the simple shall slay them, and the prosperity of fools shall destroy them.

But whoso hearkens unto me shall dwell safely, and shall be quiet from fear of evil".

When I truly began studying the Bible, I was literally given a lot of the knowledge because I began <u>proving</u> scriptures against other like scriptures, and before I realized it I was getting a clear picture of what the Bible was really telling me (just as the above <u>underlined</u> scripture indicates), *"Turn you at my reproves: behold, I will pour out my spirit unto you, I will make known my words unto you"*. I not only found out that the christian religion was the most paganism religion this world has ever witnessed but I can also prove it by using scriptures, as you will find this out as you read this book.

This christian religion was given to us, via God's permission, by King Saul/Saul called Paul/Charlemagne, and that the christians' christ is nothing more than <u>an imaginary figure</u> of this same King Saul/<u>next and last pope</u> of this pagan christian religion that he is in fact the master builder of, as stated in <u>1 Cor. 3:10-11</u> scriptures, in the New Testament times when he was called Paul. This pagan religion is described in <u>Ezekiel 20:24-26</u> scripture, which was given to us not <u>for our good</u> but <u>for a punishment</u> that will bring us to total desolation, just as this above quoted set of scriptures indicate. This is the reason for all the corruption throughout our nations, with the crime rate soaring out of control because our judgements are so out of wrack, and us taxpayers are the ones paying for the prisoners' room and board, guarding, even paying the prisoners for the work they do within the jail, a mess they themselves have made, along with their dental, medical, psychiatric sessions, and the list goes on and on. This is the main reason our taxes are so high, instead of making the criminals and/or their immediate family members pay this huge bill, they lay it on the backs of the gullible taxpayers who never committed any crimes.

Making the criminal and/or the immediate family members responsible for this huge bill will definitely encourage them to police this out-of-control member; otherwise they will be facing a potential future huge bill. All heinous crime committees should be put to death at the hands of the victim, if still alive, and at the hands of the victim's family members and close friends, on an open on stage setting, surrounded by a high heavy wire mesh fencing, where the victims, if still alive, and their loved ones can stone, kick, punch, club, and even hang this criminal without putting a hood over the criminal's head so not to hide this ugly putdown from the public witnessing this execution, even show it on the TV sets so as to reach even a larger audience. Doing it this way turns this criminal's <u>ugly crime</u> into a <u>huge positive</u> by putting the <u>fear factor</u> into, and particularly, the criminally minded individuals and naturally the rest of the people. This is the <u>scare them straight method,</u> that even God used when he told Moses to take the Sabbath breaker, who was gathering firewood for his fireplace, a chore that should have been done on a weekly workday. God told Moses to take him outside the camp and have the whole congregation stone him to death. He also used this <u>scare them straight method</u> on one Reuben tribal leader and one leader from the tribe of Levi, who challenged Moses and Aaron for the leadership role. After Moses told God about this challenge, the following day God made a deliberate approach and confronted these 2 leaders in front of the whole congregation. As a result, God opened the earth under the area these 2 leaders resided and they, their wives, their children, and all their belongings were swallowed up alive by the earth. This is reported in Numbers 16th chapter. This definitely put the <u>fear factor</u> into anyone else thinking to challenge Moses and Aaron for the leadership role. This is what's wrong with our civilization today. When the criminal goes to jail, they get free room and board and all other amenities, and after serving their allotted time are released free of any charges. The innocent taxpayers are made to pay for someone's out-of-control member's mistake, even their outrageous lawyer's expenses and the expenses paid to the court system via the government tax handouts, etc. There is absolutely no end to the total expenses wasted, and our gullible taxpayers don't even realize how bad they are being shafted via our whole justice system.

<u>Ezekiel 20:24-26</u> states, *"Because they have not executed My Judgments, but have despised My Statutes, and had polluted My Sabbaths, and their eyes were after their fathers' idols* (such as we today with all the christians' graven, painted, standing/hanging images of their pagan christ, saints, virgin mother, etc.).

*Wherefore I gave them <u>also</u> statutes that were <u>not good</u>* (all the christians' so-called holy events), *and judgments whereby they should <u>not live</u>* (via within our inept justice systems).

*And I polluted them in their own gifts* (via the christian religious events such as christmas, easter, saint day events, even the helloween gifts and goodies), *in that they caused to pass through the fire all that opens the womb* (via the aborted 1st born of our very young girls being burnt within our incinerators) *that I might make them desolate, to the end that they might <u>know</u>* (come to realize) *that I am the Lord God* (bringing this desolation upon us)".

Notice the underlined word (also), telling us that God gave to us at the beginning all the good ways to live our lives, but our ancestors strayed away from these good ways, and God punished them for their disobedience. They did return to the good ways, but in time they again and again went astray. Finally God got fed up with their continuous evil ways and finally in the days of Ezekiel, God <u>also</u> gave to us, of the House of Israel, what we have today via the hands of Charlemagne/Saul called Paul/King Saul/the devil's 1st born son/false prophet with miraculous powers reported in <u>Rev. 19:20</u>, in the years 774-804, <u>not for our good but for our punishment</u>, which is bringing us to total desolation, culminating into this last 30-biblical-year world war. The 1/3 of the Israelites to survive this end-time 30-biblical-year world war against our arch-enemies. The so-called Holy Roman Empire, God's sword, hidden today within the European Union conglomerate of nations, of which 6 of these nations are of the tribes of the House of Israel, such as France, Belgium, Netherlands, Finland, Ireland, and God forbid our mother country England. The survivors of this end-time war will enter into Daniel's extra 45 biblical years of nothingness and the 1/10th survivors will be the few blessed ones who will be gathered up by God's true Holy Messiah King David with his faithful soldiers mentioned in the 23rd chapter of 2 Samuel.

I wanted to give you the last calculations that replace the previous erroneous false predictions, to set everything into proper perspective. Hope you can understand my calculations.

Author:                                                                                              *R.A. Mueller*

# Note Page

All noted dates and times are of the Jerusalem time zone. Therefore, each area must convert dates and times according to their areas. <u>Example:</u> This book states that the place of worship at the Stonehenge site was attacked 774.778, Oct. 10th @ 9:36 from sunset of previous day, Jerusalem time zone. But after subtracting the approximate time difference of 2:15 hours from given time, really was 14 hours and approximately 13 minutes, London time zone. Naturally from sunset of previous day. For a biblical day ends and begins at sunset.

Also all scriptures using the word <u>antichrist</u> should by rights be anti-Messiah, for the Hebrew word converted to English would be referring to King David as God's Holy Messiah, definitely not Paul's pagan imaginary christ, a word interpreted from a Greek word into English. But also the christians' pagan christ is really an imaginary figure of none other than King Saul, Saul called Paul, Charlemagne, the next and last pope of the christian religion due to arrive March 20th, 2013, according to my calculations. He will also be the false prophet with miraculous powers mentioned in <u>Rev. 19:20,</u> the devil's 1st born son. In this sense therefore, it is good to be an antichrist, for you would be against Paul's pagan christ of himself, who is trying to override God's Holy Messiah, King David. Paul's disciples are anti-Messiahs/wolves dressed up in sheep's clothing, devouring all who come in contact with them, and are all those preaching the gospel of Paul's pagan christ, which is in the many christian religions, and is definitely not God's ways.

I found it very difficult to pick the right year our civilization was slated to end with the information I was able to find. With the use of <u>Daniel's 8:14</u> when the original temple was made desolate by Antiochus Epiphanes on the 15th of the 9th month in year 166 b. cue. or -166.707 and -166.734 year and this temple and altar are slated to be rebuilt and cleansed and sacrifices to be carried forth 2,300 biblical days/years in the future. 2300 * 360/365.25 = 2266.9404 Gregorian years - (-166.266) = <u>2100.6744 cue.</u> From this you can take <u>Daniel's 12:12</u> scripture of 1335 b. yrs. off, or <u>1315.811</u> Gregorian yrs. = <u>9.747 cue.</u> Charlemagne began imposing the pagan christian religion upon our ancestors, the Saxons, in the years 774-804, when he destroyed their place of worship, known today as the Stonehenge ruins, in the year 774.778, when Charlemagne made their place of worship desolate and brought their sacrificial activities to an end, and bringing Daniel's 12:11 scripture alive of the 1290 b. years or 1271.4579 Gregorian years, when God will bring us back with a 30-biblical-year war against this same so-called Holy Roman Empire, matching the same 30 biblical years it took Charles to fully impose his pagan christian religion upon our ancestors, the Saxons. This war will begin in 2016 in the month and time of Aug. 31st from sunset of previous day. This allows 9.747 Gregorian years for the survivors to be gathered up and led back to the promised land and to rebuild the temple in Jerusalem and resume the sacrifices as Daniel's 8:14 states. It will take the remnant 2,300 days or 6.297 Greg. years to rebuild the temple and have the sacrificial offerings to the Lord our God continue. This leaves only 9.747 - 6.297 = 3.45 years for King David and his men to gather up this remnant and lead them back to the promised land after Daniel's total desolation time of 30 + 45 biblical years expires.

Auther:                                                                                                                          R.A. Mueller

# Gregorian Calendar Schedule

| Calendar year/ by # of yrs in leap year = | # of leap yrs from year 0 * # of days in leap year group (1461) = | # days from day 0 / by # of days per week = # of total weeks from wk. 0 = | Combine days remaining in 1st and/or last weeks = |
|---|---|---|---|
| ↓ | ↓ | ↓ | ↓ |
| Yr. 68/4 = 17 | * 1461 = 24837 | /by 7 days = 3548.1428 | 1 day left over |
| Yr. 72/4 = 18 | * 1461 = 26298 | /by 7 days = 3756.8571 | 6 days |
| Yr. 76/4 = 19 | * 1461 = 27759 | /by 7 days = 3965.5714 | 4 days |
| Yr. -908/4 = 227 | * 1461 = 331647 | /by 7 days = 47378.142 | 1 day left over |
| Yr. -912/4 = 228 | * 1461 = 333108 | /by 7 days = 47586.857 | 6 days |
| Yr. -916/4 = 229 | * 1461 = 334569 | /by 7 days = 47795.571 | 4 days |

In the year 911 b. cue., King Jeroboam unveiled the two golden calves for the House of Israel to worship. By checking with table below, this year corresponds with our G. years of 1975 and 2003.

| | | | |
|---|---|---|---|
| Yr. 768/4 = 192 | * 1461 = 280512 | /by 7 days = 40073.142 | 1 day left over |
| Yr. 772/4 = 193 | * 1461 = 281973 | /by 7 days = 40281.857 | 6 days |
| Yr. 776/4 = 194 | * 1461 = 283434 | /by 7 days = 40490.571 | 4 days |

In the year 774 cue., in a winter month, Charlemagne attacked the Saxons' place of worship and imposed his christian religion upon them, setting up an image of the christians' pagan christ upon their Altar of God, making this altar desolate. He thereafter destroyed their place of worship, bringing an end to their daily morning and evening sacrifices. These two actions brought <u>Dan. 12:7, 11, and 12</u> scriptures alive. By checking with the table below, this year corresponds with our Gregorian calendar years of 1978 and 2006.

| | | | |
|---|---|---|---|
| Yr. 1952/4 = 488 | * 1461 = 712968 | /by 7 days = 101852.571 | 4 days left over |
| Yr. 1956/4 = 489 | * 1461 = 714429 | /by 7 days = 102061.285 | 2 days |
| Yr. 1960/4 = 490 | * 1461 = 715890 | /by 7 days = 102270.000 | 0 days |
| Yr. 1964/4 = 491 | * 1461 = 717351 | /by 7 days = 102478.714 | 5 days |
| Yr. 1968/4 = 492 | * 1461 = 718812 | /by 7 days = 102687.428 | 3 days |
| Yr. 1972/4 = 493 | * 1461 = 720273 | /by 7 days = 102876.142 | 1 day |
| Yr. 1976/4 = 494 | * 1461 = 721734 | /by 7 days = 103104.857 | 6 days |
| Yr. 1980/4 = 495 | * 1461 = 723195 | /by 7 days = 103313.571 | 4 days |
| Yr. 1984/4 = 496 | * 1461 = 724656 | /by 7 days = 103522.285 | 2 days |
| Yr. 1988/4 = 497 | * 1461 = 726117 | /by 7 days = 103731.000 | 0 days |
| Yr. 1992/4 = 498 | * 1461 = 727578 | /by 7 days = 103939.714 | 5 days |
| Yr. 1996/4 = 499 | * 1461 = 729039 | /by 7 days = 104148.428 | 3 days |
| Yr. 2000/4 = 500 | * 1461 = 730500 | /by 7 days = 104357.142 | 1 day |
| Yr. 2004/4 = 501 | * 1461 = 731961 | /by 7 days = 104565.857 | 6 days |
| Yr. 2008/4 = 502 | * 1461 = 733422 | /by 7 days = 104774.571 | 4 days |
| Yr. 2012/4 = 503 | * 1461 = 734883 | /by 7 days = 104983.285 | 2 days |
| Yr. 2016/4 = 504 | * 1461 = 736344 | /by 7 days = 105192.000 | 0 days |

Please note that our Gregorian calendar has a 4 years * 7 = 28 year duration and repeatsaccordingly.

Auther: *R.A. Mueller*

# Calculating Ages of This World from the End to the Beginning

|  |  |  |
|---|---|---|
| 2046.2358 cue. | End of 12th age or division | Mar. 27 @ 01:37 |
| + -985.62628 | Duration of each age via Gregorian calendar. |  |
| 1060.6096 | Beginning of 12th age, end of 11th age. | July 10 @ 02:44 |
| + -985.62628 | Christian leaders present signed document to military leader to pick own pope. |  |
| 74.9834 cue. | Beginning of 11th age, end of 10th age. | Dec. 24 @ 22:35 |
| + -985.62628 | Temple completely destroyed and end of the war against Roman forces. |  |
| -910.64288 b. cue. | Beginning of 10th age, end of 9th age. | July 22 @ 15:38 |
| + -985.62628 |  |  |
| -1896.2691 b. cue. | Beginning of 9th age, end of 8th age. | Apr. 07 @ 11:46 |
| + -985.62628 | Jacob's hand represents opening of 9th age; Esau's heal closing of 8th age. |  |
| -2881.8953 b. cue. | Beginning of 8th age, end of 7th age. | Nov. 22 @ 18:50 |
| + -985.62628 | God walks with Enoch and taken up to heaven. |  |
| -3867.5215 b. cue. | Beginning of 7th age, end of 6th age. | July 09 @ 08:20 |
| + -985.62628 | Adam and Eve expelled from Garden of Eden. |  |
| -4853.1477 b. cue. | Beginning of 6th age, end of 5th age. | Feb. 22 @ 21:51 |
| + -985.62628 |  |  |
| -5838.7739 b. cue. | Beginning of 5th age, end of 4th age. | Oct. 09 @ 11:22 |
| + -985.62628 |  |  |
| -6824.4001 b. cue. | Beginning of 4th age, end of 3rd age. | May 25 @ 10:29 |
| + -985.62628 |  |  |

| | | |
|---|---|---|
| -7810.0263 b. cue. | Beginning of 3rd age, end of 2nd age. | Jan. 09 @ 14:23 |
| + -985.62628 | | |
| -8795.6525 b. cue. | Beginning of 2nd age, end of 1st age. | Aug. 26 @ 03:54 |
| + -985.62628 | | |
| -9781.2787 b. cue. | Beginning of creation, first age 9782. | Apr. 11 @ 17:25 |

By adding the last and first totals which is of the Gregorian calendar -9781.2787 + 2046.2358 = 11827.515 Gregorian years, and converting them to God's biblical calendar, we arrive at 11827.515 * 365.25/360 = 12000 biblical years where each age is 1,000 biblical years in duration, as stated in 2 Esdras 14:10-14. Proving that the Lord our God has an unbending plan in motion of our current civilization, which is due to begin to expire in the year 2016.667, Aug. 31$^{th}$ with a 30-biblical-year world war against our arch-enemies, the so-called Holy Roman Empire and their allies. The present time in history we have 6 Israelite countries as members of this European Union, such as France, Belgium, and the Netherlands. I guess they haven't learned their lesson in the 2nd world war when they became easy prey by fraternizing with these countries of the Roman Empire, and if that isn't bad enough, we now have another 3 of our nations involved, such as Finland, Ireland, and, God forbid, even our mother country England. What in the world are these nations think they are gaining fraternizing with our arch-enemies? Thank God we have the United States of America next door to us, here in Canada. All I can say is, God help us Israelites when all hell breaks forth on Aug. 31st, in year 2016, and will continue on until Mar. 27st of 2046 cue., bringing an end to the 12th age of this world's civilization, where only 1/3rd of all us Israelites will survive and must try to stay alive for Daniel's extra 45 biblical years, before we are gathered up together and led back to the promised land. God help us all because of the ignorance of our leaders. I believe all related times are from the Jerusalem time zone, because all Daniel's scriptures came alive when Charlemagne attacked the Saxons' place of worship, known today as the Stonehenge ruins, located in England, in year 774.778, bringing Daniel's 12:7 and 11 scriptures alive. All the pagan Christian religious leaders and religious scholars are completely ignorant of this happening. They are still waiting for Daniel's 12:11 scripture to happen in some future date, which has already happen in Oct. 10th of year 774 cue.

Author:                                                                                               R.A. Mueller

## _Schedule of our future events to the closing of our time spent within King Saul's control._

You will find many scriptures with the word day behind a given number, such as in the book of Daniel 8:14, where it states the temple that Antiochus IV Epiphanes destroyed in Jerusalem in the year -166.707 to.734 will not be rebuilt until <u>2,300 days</u> expires. However, the Hebrew calendar to this date was 9 weeks behind time, and I had to compensate. This by rights should read biblical years/days. Meaning that this temple will be completely rebuilt in 2300 * 360 divided by 365.25 = 2266.9404 Greg. years, after it was made desolate and destroyed in year (-166.734). Therefore, in our calendar year 2266.9404 - (-166.266) = 2100.6744 Greg. calendar years, this temple will be completely rebuilt and sacrifices resumed, which is 246.156 days within the year 2100, or Sept. 3rd @ 3:45 after sundown of previous day. Please note that this is the last year of our current century. With the use of the word <u>day</u> following the 2,300 means it will take the survivors, after they are led back to the promised land, 2,300 days or 6.297 Greg. years to rebuild this temple. What is supposed to occur before the construction begins is an allotted time to <u>gather up the survivors</u> and lead them back to the promised land, Daniel's <u>45 biblical years</u> of nothingness, plus the <u>30 biblical years</u> of God's reclaiming time of us Israelites, against the so-called Holy Roman Empire armies, as it was in the 1st and 2nd world wars. These two periods add up to 75 biblical years or 73.92 Greg. years. Before this reclaiming war begins, King Saul as the last Christian pope makes his appearance and rules for 3.5 biblical years or <u>3.45 Greg. years</u>. Therefore, by subtracting the war and time of total desolation from 2100.317 - 73.92 = <u>2026.397</u>. Subtract the pope's reign of 3.45 G. years = <u>2022.947,</u> then subtract <u>6.297 G. yrs,</u> which is the 2,300 days of time allotted for the survivors to rebuild the temple, equals year <u>2016.65</u>, then subtract 3.45 which is the year we will be directly into King Saul's hand = 2013.20028 for 3.45 Gregorian years. However, Hebrew calendar was 9 full weeks behind at this particular time.

## _List of occurring past and future events in an orderly setting:_

Temple desolated via Antiochus 15th and 25th of 9th month of year 166 or -166.707 and (.734 G. yr.)

- Temple to remain desolated until 2300 b. years expires or 2266.9404 Greg. years

- Time remaining after destruction (-166.266) Greg. years = 2094.0388 Greg. years
- David and remnant rebuild temple in 6.297 Greg. years = 2094.3774 Greg. years
- David and soldiers gather remnant in 3.45 Greg years = 2090.5888 Greg. years
- Total desolate time period of 45 b. yrs or 44.353 Greg. years = 2046.2358 Greg. years
- Total reclaiming time period (WW III). 29.568788 Greg. years = 2016.667 Greg. years
- King Saul arrives for last 3.5 b. years or 3.44969 Greg. years = 2013.217Greg. years

Therefore, David will have 3.45 Greg. years to gather up all the remnant and lead them back to the land of Israel to take full advantage of the allotted time of 6.297 Gregorian years to rebuild, cleanse, and sanctify the temple and perform sacrifices to the Lord our great God Almighty. All this must be accomplished within the 1st year of the next century of year 2100.6744 on Sept. 3rd @ 3:45. Note that we will be directly within King Saul's hand when he becomes the next and last pope of the christian religion on March 20th from sundown of previous day, for the next 3.45 G. years in year 2013 Gregorian year, matching the same time it will take King David and his faithful soldiers mentioned in the second book of Samuel chapter 23 to find and gather up the remnant and lead them back to the land of Israel. King Saul shall return as christians' last pope March 20th from sunset of previous day, Jerusalem time, via biblical days which starts and ends at sundown.

Author:                                                              R.A. Mueller

## *Let's follow the proper way of the Lord our God*

The first step we must take is to observe the Sabbath day on the proper 7th day of the week, the same day the Jewish nation keep which is Saturday, from sunset Friday to sunset Saturday. The next and very important step is to prove all statements and procedures with the Old Testament scriptures, such as indicated below.

*Psalms 89:19-20 and 27:* "I have exalted one chosen out of the people. I have found *David* my servant; with my holy oil have I anointed him . . . Also I will make him my firstborn, higher than the kings of the earth". These scriptures proves Rev. 1:5 wrong; there can only be one first born and one king of kings. Paul's christ is nothing more than an imaginary figure of himself and proven within <u>Daniel's 11:31-45.</u> In verse 31 is where he and his French and German force attacked the <u>Saxons'</u> (short form for <u>Isaac's sons</u> of the House of Israel) place of worship (known today as the Stonehenge ruins) and placed upon their Altar of God an image of his christian christ, which was an image of himself as indicated in <u>vrs. 36-39</u>, which states, "*He shall exalt himself, and magnify himself above every god, and shall speak marvellous things against the God of gods*". <u>Vrs. 37</u> states, "*He shall magnify himself above all*". V<u>rs. 38-39</u> states, "*But in his estate shall he honour the God of forces: and a god whom his fathers knew not shall he honour with gold, silver, and with precious stone, and pleasant things. Thus shall he do in the most strong holds with a strange god, whom he shall acknowledge and increase with glory.*" This is definitely referring to his pagan christ of himself, who decimated their place of worship in 774.778 on Oct. 10th @ 23:17, and he continued imposing the pagan christian religion upon them thereafter onward to year 804.3468, and we will continue being within his hands for a total of 1,260 biblical years or 1241.8891 of our Gregorian years, or until 1241.8891 + 774.778 = <u>2016.667</u> of Aug. 31th from sunset of previous day, when God will begin to win us back with a 30-biblical-year world war against the so-called Holy Roman Empire nations, as it was in the 1st and 2nd world wars, matching the same amount of time it took Charlemagne/King Saul to impose his pagan christian religion upon our ancestors. In <u>Dan. 7:25</u> God stated that he will put us (*the remnant of Zion's seed who were keeping God's commandments and his Testimonies*) mentioned in <u>Rev. 12:17</u> into his hands for 1,260 biblical years. Dan. 7:20 is describing King Saul's bigness, and in verse 25 he has a mouth to match, speaking great arrogant bragging words against the most High and wears out the saints of the Most High God.

But before this world war begins, King Saul, the christians' pagan imaginary christ, must make his appearance as the last pope of the pagan christian religion for 3.5 b. years or in G. years 3.5 * 360/365.25 = 3.45 - 2016.65 = <u>2013.2 or Mar. 20th</u> from sunset of previous day, Jerusalem time. In other words King Saul can show up anytime within days of this 2013 year, as the christians' next pope and claim to be the christians' pagan christ, a religion he built as stated in <u>1 Corinthians 3:10-11</u>: "*According to the grace of God which is given unto me, as a wise masterbuilder, I have laid the foundation, and another builds thereon. But let every man take heed how he builds thereupon. For other foundation can no man lay than that is laid, which is* (of his pagan) *Jesus Christ*".

When this date of March 20th comes forth you will than know that I have been allowed to find this knowledge by none other than God himself. For God in <u>Proverbs 1:23</u> states, "*Turn you at my reproof; Behold, I will pour out my spirit unto you, I will make known my words unto you"*. Then God continues on warning the disbelievers for the next 9 verses and comes to vrs. 33 and states, *"But whoso hearkens unto me shall dwell safely, and shall be quiet from fear of evil"*.

    I can also prove the above calculations from when the original temple was made desolate by Antiochus IV in the year -166.734, and Dan. 8:14 states that this temple and site will be trodden under foot by the Gentile and heathens unto 2,300 days; then shall the sanctuary be cleansed. This 2,300 also meant biblical years where each day represents a biblical year, the word day is used because it will take King David and the recovered remnant 2300 days/365.25 = 6.297 years to completely rebuild this temple. Therefore, this temple will be completely rebuilt in year 2300 * 360/365.25 = 2266.9404 Gregorian years. Therefore, subtract -166.266 = 2100.6744 - 6.297 years to rebuild, = 2094.02 - 3.45 years to gather remnant = 2090.57—Daniel's extra 45 b. years or 44.353 Greg. years = 2046.22 - 30 b. or 29.5688 Greg. years of reclaiming war = 2016.65—King Saul's direct control of 3.45 years = 2013.2 before God begins to reclaim us back from his hand.

Temple to be built and rededicated 2300 * 360/365.25 = 2266.9404 Greg. years.
Subtract Remaining time left of b.c.e.-166.266 years = 2100.6744 Greg. years
Rebuild temple in 2,300 days or 6.297 Greg. years = 2094.3774 Greg. years
David gathering remnant 3.45 Greg. years = 2090.9274 Greg. years
Desolation time of 45 b. yrs. 44.353 Greg. years = 2046.5744 Greg. years
Reclaiming 30 b. year war 29.5688 Greg. years = 2016.0056 Greg. years
Direct control under Saul 3.45 Greg. years = 2013.2 Greg. years

2013.2 = March 20th from sunset of previous day, Saul/Paul the devil's 1st born son shows up and crowned as the christians' last pope of the christian religion he built.

    Other notable scriptures to check out such is Psalms 16:4, where David is condemning the communion ritual when he states, *"Their sorrows shall be multiplied that hasten after another god* (such as the christians' christ and all their pagan saints, virgin mother, even God's Holy Messiah, King David, for they are only human beings, etc.); *their drink offerings of blood will I not offer, nor take up their names into my lips"*.

    Also Psalms 16:10, where David is speaking to God and saying, *"For thou* (God) *will not leave my soul in hell; neither will thou suffer thine Holy One* (David) *to see corruption* (of the grave)".

    This above scripture Paul misuses in Acts 13:35 where he has God speaking to Paul's pagan christ, and in effect giving his christ power over whether God would see the corrupting powers of the grave.

In Acts 13:33 Paul/Saul is using Psalms 2 which states, *"Thou art my Son, this day have I begotten thee"*. The problem we have here is that God is only speaking to David.

In Acts 13:34, Paul says after he states God has raised his christ from the dead, now no more to return to corruption. *"He (God) said on this wise, I will give you the sure mercies of David"*. This scripture Paul uses comes from Isa. 55:3 and states, *"Incline your ears, and come unto me: hear, and your soul shall live; and I will make an everlasting covenant with you, even the sure mercies of David"*. There is absolutely no way Paul can use this scripture to legitimize his christ, with a scripture that refers to you, me, or whoever submits their life to the ways of the Lord God.

In Acts 13:35 Paul has God speaking to his christ, stating, *"Thou shall not suffer thine Holy One to see corruption* (of the grave)*"*. In doing so giving Paul's pagan christ power over God, where God the Holy One is subject to the corrupting powers of the grave. This Psalm is taken from 16:10, where it is David speaking to God, giving the power to God whether David would see the corrupting powers of the grave. Paul also states David died in Acts 13:36; Psalms 118:17-18 proves otherwise.

1 John 3:18 is stating, *"That anti-christ/Messiah shall come, even now there are many anti/Messiahs; wherefore we know it is the last time"*. John in the times of the New Testament, that Paul brought forth with his christian religion, can also be used in our days of today, and all the anti-Messiahs are all the preachers preaching the ways of this pagan christian religion, and will find this out when God begins to reclaim us back with a 30-biblical-year world war against our arch-enemies, the so-called Holy Roman Empire with their allies, beginning in year 2016.667 and ending 2046.2358, matching the same time table it took Charlemagne/King Saul to fully impose this christian religion upon our ancestors. The first ones of our ancestors who had the christian religion imposed upon them, we their modern children will be the first to be reclaimed. The last ones this christian religion was imposed upon them, we their offspring will be the last ones to be reclaimed. No one will be within the christian religious hand for more than the 1,260 biblical years. So wake up you modern day Israelites and count your blessings, and don't throw away a beautiful future.

Author:                                                                R.A. Mueller

## *Important scriptures to understand*

*Rev. 1:5* states Christians' Christ 1st born from the dead and who will be King of kings.

*Psalms 89:20 and 27* disproves *Rev. 1:5*. Psalms 89 states in *verse 19*, "I have exalted one chosen out of the people". *Verse 20 God states*, "I have found *David* my servant; with my holy oil have I anointed *him* (David)". God states in verse 27, "I will make *him* (David) my 1st born, higher than the kings of the earth". *In verse 28 God states*, "My mercy will I keep for *him* (David) for evermore, and my covenant shall stand fast with *him* (David)".

*James 2:20* calls Paul a *vain man* when he states that faith without works is dead.

*1 Peter 16-17:* "Yet if any man suffer as a *Christian* (will suffer), let him not be ashamed; but let him glorify God on this behalf. For the time is come that Judgment must begin at us, what shall the end be of *them* (the Christians) that obey not the gospel of God (but the gospel of their pagan christ)".

*Acts 13:33-37* proves Paul is a liar and deceiver by misquoting/misusing *Ps. 2, Ps. 16:10, Isa. 3.*

*Ps. 118:17-18* proves David didn't die, as Paul states in Acts 13:36.

*Ps. 16:4* proves Christians' communion is wrong.

*Daniel's 11:31* is talking about the second place of worship that the exiled House of Israel erected in the times of Ezekiel. This is the place of worship, the *Stonehenge site*, that Charlemagne, the return of King Saul for the 2nd time, the first time being in the New Testament times as Saul called Paul, to crucify God's Holy Messiah, King David, shedding David's blood as in a sacrificial offering for the forgiveness of our past and hopefully our future sins, and to build his pagan christian religion to be imposed upon our ancestors years later as a punishment upon us sinful Israelites as stated in *Ezekiel 20:24-26* to teach us a lesson we will never ever forget. We are now in the hands of King Saul, who is the devil's 1st born son, via his Christian religion, and have been ever since Charlemagne, the disguise of King Saul, began imposing this pagan Christian religion upon our ancestors via his German and French army in the year and date of 774.778 or Oct. 10th, which caused the countdown of *Daniel's 12:11* scripture ticking. This place of worship was destroyed in 774.778, and the countdown of 1260 + 30 + 45 biblical years began. King Saul will personally show up for the last 3.5 biblical years of the 1260 b. year period. Therefore, he will make his final appearance in 1256.5 * 360/365.25 = 1238.44 + 774.778 = *2013.2 on March 20th.* Then God's reclaiming time/war begins after the full 1,260 biblical years expires in year 2016.65 on Aug. 24th from sundown of previous day. This time calculates as follows, 1260 *360/365.25 = *1241.8891*. Therefore, 1241.8891 + 774.778 = the year 2016.667 is what we will call world WWIII against our arch-enemies, the so-called Holy Roman Empire and their allies. It will be for 30 biblical years and will end in 30 * 360/365.25 = 29.57 G. yrs.+2016.667 = 2046.2358. What follows this war is a desolated time period of 45 biblical years, where the survivors of the previous war must try to stay alive until God's Holy Messiah, King David, with his faithful soldiers will search all the lands for the Israelite survivors and lead them back to the promised lands. This will be after the 45-biblical-year period expires in 2046.2358 + (45 * 360/365.25) 44.353 = 2090.5888 or Aug. 2nd from sunset of previous day. King David also is allotted 6.297 years or 2,300 days for the survivors to rebuild the temple. Therefore, David has 2100.317- 6.297 = 2094.02 - 2090.57 = 3.45 years to gather up all the survivors and lead them back to the promised land to rebuild the temple in the allotted time. This temple that was destroyed in Jerusalem in the year -166.734 must be rebuilt and dedicated to the Lord our God 2,300 biblical years from this date. Therefore, the remaining time of year -166.266 +2300 * 360/365.25 = 2100.6744 Greg. year this temple must be rebuilt and dedicated to the Lord our God.

*Author:*                                                                             *R.A. Mueller*

CPSIA information can be obtained at www.ICGtesting.com
Printed in the USA
BVOW01s2007291013

334973BV00001B/17/P